Prophecy and Apocalyptic

BIBLIOGRAPHIES

Craig A. Evans
General Editor

1. The Pentateuch
2. Historical Books
3. Poetry and Wisdom
4. Prophecy and Apocalyptic
5. Jesus
6. The Synoptic Gospels
7. The Johannine Writings
8. Luke–Acts and Narrative Historiography
9. The Pauline Writings
10. Hebrews and General Epistles
11. Old Testament Introduction
12. New Testament Introduction
13. Old Testament Theology
14. New Testament Theology

BIBLIOGRAPHIES No. 4

Prophecy and Apocalyptic

An Annotated Bibliography

D. Brent Sandy and Daniel M. O'Hare

Baker Academic

Grand Rapids, Michigan

© 2007 by D. Brent Sandy and Daniel M. O'Hare

Published by Baker Academic
a division of Baker Publishing Group
P.O. Box 6287, Grand Rapids, MI 49516-6287
www.bakeracademic.com

Printed in the United States of America

Library of Congress Cataloging-in-Publication Data
Sandy, D. Brent, 1947–
    Prophecy and apocalyptic : an annotated bibliography / D. Brent Sandy and Daniel M. O'Hare.
        p.   cm.
    Includes index.
    ISBN 10: 0-8010-2601-6 (pbk.)
    ISBN 978-0-8010-2601-0 (pbk.)
    1. Bible. O.T. Prophets—Criticism, interpretation, etc.—Bibliography. 2. Prophecy—Christianity—Bibliography. 3. Apocalyptic literature—Bibliography. I. O'Hare, Daniel M., 1977– II. Title.
    Z7772.B65S26 2007
    [BS1505.52]
    016.224′06—dc22   2007026358

Contents

Series Preface   9

Authors' Preface   11

Abbreviations   17

Part 1 Prophecy

1. Information and Orientation   21
    1.1 Introductions
    1.2 Assessments of Research
    1.3 Collected Essays

2. Definition and Identification   33
    2.1 Prophecy in the Ancient Near East
    2.2 Comparative Anthropology
    2.3 Identity and Roles
    2.4 Prophetic Calls, Inspiration, and Authority
    2.5 False Prophecy
    2.6 Prophecy, Torah, and the Deuteronomic School
    2.7 Prophecy, Cult, and Psalms
    2.8 Prophecy, Kings, and Monarchy
    2.9 Prophecy and Wisdom
    2.10 Former Prophecy

2.11 Preexilic and Exilic Prophecy
2.12 Prophecy in Second Temple Judaism
2.13 Prophecy in Early Christianity

3. Conception and Communication   78
3.1 Orality, Writing, and Canon
3.2 Form, Redaction, and Genre Criticism
3.3 Poetry and Imagery
3.4 Literary Interdependence
3.5 Ideology and Theology
3.6 Syncretism and Idolatry
3.7 Covenant: Judgment and Blessing
3.8 Ethics and Social Justice
3.9 Exile and Restoration
3.10 Jerusalem and the Temple
3.11 Eschatology and Messianism
3.12 Special Studies

4. Composition and Compilation   114
4.1 Isaiah
4.2 Jeremiah
4.3 Lamentations
4.4 Ezekiel
4.5 Book of the Twelve
4.6 Hosea
4.7 Joel
4.8 Amos
4.9 Obadiah
4.10 Jonah
4.11 Micah
4.12 Nahum
4.13 Habakkuk
4.14 Zephaniah
4.15 Haggai and Zechariah
4.16 Malachi

5. Transmission and Interpretation   168
5.1 Textual History: MT, LXX, DSS, Targums, Peshitta
5.2 Prophecy in Jewish and Christian Traditions

5.3 Interpretive Issues
5.4 Literary and Rhetorical Criticism
5.5 Canonical Criticism
5.6 Feminist and Liberation Criticism
5.7 Homiletics and Contemporary Application

Part 2 Apocalyptic

6. Information and Orientation   191
    6.1 Introductions
    6.2 Assessments of Research
    6.3 Collected Essays

7. Definition and Identification   201
    7.1 Apocalyptic in the Ancient Near East
    7.2 Old Testament Origins of Apocalyptic: Cult, Wisdom,
        Prophecy
    7.3 Social Setting of Apocalyptic

8. Conception and Communication   212
    8.1 Literary Considerations
    8.2 Visions and Revelations
    8.3 Ideology and Theological Themes

9. Composition and Compilation   217
    9.1 Daniel as a Whole
    9.2 Daniel 1–6
    9.3 Daniel 7–12

10. Transmission and Interpretation   224
    10.1 Language, Texts, and Translations
    10.2 Second Temple Jewish Literature and New Testament
    10.3 Apocalyptic in Jewish and Christian Traditions
    10.4 Homiletics and Interpretive Issues

Name Index   235

Series Preface

With the proliferation of journals and publishing houses dedicated to biblical studies, it has become impossible even for the most dedicated scholar to keep in touch with the vast amount of material now available for research in all the different parts of the canon. How much more difficult then for the minister, rabbi, student, or interested layperson! Herein lies the importance of bibliographies and in particular this series, IBR Bibliographies.

Bibliographies save time by guiding students to works relevant to their research interests and by preventing the all-too-typical "wild goose chase" in the library. They thus provide the researcher with more time to read, assimilate, and write. These benefits are especially true for the IBR Bibliographies, because of three main characteristics: first, the series is conveniently laid out in line with the major divisions of the canon, with four volumes planned on the Old Testament, six on the New Testament, and four on methodology (see the listing of series titles in the front matter to this volume); second, the compiler of each volume must select only the most important and helpful works for inclusion and arrange entries under various specific topics to allow for ease of reference; third, each entry is briefly annotated in order to inform the reader more specifically about the work's contents.

Since the series is designed primarily for American and British students, the emphasis is on works written in English. Fortunately, a number of the most important foreign-language works have been translated into English, and wherever this is the case this information is included, often along with the original publication data. Again keeping in mind the needs of the student, we have decided to list the English translation before the original title.

These bibliographies are presented under the sponsorship of the Institute for Biblical Research (IBR), an organization of evangelical Christian scholars with specialties in both Old and New Testaments and their ancillary disciplines. The IBR has met annually since 1970; its name and constitution were adopted in 1973. Besides its annual meetings (normally held the evening and morning prior to the annual meeting of the Society of Biblical Literature), the institute publishes a journal, *Bulletin for Biblical Research*, and conducts regional study groups on various biblical themes in several areas of the United States and Canada. The Institute for Biblical Research encourages and fosters scholarly research among its members, all of whom are at a level to qualify for a university lectureship.

Finally, the IBR and the series editor extend their thanks to Baker Academic for its efforts to bring this series to publication. In particular, we would like to thank David Aiken for his wise guidance in giving shape to the project.

Craig A. Evans
Acadia Divinity School

Authors' Preface

This annotated bibliography consists of a front door and a foyer. That is, it provides a point of entry into the genres of Old Testament prophecy and apocalyptic and into the inner rooms associated with those disciplines. Users will find important bibliographic information, overviews of the current status of research, and potential topics for future study. The front door and foyer lead to storerooms of information awaiting exploration.

The scope of the bibliography entails fifty-one subjects under prophecy and sixteen under apocalyptic (comprised of 453 and 105 sources, respectively). For both prophecy and apocalyptic, the citations are arranged in five sections. The first section consists of introductions, assessments of the status of research, and collections of essays. The second considers definition and identification, focusing on similarities with other religious specialities and with phenomena outside the canon, on the relationship to other genres, and on historical developments. Section three looks at how the prophets and apocalyptists conceived of their messages, along with how they communicated with their audiences. Section four turns to written forms of what would become canonical Scripture, particularly in regard to composition and compilation. The final section examines how prophetic texts were transmitted and interpreted. Note that sources discussing prophecy and apocalyptic are generally listed under apocalyptic.

The bibliography follows a progression of strategic steps for research.

- *Introductions*: §1.1 and §6.1 entail introductions to prophecy and apocalyptic, respectively. For even more basic concepts and overviews, students may first wish to consult reference works such as Bible dictionaries and encyclopedias and general introductions to the Hebrew Bible.
- *Status of research*: published assessments of research can be found in §1.2 and §6.2. They provide overviews of the history, present status, and future prospects of research.
- *Collected essays*: volumes with multiple authors can be found in §1.3 and §6.3. Generally, they offer a variety of perspectives and approaches to thematic topics.

While considerable insight for interpreting specific prophetic books can be found in commentaries, for several reasons they are generally not included in this bibliography. Commentaries are more widely known and readily available than many other scholarly works. In addition, they have for the most part already been annotated in Tremper Longman III, *Old Testament Commentary Survey* (4th ed.; Baker, 2007) and in similar sources. Furthermore, excluding the many commentaries allows as much space as possible for annotating essays and monographs. The only exception to the practice of excluding commentaries is the commentary that offers a unique perspective.

The range of this bibliographical project is vast, considering the breadth of scholarly literature on prophecy and apocalyptic—covering everything from Moses to Malachi in the biblical canon and from Memphis to Mesopotamia in the ancient Near East (ANE). (For prophecy and apocalyptic in the NT, see Stanley Porter's volume in the IBR series, *Johannine Writings and Apocalyptic* [Grand Rapids: Baker Academic, forthcoming].) As a genre, prophecy ranks as the largest in the Old Testament, whether counting the number of books or the number of words. Though apocalyptic is the smallest, a disproportionate amount of research has been published on it.

With approximately 200 sources on prophecy and apocalyptic appearing annually, the benefits of a selected bibliography are self-evident. On the other hand, the process of selecting which ones merit inclusion has been daunting. It would be a challenge to select the 550 most important studies of one prophetic book only, let alone for the seventeen books from Isaiah to Malachi and for related literature in the ANE. (For example, see Thompson (#284), a bibliography listing 2,777 sources for Jeremiah.) Even for the Minor Prophets, thousands of books and articles have been written. (Compare van der Wal [#368], listing 1,220 sources for Micah.) For this bibliography, the initial collection of books and articles that seemed worthy of inclusion totaled over 1,500, a number far exceeding the threshold of usefulness for the nonscholarly user.

One consolation of limiting the number of sources included in this bibliography: the hundreds of sources not included in this print version can be accessed via **www.ibresearch.org/IBR.Studies. html**, with the citations arranged under the same subjects as in this bibliography.

Criteria for Inclusion

The following questions guided decisions about the inclusion of a particular book or article:

- Does it advance the discussion of its subject in a significant way?
- Does it reflect the breadth of issues involved?
- Does the discussion have implications that reach beyond a few specific verses or beyond an isolated issue?
- Does it reveal a turning point in the history of scholarship and have lasting value?
- Does it represent the current status of scholarship?
- Does it stimulate ideas for future research?
- Does it provide bibliographic information that leads readers to other research?

The number of articles and books that met one or more of these criteria was nevertheless far too large for this volume. In order to be more selective, we followed the simple guiding principle of including those works that are most helpful in grasping the present status of research and that are most likely to stimulate future research. Admittedly, this principle has meant a preference for recent works, especially those that guide readers to earlier works and offer up-to-date discussions, and a secondary preference for classics in the field. However, no two bibliographers would agree completely on what should be included in such a collection. To compensate for our own idiosyncrasies and inadequacies, we consulted introductory works that include recommended bibliographies in order to provide something approaching a consensus of the most valuable sources for prophecy and apocalyptic. Nevertheless, at some points this bibliography, for reasons of space, must necessarily default to being representative rather than selective, meaning that there are equally good sources not included. We make apology to many authors who would have liked to see their work included. For readers using this bibliography, hopefully what you find here will lead you to important work on the subject you are pursuing.

The objective of each annotation is to provide a summary, in a couple of sentences, of an author's main point and contribution, though clearly the necessary brevity of such annotations cannot do justice to the breadth of contents. Evaluative comments about the strengths or weaknesses of a source generally seemed unnecessary, since inclusion in this bibliography is in itself a statement about the work's value.

To avoid overlap and to increase the number of sources that could be cited, books and articles are generally listed once. For example, an essay on Ezekiel's imagery does *not* appear twice—under "Poetry and Imagery" and under "Ezekiel." This means users will need to look under more than one subtopic to find all that might pertain to their specific search. Cross-references are provided to point readers to other related categories in the bibliography.

Books consisting of collected essays posed special problems. Should there be one annotation, with a summary of the contents? Or should the titles and authors of the essays be listed in the annotation? Or should each essay be annotated separately? The conclusion was to set aside the desire for consistency and treat each volume of essays and the individual essays on their own merit. Thus, in some cases, titles of essays are listed, and in other cases contents are summarized. Generally, if the title and author of an essay is cited in the annotation of a collection of essays, it is not annotated separately. Some exceptions were made for noteworthy articles of broad interest.

No systematic attempt was made to include sources in this bibliography published after 2005.

Acknowledgments

Various libraries have offered resources that were indispensable in preparing this bibliography. They include libraries on the campuses of Associated Mennonite Biblical Seminary, Biblical Theological Seminary, Concordia Seminary (Fort Wayne), Duke University, Midwestern Baptist Theological Seminary, the University of Notre Dame, and most importantly, Grace College and Seminary. Special thanks to the administration of Grace College and Seminary for their support of this project, to Bill Darr and the staff of Morgan Library, and to the following student assistants: Dan Kramer, Ben Thomas, and Kevin Becker.

Abbreviations

ANE	Ancient Near East(ern)
BZAW	Beihefte zur Zeitschrift für die alttestamentliche Wissenschaft
CurBS	*Currents in Research: Biblical Studies*
DH	Deuteronomistic Historian
DSS	Dead Sea Scrolls
HSM	Harvard Semitic Monographs
HTR	*Harvard Theological Review*
ICC	International Critical Commentary
Int	*Interpretation*
IRT	Issues in Religion and Theology
JBL	*Journal of Biblical Literature*
JETS	*Journal of the Evangelical Theological Society*
JSJSup	Supplements to the Journal for the Study of Judaism
JSOT	*Journal for the Study of the Old Testament*
JSOTSup	Journal for the Study of the Old Testament: Supplement Series
JSPSup	Journal for the Study of the Pseudepigrapha: Supplement Series
LXX	Septuagint
MT	Masoretic Text
OBT	Overtures to Biblical Theology
OTG	Old Testament Guides
SBLDS	Society of Biblical Literature Dissertation Series
SBLSymS	Society of Biblical Literature Symposium Series
SBT	Studies in Biblical Theology
SJOT	*Scandinavian Journal of the Old Testament*
VT	*Vetus Testamentum*
VTSup	Supplements to Vetus Testamentum
ZAW	*Zeitschrift für die alttestamentliche Wissenschaft*

Part 1

PROPHECY

1

Information and Orientation

1.1 Introductions

The introductions to the prophets annotated below are recommended for upper-level college students, graduate students, and ministers (see also ##56, 58, 60, 67, 124–25, 194). Introductions suitable for general audiences are noted at the end of this section. Other places to find introductory material are commentaries and Bible companions. For example: D. L. Petersen, "Introduction to Prophetic Literature," in *The New Interpreter's Bible: General Articles and Introduction, Commentary, and Reflections for Each Book of the Bible . . .* , ed. L. E. Keck et al. (Nashville: Abingdon, 2001), 6:1–23; R. R. Wilson, "The Prophetic Books," in *The Cambridge Companion to Biblical Interpretation*, ed. J. Barton (Cambridge: Cambridge University Press, 1998), 212–25; K. Koch, "Latter Prophets: The Major Prophets," and J. L. Crenshaw, "Latter Prophets: The Minor Prophets," in *The Blackwell Companion to the Hebrew Bible*, ed. L. G. Perdue (Oxford: Blackwell, 2001), 353–68 and 369–81, respectively. Introductions to the OT are also helpful sources for prophecy and in some cases have been influential. Recent introductions include W. Brueggemann, *An Introduction to the Old Testament:*

The Canon and Christian Imagination (Louisville: Westminster John Knox, 2003). For other introductions, see E. C. Hostetter, *Old Testament Introduction*, IBR Bibliographies 11 (Grand Rapids: Baker Academic, 1995).

1   A. J. Heschel. *The Prophets*. 2 vols. in one. New York: Harper & Row, 1962. Reprinted Peabody, MA: Hendrickson, 1999.
     Classic discussion of "what it means to think, feel, respond and act as a prophet" (1.ix), with primary focus on the literary prophets of the eighth and seventh centuries. A major theme of the book is that the divine involvement in history means the prophets do not simply preach morality but share in the divine pathos, the intimate relationship between God and creation. Divine pathos is best understood as a sure intention that moves toward an assured purpose.

2   J. D. Newsome. *The Hebrew Prophets*. Atlanta: John Knox, 1984.
     Widely used as a textbook. After an introductory chapter on the history of prophecy before Amos, N. discusses the historical context, message, theology, and some representative passages of each of the prophets. The final chapter is "The Enduring Value of the Prophets' Work." An appendix considers the book of Daniel.

3   W. A. VanGemeren. *Interpreting the Prophetic Word*. Grand Rapids: Academie, 1990.
     Thorough introduction to the message of the prophets, encouraging readers to hear the prophetic testimony of God's redemptive purposes and to be sensitive to the spirit of restoration. Includes chapters on the development of prophetism, on the prophetic tradition, on prophetic motifs, and on living the prophetic word. Treats each of the Minor Prophets in canonical order, followed by the major prophets (including Daniel).

4   G. V. Smith. *An Introduction to the Hebrew Prophets: The Prophets as Preachers*. Nashville: Broadman and Holman, 1994.
     Uses communication theory and the sociology of knowledge to analyze how the prophets sought to transform the thinking

and behavior of their audiences. While providing introductory information for each of the prophets (in chronological order), the special focus is on the persuasive techniques and theology of the prophets, and the sociology of affecting change in people.

5   J. Blenkinsopp. *A History of Prophecy in Israel*. Philadelphia: Westminster, 1983. Revised and enlarged edition: Louisville: Westminster John Knox, 1996.
     Influential introduction to prophecy, tracing the development of the concept and practice of prophecy in Israel and Judah from a sociohistorical perspective. Attention is given to the figures behind the books in an attempt to construct a kind of biography for major prophetic figures. Includes bibliography for each of the prophets, as well as an introduction that situates the prophets of the Hebrew Bible in their ANE context. (See #58.)

6   A. Rofé. *Introduction to the Prophetic Literature*. Translated by Judith H. Seeligmann. Sheffield: Sheffield Academic Press, 1997. Original title: *Mavo le-sifrut ha nevu'ah*. Jerusalem: Akademon, 1992.
     Provides a general introduction to prophetic literature, focusing on the problems encountered in reading the prophets and offering suggestions toward solutions. Includes discussion of oral forms, redaction, genres, structure, social functions, literary criticism, and apocalyptic.

7   D. E. Gowan. *Theology of the Prophetic Books: The Death and Resurrection of Israel*. Louisville: Westminster John Knox, 1998.
     Summarizes the message of each of the prophetic books in light of the historical setting and the developing theology of the destruction and restoration of Israel. Observes that the prophets cluster around three events: the fall of Samaria, the fall of Jerusalem, and the return of the exiles. More than providing introduction, G. traces the developing theology of the prophets.

8   O. H. Steck. *The Prophetic Books and Their Theological Witness*. Translated by J. D. Nogalski. St. Louis: Chalice, 2000.

Original title: *Prophetenbücher und ihr theologisches Zeugnis: Wege der Nachfrage und Fährten zur Antwort.* Tübingen: Mohr Siebeck, 1996.

Discusses a method for working backward from the final form of a prophetic book to earlier versions of it, while not minimizing the path each book took in the process of changing to meet new needs. The second part of the work is concerned with exegesis of the prophetic corpus and examines fundamental facets of prophetic interpretation, especially as they concern theological aspects of the transmission process.

9   V. H. Matthews. *Social World of the Hebrew Prophets.* Peabody, MA: Hendrickson, 2001.

Takes as its premise that "as we explore the social world of the Hebrew prophets, we must first recognize that these persons, both male and female, spoke within their own time, to an audience with a frame of reference very different from ours" (1). After an introduction to historical geography and the nature of a prophet, M. provides a chronological overview of the Hebrew prophets and their books.

10   R. B. Chisholm Jr. *Handbook on the Prophets.* Grand Rapids: Baker Academic, 2002.

Summarizes the message of the prophets (including Daniel). After a brief introduction to each prophet, C. provides a pericope-by-pericope explanation, analyzing structure and themes. Includes extensive bibliography, primarily of works published since 1990.

11   J. G. McConville. *Exploring the Old Testament: A Guide to the Prophets.* Downers Grove, IL: InterVarsity/London: SPCK, 2002.

Especially useful as a textbook, this work has chapters on each of the books from Isaiah to Malachi, emphasizing the canonical form of the books. Introduces readers to critical and interpretive literature on the prophets, with bibliography included in each chapter. Focuses on issues of interpretation, theological themes, and rhetorical intention. Includes interactive sidebars, encouraging informed engagement with and further investigation into the prophetic books.

12   D. L. Petersen. *The Prophetic Literature: An Introduction.* Louisville: Westminster John Knox, 2002.
A thorough introduction to the writings of the prophets in light of recent research and likely to become a standard textbook. Addresses questions crucial for understanding prophetic literature, including definitions, origins, social setting, poetic speech, literary features, compilation and redaction, and ethical and theological issues. Discusses each of the prophetic books in terms of setting, structure, and theology. Finds that "each intermediary enacted the role of prophet in particular ways, such that the literature attesting the prophetic behavior was itself unique" (239).

13   R. R. Hutton. *Fortress Introduction to the Prophets.* Minneapolis: Fortress, 2004.
Provides a brief introduction to the preexilic prophets and Jeremiah, focused around five frequently asked but "fundamentally insoluble" questions basic to study of the prophets. Each of the preexilic prophets is treated in a single chapter, while Jeremiah absorbs the remaining half of the book.

The following introductions are recommended for general readers: J. F. A. Sawyer, *Prophecy and the Biblical Prophets* (New York: Oxford University Press, 1993); D. J. Zucker, *Israel's Prophets: An Introduction for Christians and Jews* (New York: Paulist, 1994); J. H. Eaton, *Mysterious Messengers: A Course on Hebrew Prophecy from Amos Onwards* (London: SCM Press, 1997; Grand Rapids: Eerdmans, 1998); J.-P. Prévost, *How to Read the Prophets* (New York: Continuum, 1997); M. McKenna, *Prophets: Words of Fire* (Maryknoll, NY: Orbis, 2001); N. Podhoretz, *The Prophets: Who They Were, What They Are* (New York: Simon & Schuster, 2002); M. J. Williams, *The Prophet and His Message: Reading Old Testament Prophecy Today* (Phillipsburg, NJ: P & R, 2003).

1.2 Assessments of Research

The following sources survey the breadth and depth of scholarship on the prophets. (Note that any essay that surveys scholarship on a specific prophet may be found in chap. 4 under the heading of that prophet.) Though rarely ending in broad consensus, the issues being considered have led to many important insights. Underlying questions include: What gave rise to the phenomenon of prophecy and prophets? In what sense was Moses the prototype for a prophet? What is the relationship between biblical prophets and similar religious figures in the ANE? How did prophets function in their society, particularly in relation to the covenant and to priests and kings? How did the nonwriting prophets differ from those whose prophecies were recorded? Did the definition of "prophecy" and "prophet" change over time? Do written forms of prophecy necessarily represent the oral messages of the prophets? How were the prophetic writings collected, edited, and passed down? What is the enduring significance of the prophets for various faith communities? (See also ##20, 24, 54, 64–65, 168.)

14   W. H. Schmidt. "The Form of Prophecy." Pp. 188–90 in *Old Testament Introduction*. Translated by M. J. O'Connell. New York: Crossroad, 1984. Original title: *Einführung in das Alte Testament*. Berlin: de Gruyter, 1979. Reprinted as "Contemporary Issues" in *The Place Is Too Small for Us: The Israelite Prophets in Recent Scholarship*, pp. 579–81. Edited by R. P. Gordon. Sources for Biblical and Theological Study 5. Winona Lake, IN: Eisenbrauns, 1995.
    Identifies and interacts with five questions about which debate continues in modern research. How are writing prophets indebted to earlier cultic, legal, and wisdom traditions? How are commonalities between the eighth-century writing prophets best explained? How are announcements of coming events and comprehension of the present situation linked? Does the prophetic announcement of coming doom imply certain judgment or merely a threatening possibility if disobedience persists? How is the inconsistent use of oracles of doom and salvation among different prophets best understood?

15   W. G. Hupper. *An Index to English Periodical Literature on the Old Testament and Ancient Near Eastern Studies*. 8 vols. American Theological Library Association Bibliography Series 21. Lanham, MD: Scarecrow, 1987–99.
    For the prophets, see in particular bibliographical articles and studies (1.1.2 and 1.2.4); literary criticism (3.2.10–11); exegetical studies (3.5.3.2); and theological studies (5.3–4). The eight volumes consist of 4,600+ pages and 50,000+ citations

of articles culled from over 600 journals, annuals, and proceedings. "One of the main objectives of this index was to
concentrate particularly on nineteenth-century literature
which for the most part has been neglected" (I, xvi). The
citations are listed in 1,157 classifications and within the classifications the entries are arranged chronologically. Though
only English titles are included, H. sought to be exhaustive,
including material found in less well-known places, such as
third-world publications.

16   J. L. Mays, D. L. Petersen, and K. H. Richards (eds.). *Old Testament Interpretation: Past, Present and Future: Essays in Honor
of Gene M. Tucker*. Nashville: Abingdon, 1995.
Includes four essays on prophecy describing the contours of
present scholarship and forecasting future directions of research. For an annotated essay, see Darr (#168). Other essays
are "The Former Prophets: Reading the Books of Kings" (R. R.
Wilson); "The World and Message of the Prophets: Biblical
Prophecy in Context" (P. D. Miller Jr.); "Formation and Form
in Prophetic Literature" (M. A. Sweeney).

17   D. W. Baker. "Israelite Prophets and Prophecy." Pp. 266–94 in
*The Face of Old Testament Studies: A Survey of Contemporary
Approaches*. Edited by D. W. Baker and B. T. Arnold. Grand
Rapids: Baker Academic, 1999.
Extensive survey of the scholarly literature of the previous
three decades, divided into four areas: precomposition, composition, transmission, application. Within each area pertinent
questions are answered in light of current scholarship. Questions include, Where did the prophets fit in their society? With
whom do the prophets compare, both in their own time and
in recent periods? How did the prophetic messages move from
speech to text? What use for us today are the prophets? Relevant bibliographic information is provided in the footnotes.

18   R. R. Wilson. "Current Issues in the Study of Old Testament
Prophecy." Pp. 38–46 in *Inspired Speech: Prophecy in the Ancient Near East: Essays in Honor of Herbert B. Huffmon*. Edited
by J. Kaltner and L. Stulman. JSOTSup 378. London: T & T
Clark, 2004.

Identifies three major challenges to traditional views about
prophecy and observes that these questions are still unresolved:
(1) What was the path from the prophet's original oracle to the
final written form of the prophetic text? (2) To what extent
did the particular social setting in which a prophet functioned
shape the prophetic oracles? (3) In light of prophetic materials
from the ANE, were the Israelite prophets distinctive in character and theological values? Focuses on one of these issues, the
relationship between oral and written literature, and contends
that there were good reasons for recording prophetic oracles,
with oral transmission playing a key role in preservation.

1.3 Collected Essays

The collected essays below are of broad interest for the study of
prophecy, though individual essays generally address specific topics. They embody the wealth of scholarly research on the prophets.
In addition to sources below, collections of essays are included in
appropriate sections throughout this bibliography. Note that some
essays from these collections are annotated separately, based on
whether they meet the criteria described in the preface. If so, they
are cross-referenced by their identifying number.

19   H. A. McKay and D. J. A. Clines (eds.). *Of Prophets' Visions
and the Wisdom of the Sages: Essays in Honour of R. Norman
Whybray on His Seventieth Birthday.* JSOTSup 162. Sheffield:
Sheffield Academic Press, 1993.
Seventeen essays, eight on prophecy. For annotated essays, see
Coggins (#81), Grabbe (#41), and Mayes (#73). Other essays
include: "Prophecy and Society in Israel" (A. D. H. Mayes);
"From Mari to Moses: Prophecy at Mari and in Ancient Israel"
(R. P. Gordon); "First and Last in Isaiah" (H. G. M. Williamson);
"Mother Zion, Father Servant: A Reading of Isaiah 49–55"
(K. Jeppesen); "Metacommentating Amos" (D. J. A. Clines).

20   R. P. Gordon (ed.). *The Place Is Too Small for Us: The Israelite
Prophets in Recent Scholarship.* Sources for Biblical and Theological Study 5. Winona Lake, IN: Eisenbrauns, 1995.
This collection of previously published essays is fundamentally important for research on the prophets, serving as an

essential starting point for many topics. The essays are arranged in seven sections, each with an introduction: Near Eastern Background, Message of the Prophets, Art of Prophecy, Prophecy and Society, Developing Tradition, Prophecy after the Prophets, and Future Directions. For annotated essays, see Stacey (#238), Houston (#422), Newsom (#166), Day (#177), Auld (#48), Wilson (#80), Overholt (#52), Blenkinsopp (#249), Clements (#147), Childs (#438), and Deist (#51). Other essays are of similar scope and quality.

21   R. E. Clements. *Old Testament Prophecy: From Oracles to Canon.* Louisville: Westminster John Knox, 1996.
    Includes an original summary of the interpretation of prophecy from 1965–1995. The remainder of the essays (originally published 1977–1993) are reprinted without revision. They are arranged in six parts, treating the following topics: Amos and the politics of Israel; Isaiah's prophecies to Hezekiah; the messianic hope; Second Isaiah's development of Isaiah's themes; the unity of Isaiah; Jeremiah and Deuteronomistic history; Jeremiah as prophet of hope; tradition in Ezekiel; the redaction of Ezekiel; the prophets and canonicity; the origin of apocalyptic; apocalyptic and literacy; and apocalyptic and canon.

22   P. R. Davies (ed.). *The Prophets: A Sheffield Reader.* The Biblical Seminar 42. Sheffield: Sheffield Academic Press, 1996.
    For annotated essays, see Auld (#48), Overholt (#52), Barstad (#54), Carr (#256). Other essays include: "Beyond Tradition-History: Deutero-Isaianic Development of First Isaiah's Themes" (R. E. Clements); "Second Isaiah—Prophet of Universalism" (J. Blenkinsopp); "Jeremiah as Prophet of Nonviolent Resistance" (D. L. Smith); "Second Isaiah: Prophet to Patriarchy" (B. W. Stone); "Daughter of Zion and Servant of the Lord in Isaiah: A Comparison" (J. F. A. Sawyer); "Insiders and Outsiders in the Book of Jeremiah: Shifts in Symbolic Arrangement" (L. Stulman); "Portraying Prophecy: Of Doublets, Variants and Analogies in the Narrative Representation of Jeremiah's Oracles—Reconstructing the Hermeneutics of Prophecy" (A. R. P. Diamond).

23   S. B. Reid (ed.). *Prophets and Paradigms: Essays in Honor of Gene M. Tucker.* JSOTSup 229. Sheffield: Sheffield Academic Press, 1996.
Of the fourteen essays in this volume, ten are on prophecy. For annotated essays see Davies (#61), Overholt (#117), Gottwald (#192), and Melugin (#426). Other essays include: "Hosea as a Canonical Problem: With Attention to the Song of Songs" (M. J. Buss); "The Social Location of the Prophet Amos in Light of the Group/Grid Cultural Anthropological Model" (G. Ramírez); "Studying Prophetic Texts against Their Original Backgrounds: Pre-Ordained Scripts and Alternative Horizons of Research" (E. Ben Zvi).

24   Y. Gitay (ed.). *Prophecy and Prophets: The Diversity of Contemporary Issues in Scholarship.* SBL Semeia Studies. Atlanta: Scholars Press, 1997.
For annotated essays, see Petersen (#64), Clements (#75), and Rendtorff (#440). Other essays include: "The Projection of the Prophet: A Rhetorical Presentation of the Prophet Jeremiah (According to Jer 1:1–19)" (Y. Gitay); "Between God and Man: Prophets in Ancient Israel" (D. N. Freedman); "Freeing the Imagination: The Conclusion to the Book of Joel" (J. L. Crenshaw); "Prophet and Prophecy: An Artistic Dilemma" (Z. Gitay).

25   D. E. Orton (ed.). *Prophecy in the Hebrew Bible: Selected Studies from Vetus Testamentum.* Brill's Readers in Biblical Studies 5. Leiden: Brill, 2000.
Nineteen essays published in the last third of the twentieth century, selected to reflect a broad range of scholarly insights on "the nature of prophecy in the cultural context of the ANE, the issue of true and false prophecy in biblical perspective, the genres of the prophetic texts and central features of the main prophetic books" (vii). For annotated essays see Parker (#28), Haran (#122), Sweeney (#378), and Mason (#387). Other essays are of similar scope and quality.

26   J. Kaltner and L. Stulman (eds.). *Inspired Speech: Prophecy in the Ancient Near East: Essays in Honor of Herbert B. Huffmon.* JSOTSup 378. London: T & T Clark, 2004.

Thirty-one essays, the majority on prophecy. For annotated essays, see Nissinen (#36), van der Toorn (#150), and Wilson (#18). Other essays include: "False Prophecy Is True" (D. N. Freedman and R. Frey); "When the God of Israel 'Acts-Out' His Anger: On the Language of Divine Rejection in Biblical Literature" (B. A. Levine); "What's in a Name? Cyrus and the Dating of Deutero-Isaiah" (M. Eng); "Visions of Peace in Isaiah" (D. A. Leiter); "The Spiritual Journey of Jonah: From the Perspective of C. G. Jung's Analytical Psychology" (J. Park); "Harder than Flint, Faster than Eagles: Intensified Comparatives in the Latter Prophets" (E. A. Seibert); "Jeremiah as a Polyphonic Response to Suffering" (L. Stulman); "The Royal Family in the Jeremiah Tradition" (A. Varughese).

2

Definition and Identification

2.1 Prophecy in the Ancient Near East

In addition to biblical materials, approximately 140 texts from the ANE refer to prophetic phenomena or record a prophetic message. These include letters, oracle reports, cultic texts, word lists, and other genres. The two largest collections come from Mari (fifty letters with prophetic quotations) and Nineveh (twenty-nine oracles on clay tablets and more than twenty documents referring to prophets). The distribution of prophetic texts in the ANE ranges from the eighteenth-century BC Mari documents to the seventh-century BC Assyrian and Arabian documents. For comparative study, cited below are the Mari letters, published by Durand (#27), and the Assyrian prophetic oracles, published by Parpola (#30). For a wider selection of ANE prophetic texts, see Nissinen (#35). This material is particularly relevant to the question of the origins of biblical prophecy. While similarities between biblical and ANE prophecy are informative, many scholars continue to stress the uniqueness of biblical prophecy. See also ##19, 25, and 104.

27   J.-M. Durand. *Archives épistolaires de Mari I/1.* Archives roy-
      ales de Mari 26. Paris: Éditions Recherches sur les Civilizations,
      1988.
      Comprehensive treatment of prophecy at Mari, complete
      with texts and a thorough introduction to the diverse tasks
      subsumed under the rubric of divination (3–68). One interest-
      ing text appears to be a loyalty oath sworn by the diviner to
      the king that he would divulge to the king all that he learned
      (13–15). Also treats the subject of prophetic dreams. In this
      collection of texts is the first attested use of the word *nabûm*,
      cognate to the Hebrew *nabî'* (prophet).

28   S. B. Parker. "Official Attitudes Toward Prophecy at Mari and
      in Israel." *VT* 43 (1993) 50–68. Reprinted in *Prophecy in the
      Hebrew Bible: Selected Studies from Vetus Testamentum*, pp.
      245–70. Compiled by D. E. Orton. Brill's Readers in Biblical
      Studies 5. Leiden: Brill, 2000.
      Investigates the notion of prophecy at Mari on five fronts: How
      do officials in the service of the king describe the prophecy that
      comes to their attention? What supplementary information
      do these officials give to explain prophecy? In their quotation
      of prophecy, what do Mari officials imply about its reliability?
      What do Mari letters suggest about the officials' perceptions of
      prophecy, especially concerning interpretation or evaluation?
      What do these letters tell us about what response the officials
      expect from the king? Concludes that a cautious use of parallels
      between prophecy at Mari and in Israel can prove helpful.

29   A. Jeffers. *Magic and Divination in Ancient Palestine and
      Syria.* Studies in the History and Culture of the Ancient Near
      East 8. Leiden: Brill, 1996.
      Responds to the apparent suppression of evidence in the Pen-
      tateuch concerning magic and divination. Collects "all traces
      of magic and divination in the Old Testament and in the
      closely connected (geographically and otherwise) Northwest
      Semitic world" (xiii). Concludes that Israel's leaders were
      expected to be able to discern the will of God for specific
      crises, so they sooner or later turned to magico-divinatory
      methods. The canon, however, condemns such techniques
      and relegates them to foreign influence, probably influenced
      by later ideas about a "pure" Yahwism.

30   S. Parpola. *Assyrian Prophecies.* State Archives of Assyria
      Studies 9. Helsinki: Helsinki University Press, 1997.
      Presents a new text (with transliteration and translation) of
      the corpus of seventh-century BC prophecies addressed to
      Assyrian kings, many of which share affinities with biblical
      prophecies. Argues that Aššur, the state god of Assyria, can
      be compared to the Hebrew concept of Yahweh and that Ištar
      functions as an analogue to the Christian conception of the
      Holy Spirit. Adduces parallels between Christian and Jewish
      tradition, especially the kabbalah.

31   R. M. Berchman (ed.). *Mediators of the Divine: Horizons of
      Prophecy, Divination, Dreams and Theurgy in Mediterranean
      Antiquity.* South Florida Studies in the History of Judaism 163.
      Atlanta: Scholars Press, 1998.
      Provides nine essays on "the horizons of prophecy, divina-
      tion, dreams and theurgy" (2): "Prophecy and Divination in
      Archaic Greek Literature" (A. Karp); "In the View of Rabbinic
      Judaism, What, Exactly, Ended with Prophecy" (J. Neusner);
      "To See the Light: A Gnostic Appropriation of Jewish Priestly
      Practice and Sapiential and Apocalyptic Visionary Lore" (J. D.
      Turner); "Arcana Mundi: Magic and Divination in the *De Som-
      niis* of Philo of Alexandria" (R. M. Berchman); "Iamblichean
      Dream Theory" (J. F. Finamore); "The Veiled Thoughts of
      the Therapeutae" (D. M. Hay); "Prophecy in the Targumim"
      (B. Chilton); "Prophecy and Patriarchs in Eusebius' Apolo-
      getic" (E. V. Gallagher); and "Divination in the Neoplatonism
      of Iamblichus" (G. Shaw).

32   A. Malamat. *Mari and the Bible.* Studies in the History and
      Culture of the Ancient Near East 12. Leiden: Brill, 1998.
      A collection of previously published and revised articles,
      including ten relevant to prophecy: "Intuitive Prophecy: A
      General Survey"; "Prophetic Revelations in Mari and the
      Bible: Complementary Considerations"; "Episodes Involving
      Samuel and Saul and the Prophetic Texts from Mari"; "A
      Mari Prophecy and Nathan's Dynastic Oracle"; "Parallels
      between the New Prophecies from Mari and Biblical Proph-
      ecy"; "New Light from Mari (Archives royales de Mari 26)
      on Biblical Prophecy"; "The Secret Council and Prophetic
      Involvement in Mari and Israel"; "New Mari Documents

and Prophecy in Ezekiel"; "A New Prophetic Message from
Aleppo and its Biblical Counterparts"; and "Deity Revokes
Kingship: Towards Intellectual Reasoning in Mari and the
Bible."

33   M. Nissinen. *References to Prophecy in Neo-Assyrian Sources.*
State Archives of Assyria Studies 7. Helsinki: University of
Helsinki, 1998.

A companion to Parpola's *Assyrian Prophecies* (see above,
#30), this collection of texts from the reigns of Esarhaddon
and Ashurbanipal describe prophetic oracles and intermediation. Factors that facilitate identification of a prophetic text
include whether the text specifically mentions a prophet,
usually either an ecstatic (*mahhû*) or a shouter (*raggimu*), and
where an allusion to the speech of the deity exists, in the
absence of the mention of other means of divination.

34   M. Nissinen (ed.). *Prophecy in Its Ancient Near Eastern Context: Mesopotamian, Biblical, and Arabian Perspectives.* SBL-
SymS 13. Atlanta: SBL, 2000.

Seven essays in two sections: methods and sources. For an-
notated essays, see Grabbe (#44) and Petersen (#66). Other
essays include: *"Comparare necesse est?* Ancient Israel-
ite and Ancient Near Eastern Prophecy in a Comparative
Perspective" (H. M. Barstad); "A Company of Prophets:
Mari, Assyria, Israel" (H. B. Huffmon); "Mesopotamian
Prophecy between Immanence and Transcendence: A Com-
parison of Old Babylonian and Neo-Assyrian Prophecy"
(K. van der Toorn); "The Socioreligious Role of the Neo-
Assyrian Prophets" (M. Nissinen); and "Arabian Prophecy"
(J. Hämeen-Anttila).

35   M. Nissinen. *Prophets and Prophecy in the Ancient Near East.*
Society of Biblical Literature Writings from the Ancient World
12. Atlanta: SBL, 2003.

A guide to the study of ANE prophecy with representative
documents and sources from the ANE. Includes letters and
other documents from Mari, the Ešmunna oracles, the Nineveh oracles, and other West Semitic, Neo-Assyrian and cu-
neiform sources. The texts are given in transcription and are
accompanied by new translations. Facilitates comprehensive

understanding of the prophetic phenomenon with chronological charts, maps, a glossary, and bibliography, and encourages comparative study.

36 M. Nissinen. "What Is Prophecy? An Ancient Near Eastern Perspective." Pp. 17–37 in *Inspired Speech: Prophecy in the Ancient Near East. Essays in Honor of Herbert B. Huffmon.* Edited by J. Kaltner and L. Stulman. JSOTSup 378. London: T & T Clark, 2004.

Asks whether prophecy should be defined according to how it functioned in the OT—leaving ANE phenomena to be judged by the biblical standard—or whether it should be defined by its function in the ANE. Considers various elements of a definition of prophecy (transmitting and interpreting the divine will, intermediation between a deity and an audience, prediction, relationship to divination, and the social role and function of prophets), concluding that a single definition of prophecy is impossible. Prophecy was a process rather than an entity; it was functional (i.e., acting as the mouthpiece of a deity/deities) rather than institutional; and it was intermediation rather than prediction. Sees an important distinction between "Hebrew" and "biblical" prophecy, the latter being the literary representation of the former. Includes extensive bibliography of ANE prophetic documents.

37 K. Sparks. "Intermediary Texts: Omens and Prophecies." Pp. 216–39 in *Ancient Texts for the Study of the Hebrew Bible: A Guide to the Background Literature.* Peabody, MA: Hendrickson, 2005.

Review of prophetic and mantic texts from the ANE, complete with current bibliographic material and brief summaries of Mesopotamian, Egyptian, and West Semitic texts. Concludes with six observations on debates about the relationship of biblical prophecy to prophetic intermediation in its cultural milieu.

2.2 Comparative Anthropology

The methods of cultural anthropology (also known as social anthropology) have been applied to the study of the prophets for the last several decades. It involves the study of contemporary, preindustrial societies and their diviners, healers, shamans, priests, and the like, who mediate between the supernatural and the natural worlds. Those intermediaries are then compared to the biblical prophets. While not providing direct evidence for biblical prophecy, cultural anthropology often suggests fresh models of how the prophets related to their society.

38   R. R. Wilson. *Prophecy and Society in Ancient Israel.* Philadelphia: Fortress, 1980.

Illustrates how material from comparative anthropological studies may be used to elucidate the societal role of prophecy in the biblical period. Using the title "intermediary" to describe the role of prophets in the different societies examined, Wilson surveys the entire range of biblical testimony about prophecy but focuses on Israelite prophecy rather than its Judean counterpart, since more can be gleaned about the role of prophets in society in the northern traditions. Concludes that some prophets operated outside the political establishment as severe critics while others remained inside, seeking gradual social change.

39   T. W. Overholt. *Prophecy in Cross-Cultural Perspective. A Sourcebook for Biblical Researchers.* Society of Biblical Literature Sources for Biblical Study 17. Atlanta: Scholars Press, 1986.

Provides primary sources describing prophet-like figures from diverse cultures and time periods, designed to permit comparisons with biblical prophets. The largest collection of sources is from American Indians, but also includes other cultures from the Arctic, Africa, India, and the Pacific. Concludes with chapters on oral transmission and methodology for comparative studies.

40   T. W. Overholt. *Channels of Prophecy: The Social Dynamics of Prophetic Activity.* Minneapolis: Fortress, 1989.

Using comparative data drawn from Native American prophecy, O. constructs his own model for interpreting biblical prophecy, including interaction between the intermediary and the divine and between the intermediary and his society. Characterizes prophecy as a form of divination and suggests that this divining activity did not cease after the exile. Investigates the possibility of prophetic activity in the present by investigating one example of modern Christian "prophecy" (D. Wilkerson's *The Vision*) and channeling in the media.

41 L. L. Grabbe. "Prophets, Priests, Diviners and Sages in Ancient Israel." Pp. 43–62 in *Of Prophets' Visions and the Wisdom of the Sages: Essays in Honour of R. Norman Whybray*. Edited by H. A. McKay and D. J. A. Clines. JSOTSup 162. Sheffield: Sheffield University Press, 1993.
Compares and contrasts with the prophets of Israel religious specialists found among North American Indians and African tribes, concluding that "much that was once taken to be characteristic of the canonical prophets can be found in many different cultures around the world" (59). Applauds various insights gained from social anthropology, especially in regard to the prophets.

42 F. H. Cryer. *Divination in Ancient Israel and Its Near Eastern Environment: A Socio-Historical Investigation*. JSOTSup 142. Sheffield: JSOT Press, 1994.
Analysis of magic and other forms of divination among the Azande of the Sudan, in the ANE, and in Israel, concluding that magic was more common among the populace than in the upper echelons of society. Prophetic use of divination can be inferred from their writings, even though explicit references are infrequent. A distinction existed between priestly and prophetic divination, though in actuality, probably not distinguished as sharply as the OT suggests.

43 T. W. Overholt. *Cultural Anthropology and the Old Testament*. Guides to Biblical Scholarship, Old Testament Series. Minneapolis: Augsburg Fortress, 1996.
Applies contemporary anthropological theory to a study of the Elijah-Elisha narratives in order to understand better the culture of ancient Israel. Notes four instances of tension between these narratives and the Deuteronomistic history: resuscitation, blaming the prophets, blaming God, and the prophet as healer. These elements arise from a shamanistic rather than Deuteronomistic ideology. Also examines Elijah and Elisha's roles in Israelite society and the role of divination.

44   L. L. Grabbe. "Ancient Near Eastern Prophecy from an Anthropological Perspective." Pp. 13–32 in *Prophecy in Its Ancient
Near Eastern Context: Mesopotamian, Biblical, and Arabian
Perspectives.* Edited by M. Nissinen. SBLSymS 13. Atlanta:
SBL, 2000.
Discusses the value and limits of cultural anthropology
and offers examples of an anthropological method for com-
paring the phenomenon of prophecy in the ANE and the
Bible. Topics explored include: modes of revelation, prophetic lifestyle, testing the prophets, literary prophecies,
stereotypical language, prophetic calls, and reactions to
failed prophecies.

45   A. M. Kitz. "Prophecy as Divination." *Catholic Biblical Quarterly* 65 (2003) 22–42.
Offers a preliminary working model of biblical prophecy as
one of many divinatory techniques known from the ANE.
Provides a chart of divination methods with strengths, from
mild to strong, focused on three separate categories (things,
animals, and people). Suggests that in the Hebrew Bible the
human attempt to interpret omens without help from God
was avoided, while elsewhere human skill in interpreting
these signs was emphasized.

2.3 Identity and Roles

Because the term *prophecy* may be used in different ways, in
respect both to biblical prophecy and to the diversity of phenomena
in the ANE, a single definition is unattainable. Nevertheless, according to many scholars the fundamental notion is intermediation—an
individual reportedly receiving a supernatural revelation and being
commissioned to communicate that message to an audience (but
see Balentine [#49]). Contrary to the current popular conception,
the predictive element in prophecy in the biblical world was secondary. The primary focus was revealing the divine will for the
present. Though prophecy may be considered a form of divination,
the method of receiving the prophetic message generally entailed a
vision, a theophany, a dream, or a direct voice from heaven, instead
of finding significance in the celestial bodies or entrails of animals.
Ecstasy is sometimes associated with prophecy, but references to

God's Spirit falling on a messenger and making that person God's instrument are more common in the OT. The social role of prophets varied widely, some apparently being solitary voices, while others had positions in the cult and/or in the royal courts. Until recently, the traditional view credited the prophets with playing a major role in the creation of ethical monotheism. Much of scholarship in the twentieth century challenged that view, arguing that the notion of biblical prophecy came about later in the exilic period, as compilers reworked the tradition, and that in early periods the so-called prophets were only poets. That thinking is based, in part, on the apparent differences between the former prophets and the writing prophets. In response to the question of the cessation of prophecy in the Second Temple period, most scholars now argue that prophecy continued, though in altered forms.

46 R. R. Wilson. "Prophecy and Ecstasy: A Reexamination." *JBL* 98 (1979) 321–37. Reprinted in *Community, Identity, and Ideology: Social Science Approaches to the Hebrew Bible*, pp. 404–22. Edited by C. E. Carter and C. L. Meyers. Winona Lake, IN: Eisenbrauns, 1996.

After briefly tracing scholarship on prophetic ecstasy, W. defines ecstasy in the Hebrew prophets as possession by God, which assumes many diverse forms, although it often is manifested stereotypically within a given group. Suggests that the hithpael of *nābî'* described characteristic prophetic behavior, which changed throughout the history of Israel according to the prophet's cultural, social, and geographical location.

47 D. L. Petersen. *The Roles of Israel's Prophets*. JSOTSup 17. Sheffield: JSOT Press, 1981.

Peterson expands on Max Weber's distinction of charisma and office by using role-theory to examine the roles played by prophets in Israel and Judah. Although differences between Judah and Israel led Judah to call their intermediaries "seers," while Israel called them "prophets," the role played by each was the same. This role extends only to what P. calls the "central" prophets (e.g., Amos, Hosea, Isaiah, Micah), who recognize the supremacy of Yahweh. On the other hand, the peripheral prophets, such as Elijah and Elisha, function on behalf of a deity the society sees as peripheral.

P. stresses the variety of roles encompassed in the summary term "prophecy."

48 A. G. Auld. "Prophets Through the Looking Glass: Between Writings and Moses." *JSOT* 27 (1983) 3–23. Reprinted in *The Place Is Too Small for Us: The Israelite Prophets in Recent Scholarship*, pp. 289–307. Edited by R. P. Gordon. Sources for Biblical and Theological Study 5. Winona Lake, IN: Eisenbrauns, 1995. Reprinted in *The Prophets: A Sheffield Reader*, pp. 22–42. Edited by P. R. Davies. Biblical Seminar 42. Sheffield: Sheffield Academic Press, 1996.

Argues, based on literary layers discerned in the book of Jeremiah, that the term "prophet" was applied to intermediaries late in the process of editing, and that previously, these figures were not prophets but only poets. Thus, the notion of prophecy is anachronistically applied by later editors who added prophetic narratives to the earlier poetry in order to explain it. For responses from R. P. Carroll and H. G. M. Williamson, with a rejoinder by Auld, see the subsequent essays in *JSOT* 27 or in the *Sheffield Reader*.

49 S. E. Balentine. "The Prophet as Intercessor: A Reassessment." *JBL* 103 (1984) 161–73.

Argues that the idea of a prophet as an intercessor is not supported by the biblical evidence. Analyzing three specific terms which denote intercessory prayer, B. finds that only Jeremiah is represented as a specifically prophetic intermediary. Prophets did not have a unique privilege of calling on the Lord's name, contrary to the arguments of Johnson (#95). Also examines Jeremiah's role as a prophetic intercessor, noting the repeated divine command not to intercede for the people. Concludes that prophetic intercession may have been a northern (Israelite) phenomenon among early prophets, but that communicating the divine message received greater priority.

50 D. L. Petersen (ed.). *Prophecy in Israel: Search for an Identity.* IRT 10. Philadelphia: Fortress, 1987.

Collection of influential essays originally written from the 1920s to the 1980s on the question, "What is a prophet?" P.'s introduction surveys scholarship on Israelite prophecy. Other essays are: "The Prophets as Writers and Poets" (H. Gunkel, 1923 [#156]); "Cult and Prophecy" (S. Mowinckel, 1922); "The Prophet" (M. Weber, 1922); "The Prophet as Yahweh's Messenger" (J. F. Ross, 1962); "Assyrian Statecraft and the Prophets of Israel" (J. S. Holliday Jr., 1970); "Justice: Perspectives from the Prophetic Tradition" (J. L. Mays, 1983 [#210]); and "The Role of the Prophets and the Role of the Church" (G. M. Tucker, 1981). Gunkel's chapter has been reprinted in K. C. Hanson (ed.), *Water for a Thirsty Land: Israelite Literature and Religion* (Minneapolis: Fortress, 2001), 85–133.

51   F. E. Deist. "The Prophets: Are We Heading for a Paradigm Switch?" Pp. 1–18 in *Prophet und Prophetenbuch: Festschrift für Otto Kaiser zum 65 Geburtstag*. Edited by V. Fritz, K.-F. Pohlmann, and H.-C. Schmidt. BZAW 185. Berlin: de Gruyter, 1989. Reprinted in *The Place Is Too Small for Us: The Israelite Prophets in Recent Scholarship*, pp. 582–99. Edited by R. P. Gordon. Sources for Biblical and Theological Study 5. Winona Lake, IN: Eisenbrauns, 1995.

Offers a brief description of the dominant paradigm for research in the prophets, which is concerned with uncovering the inherent meaning of a text, and new evidence that undermines this paradigm. Suggests that a sociological and anthropological paradigm is in the process of replacing the exegetical model currently in use, which is based on an over-romantic conception of the prophets.

52   T. W. Overholt. "Prophecy in History: The Social Reality of Intermediation." *JSOT* 48 (1990) 3–29. Reprinted in *The Place Is Too Small for Us: The Israelite Prophets in Recent Scholarship*, pp. 354–76. Edited by R. P. Gordon. Sources for Biblical and Theological Study 5. Winona Lake, IN: Eisenbrauns, 1995. Reprinted in *The Prophets: A Sheffield Reader*, pp. 61–84. Edited by P. R. Davies. The Biblical Seminar 42. Sheffield: Sheffield Academic Press, 1996.

Against Auld (#48), who argues that those called prophets in the OT were not thought of as prophets until the time of the exile, O. reasons that the wide distribution of intermediation in the ANE indicates that it is likely that those described as biblical prophets actually acted as prophets. Finds support

as well in the acknowledgment of the editors who produced
the anthologies of the prophets. This enables "us to affirm
that the named individuals of the Hebrew Bible actually *were*
prophets, both in their own eyes and in the judgment of at
least some of their contemporaries" (83). For responses from
A. G. Auld and R. P. Carroll, with a rejoinder by Overholt,
see the subsequent essays in *JSOT* 48 or in the *Sheffield
Reader.*

53   Y. Muffs. "Who Will Stand in the Breach? A Study of Prophetic
Intercession." Pp. 9–48 in *Love and Joy: Law, Language and
Religion in Ancient Israel.* Jerusalem/New York: Jewish Theological Seminary of America, 1992.
Examines the nature of prophetic intercession by using the
biblical accounts of Abraham, Moses, Samuel, Jeremiah, and
Ezekiel as test cases. Taking up the problem of deferred punishment, M. argues for three stages in the Israelite conception
of punishment. The first stage sees sin as a sickness that
must be destroyed and cannot be atoned for; the second sees
repentance as generating the possibility of deferring punishment to a later generation; and the third stage sees genuine
repentance as opening the possibility for forgiveness. M. also
describes Mesopotamian parallels of prophetic intercession
and concludes with a brief treatment of the methods of controlling divine anger.

54   H. M. Barstad. "No Prophets? Recent Developments in Biblical
Prophetic Research and Ancient Near Eastern Prophecy." *JSOT*
57 (1993) 39–60. Reprinted in *The Prophets: A Sheffield Reader,*
pp. 106–26. Edited by P. R. Davies. The Biblical Seminar 42.
Sheffield: Sheffield Academic Press, 1996.
In response to the ongoing debate as to what extent the biblical prophets were prophets in their own day or became
prophets in the course of the developing literary tradition,
and to what extent history can be gleaned from the prophetic
corpus (see Auld [#48] and Overholt [#52]), B. argues that a
phenomenological approach is better than a strictly historical
one. Furthermore, it is entirely plausible that the prophetic
books preserve authentic prophetic oracles. He characterizes
his approach as "positive skepticism" in contrast to "negative skepticism."

55 D. E. Fleming. "The Etymological Origins of the Hebrew *nābî':* The One Who Invokes God." *Catholic Biblical Quarterly* 55 (1993) 217–24.

Explains the etymology of *nābî'* in the active voice as one who calls or invokes God, based on recent insights from Mari and Emar. In a letter from Mari, Tebi-gerīšu writes King Zimri-Lim that he has convened a group of Hanean *na-bi-i* to ascertain the king's well-being through their skills. In another analogy, both *na-bi-i* and *munabbiātu* appear to have been intermediaries who invoked the gods through a variety of means. In light of these parallels, F. argues that the etymology of *nābî'* must be active, i.e., a "namer" of God. This active sense may be reflected in 1 Kings 18:24, 26 and 2 Kings 5:3.

56 B. Peckham. *History and Prophecy: The Development of Late Judean Literary Traditions.* Anchor Bible Reference Library. New York: Doubleday, 1993.

Reconstructs the history of Israel and how that history was recorded and interpreted in the biblical record. On the assumption that none of the record was composed before 700 BC, the prophets had an integral role in the shaping of history. "Isaiah, Amos, and Hosea shaped the prophetic response to history. They were the models of prophetic form and became the heroes of the prophetic age" (206). "Jeremiah reconciled prophetic and historiographic traditions in a dramatic display of the nation's apostasy and repentance" (338). "Ezekiel described the chaos and tried to imagine the new creation" (472). "III Isaiah was a compendium of all prophecy and heralded the end of the prophetic tradition" (719).

57 P. S. Alexander. "'A Sixtieth Part of Prophecy': The Problem of Continuing Revelation in Judaism." Pp. 414–33 in *Words Remembered, Texts Renewed: Essays in Honor of John F. A. Sawyer.* JSOTSup 195. Sheffield: Sheffield Academic Press, 1995.

Analyzes the problem of the cessation of prophecy, noting that in the Second Temple period and in the Talmudic period, many believed that prophecy had ceased, yet prophetic revelation persisted in various ways. Concludes that "the cessation of prophecy is a historical fiction" (431) and that there was no point at which the prophetic era ended and the scribal era began. Prophetic and scribal authority existed side by side.

58   J. Blenkinsopp. *Sage, Priest, Prophet: Religious and Intellectual Leadership in Ancient Israel*. Louisville: Westminster/John Knox, 1995.

Serves as a short investigation of the development of prophecy in Israel and Judah (see #5), focusing on the various functions that have been "subsumed under the rubric of prophecy" (115). The movement from dissent to official recognition of the prophets was one expression of the "intellectual leadership" of the OT.

59   R. P. Gordon. "Where Have All the Prophets Gone? The 'Disappearing' Israelite Prophet against the Background of Ancient Near Eastern Prophecy." *Bulletin for Biblical Research* 5 (1995) 67–86.

Challenges the notion of the "disappearing prophet," arguing for self-awareness as prophets. Consideration of the terminology for prophets suggests that Amos and Hosea considered themselves prophets. The prophets understood their role to include admission to the divine council and intercession between God and his people. Compares and contrasts Israelite prophecy with prophecy in the ANE.

60   L. L. Grabbe. *Priests, Prophets, Diviners, Sages in Ancient Israel: A Socio-Historical Study of Religious Specialists in Ancient Israel*. Valley Forge, PA: Trinity International, 1995.

Offers a historical and sociological analysis of king, priest, prophet, diviner, and wisdom figure. Concludes that prophets should be identified by their function and role in society, not terminology (116–17); that no qualitative distinction can be made between OT prophets and those of Mesopotamia and other premodern cultures (117); that the uniting characteristic of prophets is in receiving and announcing messages from Yahweh (183); and that prophets mixed religious and political elements in the same message (184).

61 P. R. Davies. "The Audiences of Prophetic Scrolls: Some Suggestions." Pp. 48–62 in *Prophets and Paradigms: Essays in Honor of Gene M. Tucker.* Edited by S. B. Reid. JSOTSup 229. Sheffield: Sheffield Academic Press, 1996.
Focuses on who read the books of the prophets and for whom they were intended. Concludes "that there was not necessarily any audience at all, either in the mind of the producers of these scrolls or in the subsequent owners of them" (60). "The simple wish to preserve one's words is adequate to explain the form of many of the prophetic scrolls" (62).

62 B. D. Sommer. "Did Prophecy Cease? Evaluating a Reevaluation." *JBL* 115 (1996) 31–47.
Reacting to scholars such as Aune and Overholt, S. argues that Second Temple Judaism understood prophecy as a thing of the past. Adduces Second Temple texts that support his view, showing that even when prophets are mentioned their legitimacy comes under question. Texts that describe prophecy in the Second Temple period disclose changes from earlier prophetic forms in the Hebrew Bible.

63 J. R. Levison. "Did the Spirit Withdraw from Israel? An Evaluation of the Earliest Jewish Data." *New Testament Studies* 43 (1997) 35–57.
Challenges the prevalent view that the Holy Spirit—the spirit that inspired prophecy—permanently withdrew from Israel when Haggai, Zechariah, and Malachi left the scene. Additionally, the wide variety of activities subsumed under the rubric of "prophecy" should suggest caution in proclaiming that prophecy ceased in Second Temple Judaism.

64 D. L. Petersen. "Rethinking the Nature of Prophetic Literature." Pp. 23–40 in *Prophecy and Prophets: The Diversity of Contemporary Issues in Scholarship.* Edited by Y. Gitay. SBL Semeia Studies. Atlanta: Scholars Press, 1997.
Calls for reconceptualization of the literature of the prophets and proposes a five-fold typology for prophetic literature, based on various Hebrew words for "prophet": diviner, visionary, prophet (one informed by auditory experience), the man of God, and prophetic historians. Concludes that there is more diversity in prophetic activity than is commonly recognized.

65   J. R. Linville. "On the Nature of Rethinking Prophetic Literature: Stirring a Neglected Stew. A Response to David L.
Petersen." *Journal of the Hebrew Scriptures* 2 (1998–99). http://
www.arts.ualberta.ca/JHS/Articles/article9.pdf
Responding to a paper by Petersen (#64), L. critiques the proposed five ideal role types. In contrast to Petersen, L. identifies four paradigms for prophetic study: the theological, the
historical-critical (which sees the Hebrew Bible as a generally
reliable historical source), final-form analyses, and the con-
structionist, which sees the Hebrew Bible not as a historical
source but as a construct of later writers. Argues for a con-
structionist approach to the prophetic literature.

66   D. L. Petersen. "Defining Prophecy and Prophetic Literature."
Pp. 33–44 in *Prophecy in Its Ancient Near Eastern Context:
Mesopotamian, Biblical, and Arabian Perspectives.* Edited by
M. Nissinen. SBLSymS 13. Atlanta: SBL, 2000.
Reviews six definitions of what a prophet was: one who
experienced deity in an intense way, spoke or wrote in a distinctive way, acted in a particular social setting, possessed
distinctive personal qualities, acted as an intermediary, or
who had a distinctive message. Finds that the prophet as
intermediary is the only definition comprehensive enough
to encompass prophecy in the ANE. Concludes that there
were different types of mediation, leading to different types
of literature.

67   W. Brueggemann. *The Prophetic Imagination.* Philadelphia:
Fortress, 1978. Second edition: Minneapolis: Fortress, 2001.
Classic collection of essays, each revised and updated from
original publication (now with a new preface, underscoring
changes in B.'s perspective since the first edition). Argues that
the primary prophetic task of Moses, of all the prophets, and
of Jesus (and hence, of modern prophets, too) is "to nurture,
nourish and evoke a consciousness and perception alternative to the consciousness and perception of the dominant
culture around us" (3).

68   J. C. de Moor (ed.). *The Elusive Prophet: The Prophet as a
Historical Person, Literary Character and Anonymous Artist.*
Old Testament Studies 45. Leiden: Brill, 2001.

Papers from a joint meeting of the Society for Old Testament Study and Oudtestamentisch Werkgezelschap in Nederland and België (2000). The meeting was entitled "Person or Personage? The Prophet as a Historical Person and/or a Literary Character." Essays include: "From King to Prophet in Samuel and Kings" (A. G. Auld); "Prophets in the Books of Chronicles" (P. C. Beentjes); "Personifications and Prophetic Voices of Zion in Isaiah and Beyond" (U. Berges); "A Prophet in Desperation? The Confessions of Jeremiah" (C. Bultmann); "Threading as a Stylistic Feature of Amos" (T. A. Collins); "Israelite Prophecy: Characteristics of the First Protest Movement" (T. L. Fenton); "The Portrayal of Moses as Deuteronomic Archetypal Prophet in Exodus and Its Revisal" (W. Johnstone); "Blowing the Same Shofar: An Intertextual Comparison of Representations of the Prophetic Role in Jeremiah and Ezekiel" (H. Leene); and "Ezekiel as Priest in Exile" (A. Mein).

2.4 Prophetic Calls, Inspiration, and Authority

Several highly developed call narratives (Isa. 6; Jer. 1; and Ezek. 1–3) underscore the importance of divine commissioning, which lends the prophet legitimacy despite the unpopularity of his social critiques. Weber (#69) championed the idea of prophetic charisma opposing the normal societal authority structures, but Hutton (#74) has questioned this claim. Resistance to the divine call is a standard element of call narratives as Glazov (#77) demonstrates. In addition to the prophetic call, the power of the message itself also constituted a source of the prophet's power (Hutton [#74] and Leavitt [#76]).

69 M. Weber. "The Prophet." Pp. 46–59 in *The Sociology of Religion*. Boston: Beacon Press, 1963. Reprinted in *Prophecy in Israel: Search for an Identity*, pp. 99–111. Edited by D. L. Petersen. IRT 10. Philadelphia: Fortress, 1987.

Classic definition of a prophet as one who possesses charisma, by which the prophet gains authority apart from normal authority structures. For example, Elisha's charisma was evident in his group of followers. On the other hand, not all prophets were necessarily charismatic revolutionaries.

70   K. Baltzer. "Considerations regarding the Office and Call-
     ing of the Prophet." *Harvard Theological Review* 61 (1968)
     567–81.
     Key discussion of the call narratives in the prophets for what
     they reveal about the distinctiveness of Israel's prophets vis-à-
     vis prophetic phenomena in the ANE. Finds that the call narra-
     tives functioned as installations of the prophets and compares
     them with viziers in the ANE. Concludes that the prophetic
     office is a result of a long historical development.

71   S. H. Blank. "'Of a truth the Lord hath sent me': An Inquiry into
     the Source of the Prophet's Authority." Pp. 1–19 in *Interpreting
     the Prophetic Tradition: The Goldenson Lectures, 1955–1966.*
     Edited by H. M. Orlinsky. Library of Biblical Studies. Cincin-
     nati: Hebrew Union College Press/New York: KTAV, 1969.
     Examines the book of Jeremiah for the sources of that proph-
     et's authority. Finds six ways that Jeremiah's authority is
     confirmed: fulfilled prophecy, the certainty of his experience
     that he speaks for God, the unpopularity of his message, the
     reluctance of the prophet to proclaim a message that is at odds
     with himself, its orthodox character, and the consonance of
     his message with the character of God.

72   A. Cooper. "Imaging Prophecy." Pp. 26–44 in *Poetry and Proph-
     ecy: The Beginnings of a Literary Tradition.* Edited by J. L.
     Kugel. Ithaca, NY: Cornell University Press, 1990.
     Addresses the question of divine inspiration in the prophets.
     Is it literally true? Is it a metaphor? Is it a delusion? What
     does it mean? "My inclination is to suspend explanation
     and to discard facile distinctions—between true and false
     prophets, between prophecy and poetry, between imagination
     and reality—rather than to seek labels that foster an illusion
     of understanding" (44).

73   A. D. H. Mayes. "Prophecy and Society in Israel." Pp. 25–42 in
     *Of Prophets' Visions and the Wisdom of the Sages: Essays in
     Honour of R. Norman Whybray on His Seventieth Birthday.*
     Edited by H. A. McKay and D. J. A. Clines. JSOTSup 162.
     Sheffield: Sheffield Academic Press, 1993.
     Considers the notion of a supernatural call to a prophetic min-
     istry and the notion of supernatural revelation to be idealistic.

Though the terms *charisma* and *ecstasy* are not without problems, M. considers them to reflect more accurately the phenomenon of prophecy. Also reviews the relationship of prophecy to Israel's cult.

74 R. R. Hutton. *Charisma and Authority in Israelite Society.* Minneapolis: Fortress, 1994.
Questions the bifurcation of charisma and institution by reviewing six types of leaders in ancient Israel (judges, kings, prophets, priests, sages, and Mosaic authority) and argues that charisma and institution are involved in each type. Includes a review of the history of scholarship from Weber to 1994 (chap. 1).

75 R. E. Clements. "Max Weber, Charisma and Biblical Prophecy." Pp. 89–108 in *Prophecy and Prophets: The Diversity of Contemporary Issues in Scholarship.* Edited by Y. Gitay. SBL Semeia Studies. Atlanta: Scholars Press, 1997.
Reflects on the notion of charisma and its relationship to the success of the prophets. Argues that the prophets whose writings were preserved had special charisma. Explores the possibility that compilers made significant changes and added considerable content to the prophetic material.

76 J. Leavitt. "Poetics, Prophetics, Inspiration." Pp. 1–60 in *Poetry and Prophecy: The Anthropology of Inspiration.* Edited by J. Leavitt. Ann Arbor: University of Michigan Press, 1997.
Provides a general introduction to the relationship between poetry and prophecy, both conceived broadly, inquiring into their overlapping qualities and the history of their interaction in ancient and modern times. Notes trends that are erasing boundaries between the two fields. Includes a substantial bibliography relevant to the subject.

77 G. Y. Glazov. *The Bridling of the Tongue and the Opening of the Mouth in Biblical Prophecy.* JSOTSup 311. Sheffield: Sheffield Academic Press, 2001.
Examines the reluctance to speak as expressed in the call narratives of Moses, Isaiah, Jeremiah, and Ezekiel against mouth-opening motifs in the ANE. Focuses on the reasons for the reluctance to speak and the keys to the prophet speaking.

Finds that Jeremiah "became a silent suffering servant" (359) as did Ezekiel, because they bore the grief and sorrow of the people. The suffering servant motif of the call narratives comes to fruition in the suffering servant of Isa. 53:7.

2.5 False Prophecy

Though Deut. 13:1–5 established criteria for identifying false prophecy, the issue was more complex than the simple fulfillment of the prophetic word. True prophets sometimes proclaimed things that did not come true for several reasons. The prediction could be subsequently reversed; the fulfillment could be delayed so that neither the prophet nor the immediate hearers saw the event(s) come to pass in their lifetime; or the hearers could misunderstand what the prophet intended. Fundamentally, the populace decided between true and false prophets based on acknowledgment of the deity and the prophet who faithfully represented the deity. But some audiences were not always correct in their assessment. The challenge of distinguishing between true and false prophecy was unavoidable, especially in the event of diametrically opposed prophetic claims (e.g., Hananiah and Jeremiah). See also #25 and #26.

78   J. L. Crenshaw. *Prophetic Conflict: Its Effect upon Israelite Religion.* BZAW 124. Berlin: de Gruyter, 1971.
Seeks to understand prophecy in light of its conflict with false prophecy, concluding that tension in prophecy is inherent because of the mystery of divine revelation and the challenge of human communication, and because of the tension between divine sovereignty and human limitations. No means of self-validation was adequate to authenticate true prophecy, resulting in polarization both among prophets and between audiences and prophets.

79   R. P. Carroll. *When Prophecy Failed: Cognitive Dissonance in the Prophetic Traditions of the Old Testament.* New York: Seabury, 1979.
Addresses the issue of fulfilled and nonfulfilled prediction, applying L. Festinger's cognitive dissonance theory, where elements that produce ambiguity or conflict are minimized by various mechanisms. Illustrates the applicability of cognitive

dissonance through an exegesis of selected texts (in Isaiah, Haggai, and Zechariah) relative to how readers understood apparently disconfirmed texts. Identifies factors that modified the effect of cognitive dissonance on prophecy: divine deception, prophetic conflict, the demonic, and the rise of apocalyptic.

80   R. R. Wilson. "Interpreting Israel's Religion: An Anthropological Perspective on the Problem of False Prophecy." Pp. 67–80 in *Sociological Approaches to the Old Testament.* Philadelphia: Fortress, 1984. Reprinted in *The Place Is Too Small for Us: The Israelite Prophets in Recent Scholarship*, pp. 332–44. Edited by R. P. Gordon. Sources for Biblical and Theological Study 5. Winona Lake, IN: Eisenbrauns, 1995.
Briefly reviews past scholarship on false prophecy, after which W. argues that prophecy can be a method by which individuals outside the center of power in a society can attempt to change society in their favor. Accusations of witchcraft can silence those at the margins of society or conversely can be used effectively against those at the center. Finds that sociological considerations, not theological ones, were decisive for determining who was deemed a false prophet, and tests this hypothesis using the story of Jeremiah and Hananiah.

81   R. J. Coggins. "Prophecy—True and False." Pp. 80–94 in *Of Prophets' Visions and the Wisdom of the Sages: Essays in Honour of R. Norman Whybray on His Seventieth Birthday.* Edited by H. A. McKay and D. J. A. Clines. JSOTSup 162. Sheffield: Sheffield Academic Press, 1993.
Reviews the data for the vilification of certain prophets in light of the role of prophets as presented in the Deuteronomistic literature. Finds that charges of false prophecy were often based on ideological rivalry, "particularly the recognition of the need within the religious community to legitimate certain voices and to exclude others—factors that make objective assessment extremely elusive" (93).

82   J. E. Brenneman. *Canons in Conflict: Negotiating Texts in True and False Prophecy.* Oxford: Oxford University Press, 1997.
Synthesizes canonical criticism and canon formation. "The foil for such a study falls on questions raised by conflicting biblical

passages, in this case intentionally on the warring 'plowshare' oracles of Isa. 2:2–4 (Mic. 4:1–4) against Joel 3:9–12 (MT 4:9–12). Each prophet imagines a very different end to history. Can Joel and Isaiah both be true prophets . . . ?" (viii). "The question of who a true prophet was in contradistinction to a false one was shown to be a function of the interpretive community of a particular prophet in a particular setting" (137).

83   D. Epp-Tiessen. "The Lord Has Truly Sent the Prophet." Pp. 175–85 in *Reclaiming the Old Testament: Essays in Honour of Waldemar Janzen*. Edited by G. Zerbe. Winnipeg: CMBC, 2001.

Against the thesis that uncertainty about true and false prophets led to the demise of the prophetic movement in ancient Israel, E.-T. argues that the Israelite community placed high value on the words of some prophets. Though no foolproof criteria could distinguish between true and false prophecy (even as communities of faith today may struggle to determine who truly speaks for God), E.-T. offers four criteria for identifying true prophets.

2.6 Prophecy, Torah, and the Deuteronomic School

A consideration of the relationship of the prophets to the Pentateuch entails several issues. According to Deut. 34:10, Moses was the preeminent prophet. Was that intended to define the prophetic paradigm, or did the function of prophets change over time? To what extent did the prophets borrow from the Pentateuch and carry on the legal traditions? Were the prophets largely responsible for the Israelites' ethical monotheism or did they inherit it? Along these lines, the relationship of the writing prophets to the Deuteronomistic Historian (DH) raises an important issue: though focusing on the time period of the writing prophets, DH only mentions Isaiah and Jonah, and the latter only in passing. Instead, DH gives considerable coverage to prophets otherwise unattested in the OT (e.g., Elijah, Elisha, Nathan, Ahijah, Huldah).

84   J. Blenkinsopp. *Prophecy and Canon: A Contribution to the Study of Jewish Origins*. Notre Dame, IN: University of Notre Dame Press, 1977.

Seeks to work out the relationship between Torah and prophecy. Finds that the prophetic corpus relates back to the paradigmatic prophet Moses and looks forward to the coming future prophet, as evidenced by the end of the Pentateuch (Deut. 34:10) and the end of the prophets (Mal. 3:22–24). In effect, prophecy was commentary on Torah, and the prophets mediated the covenant between Yahweh and the chosen people.

85 A. Hurvitz. *A Linguistic Study of the Relationship between the Priestly Source and the Book of Ezekiel: A New Approach to an Old Problem.* Cahiers de la Revue Biblique 20. Paris: Gabalda, 1982.

Takes up the question of the relationship of the Priestly source (P) to Ezekiel by arguing that P is earlier than Ezekiel and as a consequence must be seen to be compiled during the pre-exilic period (although he admits that the period up to 550 BC is possible for its composition). Changes in grammatical forms and vocabulary from P to Ezekiel demonstrate that "in their extant versions it is P, and not Ez., which comes first in a chronological sequence" (151).

86 R. F. Person. *Second Zechariah and the Deuteronomic School.* JSOTSup 167. Sheffield: JSOT Press, 1993.

Suggests that the Deuteronomic school was responsible for the redactional addition of Zech. 9–14 to chaps. 1–8, based on the verbal allusions in chaps. 9–14, which suggest consultation of written documents, as well as the prosaic nature of the chapters. Arguing that the Deuteronomic school continued into the postexilic period, P. finds three kinds of evidence for attributing Zech. 9–14 to the Deuteronomic school: (1) it contains Deuteronomic phraseology; (2) Zech. 9–14 was strongly influenced by passages in the DH and Jeremiah; and (3) Zech. 9–14 shows strong influence of Deuteronomic influence in diction and imagery. Chapter 7 explores a possible social setting for the Deuteronomic movement in the postexilic period.

87 H. M. Barstad. "The Understanding of Israel's Prophets in Deuteronomy." *SJOT* 8 (1994) 236–51.

Concludes that Deuteronomy holds a negative conception of prophecy and that it advances itself as the culmination of revelation to the prophet Moses. Illustrates this negative conception by consideration of three passages. Deuteronomy 13 is more concerned with idolatry than prophecy. Deuteronomy 18:15–19 refers to Joshua, not to a succession of Mosaic prophets. Deuteronomy 18:9–14, 15–19, and 20–22 are placed in the same context as other forbidden activity, such as the cult of Molech, thus casting prophecy in an unflattering light.

88   E. Ben Zvi. "A Deuteronomistic Redaction in/among 'The Twelve'?: A Contribution from the Standpoint of the Books of Micah, Zephaniah and Obadiah." *Society of Biblical Literature Seminar Papers* (1997) 433–59.
     Critically examines five bases for the proposed Deuteronomic redaction of the Twelve: (1) the presence of a corpus of Deuteronomistic writings against which redaction can be judged; (2) distinct language used by the group; (3) use of "central" Deuteronomic theology; (4) appearance of the same words and expressions in the Deuteronomistic corpus and a particular book; and (5) redaction-critical hypotheses of the development of the Twelve. Finds neither shared language, affinity, nor theology between the Twelve and the Deuteronomistic corpus.

89   L. S. Schearing and S. L. McKenzie (eds.). *Those Elusive Deuteronomists: The Phenomenon of Pan-Deuteronomism.* JSOTSup 268. Sheffield: Sheffield Academic Press, 1999.
     A collection of essays considering to what extent there was a Deuteronomistic movement, who the Deuteronomist was, and the Deuteronomist's role in various portions of the canon. Includes the following articles related to the prophets: "The Deuteronomists and the Former Prophets, or What makes the Former Prophets Deuteronomistic?" (A. G. Auld); "The Deuteronomists and the Latter Prophets" (R. A. Kugler); "The Deuteronomists and the Writings" (J. L. Crenshaw); "How Did Jeremiah Become a Convert to Deuteronomistic Ideology?" (T. C. Römer); "Pan-Deuteronomism and the Book of Ezekiel" (C. L. Patton); "Micah's Deuteronomistic Redaction and the Deuteronomists' Identity" (S. L. Cook); "A Deuteronomistic Redaction in/among 'The Twelve'?: A Contribution from the Standpoint of the Books of Micah, Zephaniah and Obadiah" (E. Ben Zvi).

90   J. C. de Moor and H. F. Van Rooy (eds.). *Past, Present, Future: The Deuteronomistic History and the Prophets.* Old Testament Studies 44. Leiden: Brill, 2000.

Papers from a joint meeting of the South African and Dutch Old Testament Societies (1999). The theme of the meeting was the Deuteronomistic reshaping of Israel's history. Relevant essays include: "Who Were the Servants? A Comparative Inquiry in the Book of Isaiah and the Psalms" (U. Berges); "The End of the End, Or, What Is the Deuteronomist (Still) Doing in Daniel?" (H. J. M. van Deventer); "Ezekiel and Jeremiah: Promises of Inner Renewal in Diachronic Perspective" (H. Leene); "A Genre Shift in Biblical Prophecy and the Translator: Person Shift in Hosea" (L. J. de Regt); "Data Relevant to the Dating of the Prophecy of Obadiah" (J. Renkema); "No Need for a Prophet like Jeremiah: The Absence of the Prophet in Kings" (M. D. Terblanche).

91   T. Römer. "Is There a Deuteronomistic Redaction in the Book of Jeremiah?" Pp. 399–421 in *Israel Constructs Its History: Deuteronomistic Historiography in Recent Research.* Edited by A. de Pury, T. Römer, and J.-D. Macchi. JSOTSup 306. Sheffield: Sheffield Academic Press, 2000. Original publication: pp. 419–41 in *Israël construit son historie: L'historiographie deutéronomiste à la lumière des recherches récentes.* Le Monde de la Bible 34. Geneva: Labor et Fides, 1996.

After reviewing the history of scholarship on the Deuteronomistic role in the composition of Jeremiah, R. posits that two inquiries are necessary. He finds, regarding the compositional intentions of an eventual Deuteronomic redaction, that it was the denouncement of popular and blind confidence in the temple. Regarding the ideological and theological differences between Jeremiah and DH, he finds that "the redactors of DH and the 'historical' Jeremiah (even certain traditions circulating in regard to him) are in conflict about the significance of the exile" (418).

92   R. L. Kohn. *A New Heart and a New Soul: Ezekiel, the Exile and the Torah.* JSOTSup 358. London: Sheffield Academic Press, 2002.

Examines vocabulary and phrases shared between Ezekiel and the Priestly source (divided into ten categories), finding that

Ezekiel is familiar with P and adopts it for his own purposes, sometimes making substantive changes. Also investigates Ezekiel's affinities with Deuteronomy and DH, noting that at times Ezekiel prefers D's diction and theology to P's. Concludes that Ezekiel did not know the Torah in its final form, but he strongly anticipated it.

93 J. E. Harvey. *Retelling the Torah: The Deuteronomistic Historian's Use of Tetrateuchal Narratives*. JSOTSup 403. London: T & T Clark, 2004.
Contends that at least by the seventh century BC the DH shaped its stories based on the stories of the Tetrateuch (Gen.–Num.), which included many P narratives, although it did not yet exist in its final form. Seeks to provide an alternative to writing credulous history on the one hand and denying the possibility of any historical knowledge of ancient Israel on the other.

2.7 Prophecy, Cult, and Psalms

The relationship of prophecy to the cult and to the Psalms is framed by several questions. Did priests and prophets serve side by side in services of worship? Did priests become prophets and vice versa? Did the psalmists borrow prophetic utterances and speak as prophets? Evidence for cultic prophets is found in the Psalms though they remain anonymous. Likewise, 1 and 2 Chron. portray cultic personnel in prophetic terms. Oracles of cultic prophets may have been included in the writing prophets. At least one prophet was also a priest (Ezekiel) and Jeremiah was from a priestly family. For additional consideration of the relationship of the cult to the prophets, see Cook and Patton (#317).

94 S. Mowinckel. "Cult and Prophecy." Translated by J. L. Schaaf. Pp. 74–98 in *Prophecy in Israel: Search for an Identity*. Edited by D. L. Petersen. IRT 10. Philadelphia: Fortress, 1987. Original publication: pp. 4–29 in *Psalmenstudien III: Kultprophetie und prophetische Psalmen*. Kristiana: Jacob Cybwad, 1922.
Beginning with prophetic elements in the Psalter, Mowinckel explores the relationship between prophecy and sacrament and between seer and priest. Concludes that the cult had

prophets, which may have been the same individuals as the liturgists, making the prophets cultic officials. Locates the social setting of prophecy in the cult.

95 A. R. Johnson. *The Cultic Prophet and Israel's Psalmody.* Cardiff: University of Wales Press, 1979.
Suggests that professional prophets were closely connected to the temple liturgy, as evidenced by the Psalms, which reveal prophetic authorship and/or the prophets' liturgical functions. The first part of the work treats the cultic prophet's role in "regular worship," while the second and third parts treat the cultic prophet's intermediation in times of national and individual crisis. See also his *The Cultic Prophet in Ancient Israel.* Cardiff: University of Wales Press, 1962.

96 J. H. Eaton. *Vision in Worship: The Relation of Prophecy and Liturgy in the Old Testament.* London: SPCK, 1981.
Seeks "to examine the contribution of prophetic ministries to the great occasions of Israelite worship" by examining four elements of worship relevant to prophecy: theophany, God's speeches to his people, his dialogues and disputes with his people, and his oracles of monarchic installation or renewal (1). Concludes that prophecy seems to develop from within liturgical worship and that cult prophets helped to apply liturgical celebration to contemporary events.

97 J. M. O'Brien. *Priest and Levite in Malachi.* SBLDS 121. Atlanta: Scholars Press, 1990.
Asks: "If one accepts the Documentary Hypothesis, what does this assumption entail for reading the Book of Malachi?" (xi). An investigation of the terms *priest* and *Levite* in Malachi finds them to be synonymous and shows no hint of rivalry between priestly groups. Identifies the genre of Malachi as a prophetic lawsuit (*rîb*), helping in the interpretation of various passages and showing Malachi's indebtedness to various prophetic and nonprophetic traditions, including P and the DH. Dates Malachi from 605 to the late sixth century BC.

98 R. Tournay. *Seeing and Hearing God with the Psalms: The Prophetic Liturgy of the Second Temple in Jerusalem.* JSOTSup

118. Translated by J. Edward Crowley. Sheffield: JSOT Press, 1991. Original title: *Voir et entendre Dieu avec les Psaumes ou la liturgie prophétique du second temple à Jérusalem.* Cahiers de la Revue Biblique 24. Paris: J. Gabalda, 1988.

Proposes that the Levitical singers of the second temple constitute the first certain examples of cultic prophets who were charged with performing the oracular and theophanic portions of the Psalter. Dates most psalms to the postexilic period, even royal psalms whose composition T. interprets as reflecting a messianic anticipation. God's theophanies reveal his name and his glory, while the oracles in the psalms constitute dialogue between the Deity and his suppliant.

99   H. Gunkel. *Introduction to Psalms: The Genres of the Religious Lyric of Israel*, pp. 251–92. Completed by J. Begrich. Translated by J. D. Nogalski. Macon, GA: Mercer University Press, 1998. Original title: *Einleitung in die Psalmen: die Gattungen der religiösen Lyrik Israels.* Fourth edition. Handkommentar zum Alten Testament. Göttingen: Vandenhoeck & Ruprecht, 1985.

Classic and influential statement of prophetic influence on the Psalter, considering the theology and form of eschatology in the Psalms and its relation to the prophetic books. In addition to treating the word of rebuke, the prophetic judgment speech and other prophetic forms in the Psalms, G. is concerned with the situation of the "prophetic psalms," their historical setting and the intellectual influence of the prophets on the Psalter.

100   L. L. Grabbe and A. O. Bellis (eds.). *The Priests in the Prophets: The Portrayal of Priests, Prophets, and Other Religious Specialists in the Latter Prophets.* JSOTSup 408. Sheffield: Sheffield Academic Press, 2004.

Eleven essays reflecting the ongoing discussion about the relationship of prophet and priest: "Observations on Prophetic Characters, Prophetic Texts, Priests of Old, Persian Period Priests and Literati" (E. Ben Zvi); "The Prophetic Critique of Ritual in Old Testament Theology" (B. D. Bibb); "Prophets and Temple Personnel in the Mari Archives" (D. E. Fleming); "The Northern Voyage of Psammeticus II and Its Implications for Ezekiel 44.7–9" (J. Galambush); "A Priest

Is without Honor in His Own Prophet: Priests and Other
Religious Specialists in the Latter Prophets" (L. L. Grabbe);
"The Day of Yahweh and the Mourning of the Priests in
Joel" (J. R. Linville); "Priestly Purity and Prophetic Lunacy:
Hosea 1.2–3 and 9.7" (R. D. Nelson); "What Was the Image
of Jealousy in Ezekiel 8?" (M. S. Odell); "Layers of Meaning:
Priesthood in Jeremiah MT" (C. Patton); "The Priests in the
Book of Malachi and Their Opponents" (J. Schaper); "The
Prophet versus Priest Antagonism Hypothesis: Its History
and Origin" (Z. Zevit).

101 J. W. Hilber. *Cultic Prophecy in the Psalms*. BZAW 352. Berlin:
de Gruyter, 2005.
Examines Assyrian prophetic sources for insights into understanding cultic prophecy and the psalms. Finds that ANE
prophecies most often concern the king, suggesting that royal
psalms are the closest counterparts to Assyrian prophecy.
Concludes that the evidence of first person divine speech,
framing devices, and parallels with Assyrian prophecies con-
firm the authentic prophetic character of certain psalms.

2.8 Prophecy, Kings, and Monarchy

According to the influential theory of F. M. Cross, prophecy is
intimately connected with kingship. Prophecy rose simultaneously
with kingship and declined with the loss of the royal house. The
relationship of the prophets and the monarchy is particularly evident in the former prophets. Prophets were called on by kings to
ascertain the divine will and to interpret the meaning of events.
Some prophets stood outside the power structure and called for
revolutionary change, while others remained loyal to the monarch
and sought to effect gradual change. Some prophets sought to aid
the king by delivering messages from God and by holding him ac-
countable to God's will. Others worked at odds with the king, even
to the point of seeking his overthrow.

102 S. A. Irvine. *Isaiah, Ahaz and the Syro-Ephraimite Crisis*.
SBLDS 123. Atlanta: Scholars Press, 1990.
Examines all of the biblical and nonbiblical evidence for the
Syro-Ephraimite war and Isaiah's message during it. Argues

that Ahaz "adhered to a neutralist course throughout the episode, despite the inclination of many Judeans to join Syria and Israel in revolt against Assyria," that "nearly all of Isaiah 7–12 makes sense against the background of the Syro-Ephraimite crisis," and that "Isaiah supported Ahaz throughout the war, applauding and encouraging the king in his isolationist stand" (xv–xvi).

103 S. A. Irvine. "Isaiah's *She'ar-Yashub* and the Davidic House." *Biblische Zeitschrift* 37 (1993) 78–88.
Interacting with previous approaches to interpreting the name She'ar-Yashub based on the narrative in Isa. 7:1–9, I. suggests that the name was meant hopefully, indicating the certain survival of a remnant, which he identifies as the Davidic line of kings.

104 A. Lemaire (ed.). *Prophètes et Rois: Bible et Proche-Orient.* Paris: Cerf, 2001.
Collects eleven essays discussing the relationship between kings and prophets in the ANE. Essays include "Prophètes et rois dans le Proche-Orient amorrite" (D. Charpin); "Les Prophéties à l'époque néo-assyrienne" (P. Villard); "Prophètes et rois dans les inscriptions ouest-sémitiques (IXe-VIe siècle a. J.-C.)" (A. Lemaire); "Rois et prophètes dans le cycle d'Élie" (M. Masson); "Achab, l'exil d'Élie et les Arabes" (A. Lemaire); "Amos et Osée face aux rois d'Israël" (I. Jaruzelska); "Ésaïe, Jérémie, et la politique des rois de Juda" (H. Rouillard-Bonraisin); "Signes et oracles messianiques dans le Proto-Ésaïe" (M. Gorea-Autexier); "Le prophète critique la monarchie: le terme *nāśī'* chez Ézéchiel" (D. Bodi); "Zacharie et les autorités de son temps" (A. Sérandour); "Épilogue: La fin des prophètes?" (A. Lemaire).

105 M. Roncace. *Jeremiah, Zedekiah, and the Fall of Jerusalem.* JSOTSup 423. New York: T & T Clark, 2005.
Supplies a narratological and intertextual study of Jer. 37:1–40:6, beginning with a consideration of narratology and intertextuality and followed by a detailed examination of the ten episodes of the chosen text. Argues that Jeremiah resists simplistic reading strategies. Provides a synchronic interpretation of the text as a model for future studies of

prophetic narrative without seeking to deny the helpfulness of diachronic approaches.

2.9 Prophecy and Wisdom

Scholars have long noted the influence of different kinds of wisdom on prophets and prophetic literature, especially Amos (Terrien [#106]), Isaiah (Williamson [#111]), and Jeremiah (Baumann [#112]). This influence is evident in several areas, particularly the use of common wisdom forms. In view of the wisdom influence, Crenshaw (#107) has called for a more self-conscious methodology. Van Leeuwen (#108) has found that the wise men, especially in the royal court, often stood opposed to the prophetic message. On the other hand, in the redaction of some prophetic books, scribal wisdom influence is visible (Van Leeuwen [#109]), demonstrating the complex relationship between the two types of revelation.

106   S. Terrien. "Amos and Wisdom." Pp. 108–15 in *Israel's Prophetic Tradition: Essays in Honor of James Muilenburg*. Edited by B. W. Anderson and W. Harrelson. New York: Harper, 1962.
Finds considerable influence of wisdom traditions on Amos. In that his words and expressions reflect the language and speech habits of the sapiential circles, it is likely that the prophet was inspired by wisdom.

107   J. L. Crenshaw. "The Influence of the Wise upon Amos." *ZAW* 79 (1967) 42–52.
Including Terrien (#106) who detected wisdom influence on Amos, C. rejects previous studies as inadequate, citing improper methodology. Affirms *Mahnreden* and numerical sayings as providing evidence of indirect wisdom influence on Amos, and further notes the wisdom influence on Amos's doxologies, which he acknowledges are secondary. Holds that cultic language had a greater influence on Amos than wisdom language.

108   R. C. Van Leeuwen. "The Sage in the Prophetic Literature." Pp. 295–306 in *The Sage in Israel and the Ancient Near East*. Edited by J. G. Gammie and L. G. Perdue. Winona Lake, IN: Eisenbrauns, 1990.

Notes the influence of wisdom sages or scribes in redacting the Hebrew Bible, but seeks a more careful definition of
wisdom in order to observe its influence more closely. Finds
that the wise men in the prophetic books are almost always
the opponents of the prophets since they forget the limits of
human wisdom.

109 R. C. Van Leeuwen. "Scribal Wisdom and Theodicy in the
Book of the Twelve." Pp. 31–49 in *In Search of Wisdom: Essays in Memory of John G. Gammie*. Edited by L. G. Perdue
et al. Louisville: Westminster/John Knox, 1993.
Focuses on the "redactional logic that governs the scribal
employment of Exod. 34:6–7 to create a comprehensive prophetic theodicy" (48). Concludes that the arrangement and
editing of the first six books of the Twelve reveal a wisdom
theodicy, moving from judgment to salvation. "My analysis
assumes that the end-redaction of the *Tanakh* as a whole
was the work of scribal sages who were forerunners of Ben
Sira" (49).

110 J. Day, R. P. Gordon, and H. G. M. Williamson (eds.). *Wisdom in
Ancient Israel: Essays in Honour of J. A. Emerton*. Cambridge:
Cambridge University Press, 1995.
Summarizes the current status of scholarship on wisdom in
the OT and includes four essays on prophecy: "Amos and the
Wisdom Tradition" (J. A. Soggin); "Hosea and the Wisdom
Tradition: Dependence and Independence" (A. A. MacIntosh);
and "Jeremiah and the Wise" (W. McKane).

111 H. G. M. Williamson. "Isaiah and the Wise." Pp. 133–41 in
Wisdom in Ancient Israel: Essays in Honour of J. A. Emerton.
Edited by J. Day et al. Cambridge: Cambridge University Press,
1995.
After a brief summary of previous research, W. focuses on de-
tecting wisdom influences on Isaiah of Jerusalem, noting that
recent research has detected the influence of clan wisdom, a
broader category than court wisdom. Follows D. F. Morgan in
suggesting two areas for further research: the epistemology
of Isaiah and Israel, and Isaiah's relationship to the king's
political advisors.

112 G. Baumann. "Jeremia, die Weisen und die Weisheit: Eine
Untersuchung von Jer 9,22f." *ZAW* 114 (2002) 59–79.
Explores the connections between Jeremiah and wisdom literature, especially Proverbs, arguing that wisdom sayings are
not later additions to Jeremiah but are integral to the book.
In Jer. 8–10, wisdom is viewed as a divine attribute and not
a human skill, with the lone exception of 9:16, attributable
to the polemic of a later hand.

2.10 Former Prophecy

The extensive focus on prophecy in the former prophets (Josh.,
Judg., 1–2 Sam., and 1–2 Kings)—recording the exploits of well-known
prophets such as Elijah and Elisha and lesser-known prophets and
prophetesses such as Ahijah and Huldah—has led to the suggestion
that the authors themselves may have been prophets. However, most
scholars conclude that there were probably priestly and scribal influences as well. A comparison of the phenomenon of former prophecy
with the literature preserved by the classical prophets has led scholars
to puzzle over the differences. Scholars have detected two or three
redactional layers of the Deuteronomist tradition. Questions remain
about how accurately the prophetic books attest to the function of
Israelite prophets. The influence of Deuteronomy on the former
prophets is accepted by most scholars, with the result that the former
prophets are often referred to as the Deuteronomistic History.

113 W. F. Albright. "Samuel and the Beginnings of the Prophetic
Movement." Pp. 151–76 in *Interpreting the Prophetic Tradition: The Goldenson Lectures, 1955–1966.* Edited by Harry M.
Orlinsky. Library of Biblical Studies. Cincinnati: Hebrew
Union College Press/New York: KTAV, 1969.
Classic study arguing that the beginnings of ecstatic prophecy in Israel had "an organic connection" with Samuel. A.
contends that Samuel was "the first great religious reformer
after Moses" (166) who attempted to undermine the role of
the temple in preference for local sanctuaries and ecstatic
prophets.

114 A. Rofé. *The Prophetical Stories: The Narratives about the
Prophets in the Hebrew Bible: Their Literary Types and History.*

Publications of the Perry Foundation for Biblical Research in the Hebrew University of Jerusalem. Translated with additions by D. Levy in 1982. Jerusalem: Magnes, 1988. Original title: *Sipure ha nevi'im: ha-siporet ha-nevu'it ba-Mikra-sugyah ye-toldoteha*. Jerusalem: Magnes, 1982.
Examines narratives describing the public activities of the prophets as recorded in the books of 1 and 2 Kings and Jer. Dates the narratives based on linguistic evidence. Classifies twelve distinct genres of prophetic narratives. Seeks to understand the message of the stories in light of historical background.

115 M. Noth. *The Deuteronomistic History*. Second edition. JSOT-Sup 15. Sheffield: Sheffield Academic Press, 1991. Original publication: pp. 1–110 in *Überlieferungsgeschichtliche Studien: die sammelnden und bearbeitenden Geschichtswerke im Alten Testament*. Second edition. Tübingen: M. Niemeyer, 1957.
Foundational and critical study of the former prophets (Deut.–2 Kings) arguing that the whole was the work of a single author who drew together traditional materials and molded them together with his own commentary to make sense of the ever-worsening decline of Israelite and Judahite history. Argues that the beginning of the work was in the prologue to Deuteronomy, not Joshua, that a coherent chronological system existed for the whole, and that the author worked independently of cultic or other official concerns.

116 R. B. Coote. *Elijah and Elisha in Socioliterary Perspective*. Atlanta: Scholars Press, 1992. Reprinted Philadelphia: Fortress, 1995.
Collection of four essays that seek to "address the social nature of Elijah and Elisha and the social nature of the biblical narratives about them" (ix). Includes: "The Pre-Deuteronomistic Elijah Cycle" (J. A. Todd); "The Local Hero in Palestine in Comparative Perspective" (S. D. Hill); "The Elijah/Elisha Stories: A Socio-cultural Analysis of Prophets and People in Ninth-Century BCE Israel" (T. H. Rentería); "The Prophetic Alternative: Elisha and the Israelite Monarchy" (W. J. Bergen).

117 T. W. Overholt. "Elijah and Elisha in the Context of Israelite Religion." Pp. 94–111 in *Prophets and Paradigms: Essays in*

Honor of Gene M. Tucker. Edited by S. B. Reid. JSOTSup 229. Sheffield: Sheffield Academic Press, 1996.

Reconstructs the social and intellectual contexts of Elijah and Elisha as presented by the narratives in 1–2 Kings. Discusses the official and popular religion of the Israelites under the monarchy, concluding that Elijah and Elisha were representatives of a shamanism pervading Israelite religion in this period.

118 U. Simon. *Reading Prophetic Narratives.* Translated by L. J. Schramm. Indiana Studies in Biblical Literature. Bloomington, IN: Indiana University Press, 1997.

Offers a literary and religious reading of seven prophetic stories from Samuel through Kings, using rhetorical criticism, defined as combining a close reading, form criticism, and structural analysis. Does not address issues of historicity, composition, and revision. Most chapters were published from 1967 to 1990 in earlier forms.

119 A. G. Auld. "The Former Prophets: Joshua, Judges, 1–2 Samuel, 1–2 Kings." Pp. 53–68 in *The Hebrew Bible Today: An Introduction to Critical Issues.* Edited by S. L. McKenzie and M. P. Graham. Louisville: Westminster John Knox, 1998.

After a brief overview of the former prophets and their story, A. details scholarly opinion of the composition of the Deuteronomistic History. Includes his own opinion that "the history of Israel was gradually written backward from Kings via Deuteronomy to Genesis" (67).

120 W. J. Bergen. *Elisha and the End of Prophetism.* JSOTSup 286. Sheffield: Sheffield Academic Press, 1999.

Finds that though Elisha is consistently presented as a true prophet of Yahweh, the narratives in which he plays a part leave the reader with a negative judgment on prophecy. Though Elisha is a miracle worker, his roles are limited visà-vis other prophets. The absence of divine speech, of a sense of prophetic mission, and of opposing pagan deities subtly suggest a demise of prophetism.

121 E. Ben Zvi. "'The Prophets'—References to Generic Prophets and Their Role in the Construction of the Image of the 'Prophets of Old' within the Postmonarchic Readership/s of the Book of Kings." *ZAW* 116 (2004) 555–67.

Examines the general image of prophecy in the books of 1–2 Kings apart from specific prophets such as Elijah. Finds that the prophets were considered to be a faithful minority likely to be persecuted by evil rulers, that they were associated with transmitting Yahweh's teachings, and that their role was assumed to be reminding God's people of past failures in complying with Yahweh's expectations—leading to extreme punishment.

2.11 Preexilic and Exilic Prophecy

Although the former prophets cover the same period as the preexilic prophets, there is surprisingly little overlap between descriptions of prophecy in the two collections. Amos and the other eighth-century writing prophets are often described as inaugurating a new era of prophecy in Israel and Judah (Haran [#122]). These prophets were frequently scathing in their judgment of Israel and merciless in their descriptions of the judgment to come if hearers did not repent. The preexilic prophets devoted much attention to the correct operation of cultural institutions, such as kingship and priesthood, and provided divine guidance in the event of military crises (Grabbe [#129]). With the advent of the exile, this crisis gave impetus to a permanent paradigm shift in how Israel viewed itself and its God (Albertz [#128]; Grabbe [#126]). See also §3.9.

122   M. Haran. "From Early to Classical Prophecy: Continuity and Change." *VT* 27 (1977) 385–97. Reprinted in *Prophecy in the Hebrew Bible: Selected Studies from Vetus Testamentum*, pp. 102–14. Compiled by D. E. Orton. Brill's Readers in Biblical Studies 5. Leiden: Brill, 2000.

Isolates several features that distinguish early prophecy: (1) bands of prophets given to collective ecstasy, sometimes accompanied by instruments; (2) special places of oracular activity; and (3) attraction to permanent institutions of oracular activity, including the tent of meeting and temples. Classical prophecy, on the other hand, is marked by the written accompaniment of the oral prophecy and by the preservation of irrational ecstatic experiences in sober-minded literary expression.

123 R. R. Wilson. "Early Israelite Prophecy." *Int* 32 (1978) 3–16. Reprinted in *Interpreting the Prophets*, pp. 1–13. Edited by J. L. Mays and P. J. Achtemeier. Philadelphia: Fortress, 1987. Notes the lack of scholarly consensus concerning the character and social role of prophecy in pre-eighth-century prophecy. Past investigation has suffered from two defects: (1) the gulf between the early and writing prophets has been drawn too widely; and (2) no single model advanced has adequately explained the data. Ancient Near Eastern models, the portrait of the prophets in the Elohistic source, and the role of prophecy in the Deuteronomic history are all examined with an eye to emphasizing the complexity of traditions about prophecy.

124 K. Koch. *The Prophets.* Vol. 1: *The Assyrian Period.* Philadelphia: Fortress, 1983. Translated by M. Kohl. Original title: *Die Propheten I: Assyrische Zeit.* Stuttgart: W. Kohlhammer, 1970.
Provocative study of the rise of prophecy in the eighth century (includes Amos, Hosea, Micah, proto-Isaiah, Joel, Nahum, and Zephaniah). Seeks to understand the prophets as independent thinkers and "to work out the distinctive intellectual profiles of these mighty figures" (vii). Reconstructs (sometimes imaginatively) the historical circumstances of the prophets.

125 K. Koch. *The Prophets.* Vol. 2: *The Babylonian and Persian Periods.* Philadelphia: Fortress, 1984. Translated by M. Kohl. Original title: *Die Propheten II: Babylonisch-persische Zeit.* Stuttgart: W. Kohlhammer, 1978.
Continuation of #124 dealing with the prophets from Jeremiah to Jonah. For overview of the author's understanding of the prophets, see "Retrospect and Prospect" (189–203).

126 L. L. Grabbe (ed.). *Leading Captivity Captive: "The Exile" as History and Ideology.* JSOTSup 278. Sheffield: Sheffield Academic Press, 1998.
Papers from the European Seminar on Historical Methodology (1997), focusing on the function of the image of exile in the OT and Judaism and on the biblical and extra-biblical evidence for large deportations from the northern and southern kingdoms. Papers reflect the consensus of the participants that one or more deportations had occurred and that the

term *exile* is "heavily loaded with theological and ideological significance and thus not a neutral designation of a mere historical period or episode" (147).

127 M. A. Sweeney. "The Latter Prophets: Isaiah, Jeremiah, Ezekiel." Pp. 69–94 in *The Hebrew Bible Today: An Introduction to Critical Issues*. Edited by S. L. McKenzie and M. P. Graham. Louisville: Westminster John Knox, 1998.
Examines Isaiah, Jeremiah, and Ezekiel in their role in the Hebrew Bible, after which S. examines the history of scholarship on the prophetic books. Analyzes Isaiah, Jeremiah, and Ezekiel as to their contents and themes, incorporating recent scholarship on the works.

128 R. Albertz. *Israel in Exile: The History and Literature of the Sixth Century BCE*. Translated by D. E. Green. SBL Studies in Biblical Literature 3. Atlanta: SBL, 2003. Original title: *Die Exilszeit: 6. Jahrhundert v. Chr*. Biblische Enzyklopädie 7. Stuttgart: W. Kohlhammer, 2001.
Reconstructs the history of the exilic period based on biblical and apocryphal sources. Analyzes the literature, considering issues of authorship, social setting, collection, editing, and transmission. Finds that the period was formative for later theological developments.

129 L. L. Grabbe (ed.). *"Like a Bird in a Cage": The Invasion of Sennacherib in 701 BCE*. JSOTSup 363. London/New York: Sheffield Academic Press, 2003.
Collection of nine essays from the 2000 meeting of the European Seminar on Methodology in Israel's history: "Chronology: A Skeleton without Flesh? Sennacherib's Campaign as a Case Study" (B. Becking); "Malleability and Its Limits: Sennacherib's Campaign against Judah as a Case-Study" (E. Ben Zvi); "This Is What Happens . . ." (P. R. Davies); "Of Mice and Dead Men: Herodotus 2.141 and Sennacherib's Campaign in 701 BCE" (L. Grabbe); "701: Sennacherib at the Berezina" (E. Knauf); "On the Problems of Reconstructing pre-Hellenistic Israelite (Palestinian) History" (N. P. Lemche); "Sennacherib's Campaign of 701 BCE: The Assyrian View" (W. Mayer); "Updating the Messages: Hezekiah's Second Prophetic Story (2 Kings 19.9b–35) and the Community of

Babylonian Deportees" (N. Na'aman); and "Clio in a World of Pictures—Another Look at the Lachish Reliefs from Sennacherib's Southwest Palace at Nineveh" (C. Uehlinger). L. L. Grabbe provides an introduction and conclusion.

130 J. Middlemas. *The Troubles of Templeless Judah.* Oxford Theological Monographs. Oxford: Oxford University Press, 2005.
Examines both archaeological and textual evidence for the situation in Judah after the Babylonian destruction of Jerusalem. In contrast to the prophets (especially Jeremiah) who suggest that the situation in Judah is in total disarray, and who present their case for the remnant from the Babylonian captivity forming a new community as the true Israel, M. finds evidence in the Psalms and Lamentations for a favorable view of the Judeans in this templeless period.

2.12 Prophecy in Second Temple Judaism

With the rebuilding of the temple and the reentry of the people into the land, a concomitant change was visible in the nature of prophecy. No longer was prophecy primarily concerned with articulating a new message from God. Attention turned to interpreting previously given revelation (Barton [#132]; Schniedewind [#136]). One chief cause of this development was the difficulty in distinguishing true from false prophecy (see §2.5). Another factor in the decline of prophecy's popularity may have been a lack of literacy among the population (Blenkinsopp [#138]). Whatever the cause, some prophetic corpora deny the validity of any contemporary prophecy (Petersen [#131]), while other redactions and authors make room for contemporary prophecy in a diminished role (Gray [#134]). Any prophetic activity that did exist, however, was strongly influenced by political and social factors caused by the domination of foreign powers (Bedford [#137]; Trotter [#139]). See also §3.9–3.10 and ##62–63.

131 D. L. Petersen. *Late Israelite Prophecy: Studies in Deuteroprophetic Literature and in Chronicles.* Society of Biblical Literature Monograph Series 23. Missoula, MT: Scholars Press, 1977.
Examines the perceptions of prophecy in two bodies of literature from the postexilic period: the deutero-prophetic

collections and Chronicles. Analysis of Jer. 23:34–40; Zech. 13:2–6; and Mal. 3:1, 23–24 leads to the conclusion that these authors viewed classical prophecy as ended, even denying the validity of contemporary prophetic activity. 1 Chron. 25 and 2 Chron. 20, 29, 34:30, and 35:15 suggest that Levitical prophets differed from classical ones by participating in temple liturgy. P. also discovers evidence of power struggles and of an anachronistic conception of First Temple Levites acting as their Second Temple counterparts did, namely, with a strong prophetic role.

132 J. Barton. *Oracles of God: Perceptions of Ancient Prophecy in Israel after the Exile*. Oxford: Oxford University Press, 1986.
Argues that after the exile, from about 200 BC to AD 200 (with some flexibility on either end), a bipartite Torah and prophetic canon was envisaged, though the order of books was not fixed. Sees a sharp break between prophecy before and after the exile, with postexilic notions of prophecy shaped by reading of earlier texts (the "oracles of God"), which occurred in four modes: (1) halakah/ethics; (2) meaning of prophecy for the present day; (3) knowledge of the future without expectation of an imminent end; and (4) information about God and the heavens.

133 R. A. Mason. *Preaching the Tradition: Homily and Hermeneutics after the Exile*. Cambridge: Cambridge University Press, 1990.
Analyzes all the "addresses" in Chronicles that lack a parallel in Samuel–Kings, finding that von Rad's description of a "Levitical sermon" is untenable, but that the addresses nonetheless reflect a wide spectrum of postexilic preaching. In the book's second half, M. discusses the addresses in Ezra–Nehemiah, Haggai, Zech. 1–8, and Malachi, discovering that they too are united in their reflection of a "general practice of preaching and teaching which was familiar from the practice of the second temple" (258).

134 R. Gray. *Prophetic Figures in Late Second Temple Jewish Palestine*. New York: Oxford University Press, 1993.
Provides a study of Josephus's perceptions of prophecy both in the history of Israel and in terms of his contemporary world.

Josephus saw a difference between ancient and contemporary prophecy, since he expressed nostalgia for a holier past in closer touch with God, but did not deny the presence of analogous activity in his own time. Describes Josephus's own prophecy in two different ways, as a Jeremiah-like priest who reproves sin and as a Daniel-like wise man. Also scrutinizes Josephus's description of prophecy among the Essenes, his negative characterization of sign prophets, and his treatment of other prophetic figures.

135 T. C. Eskenazi and K. H. Richards (eds.). *Second Temple Studies. Vol. 2: Temple Community in the Persian Period.* JSOTSup 175. Sheffield: JSOT Press, 1994.

Papers from an international symposium (Rome, 1991) and from annual SBL meetings, focusing on the postexilic Judean community. Essays specifically addressing prophecy are: "So What Do We *Know* about the Temple? The Temple in the Prophets" (R. P. Carroll); "The Polemic against the Gods and Its Relevance for Second Isaiah's Conception of the New Jerusalem" (K. R. Baltzer); "Haggai's Temple Constructed, Deconstructed and Reconstructed" (D. J. A. Clines); "What Does Zechariah 1–8 Tell Us about the Second Temple?" (P. Marinković); and "Prophet and Society in the Persian Period according to Chronicles" (H. V. van Rooy).

136 J. J. M. Schniedewind. *The Word of God in Transition: From Prophet to Exegete in the Second Temple Period.* JSOTSup 197. Sheffield: Sheffield Academic Press, 1995.

In contrast to the preexilic prophets who received the word of God, postexilic prophets (like Ezra) interpreted the word of God. Since the book of Chronicles is a postexilic perspective on preexilic history, it invites comparison between the classical prophets who "received" and the inspired scribes who "interpreted." Concludes that the meaning of the "word of God" underwent a radical transformation, which had a profound impact on the development of Judaism and Christianity.

137 P. R. Bedford. *Temple Restoration in Early Achaemenid Judah.* Leiden: Brill, 2001.

Investigates the circumstances surrounding the building of the second temple and its role in Achaemenid Yehud, questioning the idea that the temple was at the center of a power struggle among competing groups in the early Persian period. Also denies that the rebuilding reflected an empire-wide Persian policy. Rather, the initiative for the completion of the rebuilding stemmed from an imperial decision to install Zerubbabel as governor of Judah. Haggai and Zech. 1–8 argue that the temple rebuilding is not rebellious, but the first step in Judah's restoration.

138 J. Blenkinsopp. "The Social Roles of Prophets in Early Achaemenid Judah." *JSOT* 93 (2001) 39–58.

Finds that the social roles of prophets in the Neo-Babylonian and Achaemenid periods are obscured by speech that recalls earlier prophetic utterance (e.g., "thus says the Lord"). In view of the paucity of literacy in these periods, none of the prophetic texts that emerged possessed mass appeal. Examination of terms used for prophets (such as *mal'ak* and *sōpeh*) demonstrate the change from prophecy to preaching. The fractious nature of the province of Judah, politically and economically, may have contributed to the rise of sectarianism.

139 J. M. Trotter. *Reading Hosea in Achaemenid Yehud*. JSOTSup 328. Sheffield: Sheffield Academic Press, 2001.

Provides a final-form reading of Hosea from the perspective of its readers in early Achaemenid Yehud (539–516 BC). Contends that combining a reader-oriented approach with a sociological analysis of the reading community enables the scholar to reconstruct a particular community's reading. Argues that the Achaemenid empire influenced and financed the reading and production of biblical texts. A more strongly monotheistic reading of Hosea emerged in this period, as did the notion of Persian Yehud as being in a "post-punishment relationship" with the deity (225).

140 G. Boccaccini. *Roots of Rabbinic Judaism: An Intellectual History, from Ezekiel to Daniel*. Grand Rapids: Eerdmans, 2002.

Examines the social groups of Second Temple Judaism. Finds three strains of thought: Zadokite, Enochic, and Sapiential. Zadokite Judaism (the priestly class) was dominant up to the time of the Maccabean revolt, controlling religious life, the temple, and the preservation and interpretation of the Torah. In general, society was "preoccupied with the stability and regularity of worship, not with the transmission of oral traditions" (203). "The modifications introduced by Daniel into the Zadokite system were essential in initiating that trajectory of thought that would ultimately give birth to Rabbinic Judaism" (207).

2.13 Prophecy in Early Christianity

In the NT prophecy was important in various ways: it defined the ministry of Jesus, John the Baptist, and leaders in the early church; Christians found strong support in the words of the OT prophets for their beliefs about Jesus; the gospels portrayed John the Baptist in ways reminiscent of Elijah, perhaps reflecting some degree of John's own self-perception (Webb [#142]); and many scholars argue that Jesus is best understood in prophetic terms (e.g., Hooker [#144]; see also Evans [#417]). Yet the roles and experience of prophets in the early church are still debated, and their continuity with previous prophetic figures is open to interpretation. Nor has a consensus emerged concerning the relation of early Christian prophecy to its Greco-Roman manifestations. The stress on the continued experience of prophecy served to set early Christianity apart from rabbinic Judaism, which generally denied its continued relevance. See also §5.2.

141 D. E. Aune. *Prophecy in Early Christianity and the Ancient Mediterranean World*. Grand Rapids: Eerdmans, 1983.
   Foundational work synthesizing "the evidence for the historical and social phenomenon of prophecy in early Christianity" (16). Topics under discussion include the nature and form of Greco-Roman prophecy (chaps. 2–3), prophecy in ancient Israel and early Judaism (chaps. 4–5), and the prophetic role and speech of Jesus (chaps. 6–7). The main focus of the work, however, is devoted to an examination of the character of early Christian prophecy, specifically its relationship to the sayings of Jesus, basic features of Christian prophetic speech, and its preservation in early Christian works.

142 R. L. Webb. *John the Baptizer and Prophet: A Socio-Historical Study.* Journal for the Study of the New Testament: Supplement Series 62. Sheffield: JSOT Press, 1991.
Analyzes John the Baptist's public role as a baptizer and prophet, finding that John created and led a Jewish sectarian movement. Portraits of John in surviving literature, the nature of his baptism in comparison with illustrations in the Hebrew Bible, Second Temple Judaism, and Qumran, and his relationship to other contemporary prophetic figures are closely analyzed and developed.

143 C. Forbes. *Prophecy and Inspired Speech in Early Christianity and Its Hellenistic Environment.* Wissenschaftliche Untersuchungen zum Neuen Testament 75. Tübingen: Mohr Siebeck, 1995. Reprinted Peabody, MA: Hendrickson, 1997.
Argues against the thesis that Greco-Roman religious parallels are helpful for describing the phenomenon or theological conception of early Christian prophecy and glossolalia. Suggests that the descriptions of prophecy in the LXX were more formative for early Christianity than those in Greek or Roman religion. The Corinthians were influenced by Palestinian wisdom speculation that they thought gave them greater status than other believers, not by their pagan pasts.

144 M. D. Hooker. *The Signs of a Prophet: The Prophetic Actions of Jesus.* Harrisburg, PA: Trinity, 1997.
Examines Jesus' prophetic and symbolic actions, finding three kinds of prophetic activity in the OT: miracles/epiphanies, prophetic drama, and proofs. After surveying descriptions of prophetic activity in Josephus and the NT, H. examines the sign of Jonah, the sign of John, and Jesus' refusal to perform signs. Analysis of the gospels reveals that although Jesus refused demands for proof of his prophetic status, his dramatic actions manifested his true nature to his followers. Concludes that understanding prophetic drama finally explains not only Jesus, but the traditions about him in the Gospels.

145 B. Witherington III. *Jesus the Seer: The Progress of Prophecy.* Peabody, MA: Hendrickson, 1999.
Despite the title, this work intends "to examine larger issues concerning the nature of prophecy and the development of

prophetic traditions, especially paying attention to the cross-cultural nature of the prophetic phenomenon" (xii). Beginning at Mari and with early Israelite prophets, W. surveys the history of Israelite prophecy down to the beginnings of Christianity. Jesus saw himself as a "messianic prophetic figure" based in part on Daniel (285).

3

Conception and Communication

3.1 Orality, Writing, and Canon

Among the records of prophetic sayings in the ancient world, the Hebrew Bible alone preserves prophecy as literature. This prophetic literature appears in various forms, from third-person historical accounts to first-person records of oracles. Traditionally, the apex of literary prophecy was considered to be the books attributed to Amos, Hosea, Micah, Isaiah, and Jeremiah, to which the nonwriting prophets, as described in the historical books, were precursors. The prophets of the exilic and postexilic periods were thought to represent the decline of prophecy. But in the twentieth century some scholars began to understand prophecy in reverse. According to these scholars, the scribes of the Second Temple period—looking back on the destruction of Jerusalem and the exile—sought ways to explain what their ancestors had undergone. They employed traditions and written sources that survived from earlier periods and created the prophetic books as we now know them.

Yet many questions remain about the biblical records of prophecy. What gave rise to Hebrew prophecy being written and then canonized? Who determined that a prophetic event would have a wider application to other audiences and should be recorded? For the prophetic events that were initially oral, what was the process that led to written forms of the prophecy? Who composed the literary form? What was the time lapse between event and record? How much interpretation was introduced by editors and scribes? See also #84.

146 T. H. Robinson. "Die prophetischen Bücher im Lichte neuer Entdeckungen." *ZAW* 45 (1927) 3–9.
Finds three phases in the development of the prophetic books: (1) a prophetic oracle is transmitted by a prophet's disciples; (2) individual oracles are compiled and arranged, including the addition of new material; (3) collections of oracles are put into final literary form. R. set the stage for decades of research on the prophets, which focused especially on the first two phases.

147 R. E. Clements. "The Prophet and His Editors." Pp. 210–20 in *The Bible in Three Dimensions: Essays in Celebration of Forty Years of Biblical Studies in the University of Sheffield.* Edited by D. J. A. Clines, S. E. Fowl, and S. E. Porter. JSOTSup 87. Sheffield: JSOT Press, 1990. Excerpted and reprinted in *The Place Is Too Small for Us: The Israelite Prophets in Recent Scholarship*, pp. 443–52. Edited by R. P. Gordon. Sources for Biblical and Theological Study 5. Winona Lake, IN: Eisenbrauns, 1995.
Reflects on the relationship editors had to a prophet and to other religious groups, and why prophets' words were recorded for later generations. Considers prophetic editors as preservationists, as originators of tradition, and as interpreters. Suggests that editors added material to form coherent written documents, possibly drawing from other prophets or fashioning their own primitive commentary in order to help correctly understand the prophet's message.

148 E. Ben Zvi and M. H. Floyd (eds.). *Writings and Speech in Israelite and Ancient Near Eastern Prophecy.* SBLSymS 10. Atlanta: SBL, 2000.
Ten essays discussing orality and writtenness. See in particular: "Transmitting Prophecy across Generations" (J. L. Crenshaw); "'Pen of iron, point of diamond' (Jer 17:1): Prophecy as Writing" (P. R. Davies). Other essays are of similar scope and quality.

149 S. Chapman. *The Law and the Prophets: A Study in Old Testament Canon Formation.* Forschungen zum Alten Testament 27. Tübingen: Mohr Siebeck, 2000.

Suggestive work that applies B. Childs's canonical criticism to the formation of the OT canon, arguing that the Law and the Prophets gained canonical force together and that the privileged position of the Torah was a product of early rabbinic thinking. Speaking of canon as a "theological grammar," C. finds that God's revelation to Israel always proceeded through both prophetic and legal means, and that this "core canon" was in a "relatively stable form" by "sometime in the fourth century (400–350 BC, i.e., before Chronicles)" (286).

150 K. van der Toorn. "From the Mouth of the Prophet: The Literary Fixation of Jeremiah's Prophecies in the Context of the Ancient Near East." Pp. 191–202 in *Inspired Speech: Prophecy in the Ancient Near East: Essays in Honor of Herbert B. Huffmon.* Edited by J. Kaltner and L. Stulman. JSOTSup 378. London: T & T Clark, 2004.

Uses Jeremiah as an example of the transition from oral to written prophecy and finds that there were in the ANE two basic motives for committing prophecy to writing: transmitting a prophecy to an audience at a different location and preserving an oracle for future use. Concludes that Jeremiah was not a literary author intent on recording his message for future generations but wrote his message (or had Baruch write it) only when circumstances prevented him from addressing his audience in person (201). Attributes the collection(s) of Jeremiah's oracles to one or more anonymous authors.

151 M. Nissinen. "How Prophecy Became Literature." *SJOT* 19 (2005) 153–72.

Traces the process from spoken to written word, posing numerous questions for future research. "Prophecy should be considered a form of social communication in which the whole community, or a fraction of it, participates. The literarization of prophecy presupposes a community that adopts, repeats, interprets, and reinterprets prophetic messages for its own purposes" (155).

152 J. Schaper. "Exilic and Post-Exilic Prophecy and the Orality/ Literacy Problem." *VT* 55 (2005) 324–42.
Applies social anthropological research to orality in exilic and postexilic prophetic texts. Proposes three categories of references to writing: "writing as a divine activity within the divine sphere, writing as practised by human beings, and writing as a divine activity bridging the gap between the divine and human spheres" (327). Finds a high degree of literacy in the upper echelons of society, leading to significant impact on Judean prophecy and to close contacts between prophets and priests/scribes in the late preexilic period and onward.

3.2 Form, Redaction, and Genre Criticism

During most of the twentieth century, form criticism held center stage in the study of prophecy, classifying forms of text (especially oral) and postulating the life setting of those forms. If the prophets were primarily speakers not writers, then it seemed appropriate for the typical oral speech forms to be the focus of research. The material added later by compilers and editors was a separate consideration, largely incidental. Redaction criticism, in turn, took a different approach, giving attention to how compilers and editors shaped texts, generally reinterpreting earlier materials for later generations. Recent decades have seen scholarship moving away from the form critical approach of analyzing short, oral forms of expression toward the larger, literary units of the canonical text, including literary and linguistic structures and social settings. The conclusion is that redactors functioned as authors, composing messages that addressed the issues of their times, while freely borrowing from earlier prophetic traditions. To understand the prophetic message and rhetorical forms evident in the final form of the text, the genre characteristics of these larger units are important. Combining form criticism and redaction criticism, scholars seek to identify layers in prophetic texts, based on inconsistencies, changes in perspective, and other factors pointing to multiple hands involved in composition. For a history of scholarship of the first half of the twentieth century regarding prophetic speech forms, see Westermann (#153, 13–89).

153 C. Westermann. *Basic Forms of Prophetic Speech*. Translated by Hugh Clayton White. Philadelphia: Westminster, 1967.

Original title: *Grundformen Prophetischer Rede.* Munich: Kaiser, 1960.

Seminal examination of prophetic judgment speeches as proclaimed to individuals and to the nation. Isolates the texts of judgment speeches, defines the form, analyzes the historical setting, and traces the development of the speeches. Includes detailed summary of scholarship from the first half of the twentieth century.

154 K. Nielsen. *Yahweh as Prosecutor and Judge: An Investigation of the Prophetic Lawsuit (Rîb-Pattern).* JSOTSup 9. Sheffield: JSOT Press, 1979.

A form-critical investigation of the prophetic lawsuit, isolating four elements common to the form. Exegesis of Isa. 1:2–3; 3:13–15; Hos. 2:4–17; 4:1–3; and Ps. 50 follows. Defines the actual *Sitz im Leben* of the prophetic lawsuit as an emergency measure in which the prophet tries to force the people to become conscious of the covenant's demands on them, perhaps during the annual New Year's Festival ceremony of covenant renewal.

155 S. Niditch. *The Symbolic Vision in Biblical Tradition.* HSM 30. Chico, CA: Scholars Press, 1983.

In contrast to other synchronic investigations of the symbolic vision, N. emphasizes the diachronic development of the form in three stages, from its early form in Amos and Jeremiah to its "baroque and narrative" form in Daniel, 2 Baruch, and 4 Ezra (12).

156 H. Gunkel. "The Prophets as Writers and Poets." Pp. 22–73 in *Prophecy in Israel: Search for an Identity.* Translated by J. L. Schaaf. Edited by D. L. Petersen. IRT 10. Philadelphia: Fortress, 1987. Original title: "Die Propheten als Schriftsteller und Dichter." Pp. 34–70 in Gunkel's *Die Propheten.* Göttingen: Vandenhoeck & Ruprecht, 1923.

A comprehensive and influential essay on the study of the prophets. Gunkel led the way in genre criticism, analyzing oral forms of prophetic speech and tracking the development from oral to written forms. He stressed that prophets should be understood more as speakers than as writers. In his introduction, Petersen comments, "It is not too much to say that this one essay presents the birth of what we know today as form and redaction criticism" (12).

157 C. Westermann. *Prophetic Oracles of Salvation.* Translated by K. Crim. Louisville: Westminster/John Knox, 1991. Original title: *Prophetische Heilsworte in Alten Testament.* Göttingen: Vandenhoeck & Ruprecht, 1987.

A complement to W.'s earlier *Basic Forms of Prophetic Speech* (#153), this volume describes four different kinds of prophetic oracles. After a treatment of oracles of salvation before the writing prophets, W. treats unconditional oracles of salvation, followed by a second type that describes God's judgment on foreign nations and consequent salvation of Israel. Discussion of conditional oracles of salvation as well as their nonprophetic counterparts concludes this exegetically informative volume.

158 P. W. Ferris. *The Genre of Communal Lament in the Bible and the Ancient Near East.* SBLDS 127. Atlanta: Scholars Press, 1992.

Compares the form and function of Hebrew public laments with similar lamentation in neighboring cultures. Finds that private expressions of grief evolved into a professional guild that was responsible for the composition and performance of the dirge. Concludes that there is insufficient evidence that the Israelites directly learned laments while in the Babylonian exile.

159 T. Collins. *The Mantle of Elijah: The Redaction Criticism of the Prophetical Books.* Biblical Seminar 20. Sheffield: JSOT Press, 1993.

Synthesizes current research on the formation of the books of the prophets. Evaluates the results and implications of redaction criticism of Isaiah, the Twelve, Ezekiel, and Jeremiah. Concludes: "The fiction that the eighth-century Isaiah uttered all the oracles in the book is an important literary device, and one of its functions is to underline the work's essential unity. This effective device should not be lightly brushed aside for the sake of historical accuracy" (55).

160 S. J. DeVries. *From Old Revelation to New: A Tradition-Historical and Redaction-Critical Study of Temporal Transitions in Prophetic Traditions.* Grand Rapids: Eerdmans, 1995.

Explores inner-biblical exegesis and redaction history via temporal formulas (such as "in that day"), which served "as a special redactional device. . . . The employment of these particular formulas at points of transition reveals much indeed about the ideology of those who first preserved and later extended the prophetic heritage" (15). Discusses how and where temporal expressions were used and in what ways they underwent development, pointing to growth in the prophetic tradition.

161 A. Schart. *Die Entstehung des Zwölfprophetenbuchs: Neubearbeitungen von Amos im Rahmen schriftenübergreifender Redaktionsprozesse.* BZAW 260. Berlin: de Gruyter, 1998.
Uses the redaction-history of Amos as a way to understand the redaction-history of the Book of the Twelve as a whole, finding six successive stages in which the core of the words of Amos (now in chaps. 3–6) became intertwined with other prophetic works. Historical developments in politics and the understanding of prophecy resulted in a work united by the use of catchwords, similar structuring, and thematic coherence.

162 A. Behrens. *Prophetische Visionsschilderungen im Alten Testament: Sprachliche Eigenarten, Funktion und Geschichte einer Gattung.* Münster: Ugarit-Verlag, 2002.
Discusses the literary type, history, and characteristic features of the prophetic vision. After a review of previous research, B. distinguishes two parts of the vision: the vision proper and dialogue between the prophet and a heavenly figure. Investigates the form and literary function of prophetic visions in Amos 7:1–8:2; 9:1–4; Jer. 1; 24:1–10; 1 Kings 22; Ezek. 1–3; 8–11; 37:1–14; Zech. 1–6; and Dan. 8–12. Emphasizes the uniqueness of prophetic visions in the Hebrew Bible against others known from the ANE.

163 S. Mowinckel. *The Spirit and the Word: Prophecy and Tradition in Ancient Israel.* Edited by K. C. Hanson. Fortress Classics in Biblical Studies. Minneapolis: Fortress, 2002.
A collection of M.'s works, published between 1922 and 1946, that apply form, tradition, and literary criticism to prophecy. Emphasizes the religious experience of the prophets, the

orality behind the written forms, the role of editors in shaping written forms, and Israelite cultic tradition.

164 M. A. Sweeney and E. Ben Zvi (eds.). *The Changing Face of Form Criticism for the Twenty-first Century.* Grand Rapids: Eerdmans, 2003.
Acknowledging the demise of traditional form criticism, these essays reflect on earlier aspects of the discipline and look forward to new strategies. M. S. Odell argues that Ezek. 1 is not a true call narrative; D. L. Petersen offers a revised version of Westermann (#153); E. Ben Zvi redefines a prophetic book; M. Floyd distinguishes between prophetic book and prophetic reading; P. K. Tull argues that the unlimited variations of prophetic forms need to be considered; and M. Sweeney contests the division of Zechariah into three parts.

3.3 Poetry and Imagery

Because poetry inherently stretches the meanings of words and the imaginations of hearers, appealing to both the left and right hemispheres of the brain, and because biblical poetry represents worldviews and mechanisms different from our own, understanding the poetry of the prophets challenges all modern readers. The last two decades of the twentieth century saw a revival of interest in Hebrew poetry, which continues in the present. Under consideration are questions regarding what distinguishes prose from poetry, how parallelism works, whether Hebrew poetry is primarily an imitation of reality or an outpouring of feelings, in what sense it has meter, the nature of poets' style, the function of metaphor, and how biblical poetry is related to poetry in the ANE. For review of recent scholarship on metaphor, see Doyle (#171, 49–144). See also ##76, 187, 334, 335, 338, and 348.

165 W. H. Bellinger Jr. *Psalmody and Prophecy.* JSOTSup 27. Sheffield: JSOT Press, 1984.
Focuses on prophetic elements in lament psalms, with a consideration of whether such psalms originated in a liturgical setting. Examines a variety of individual laments coming from cultic settings and finds that the worshippers consistently expected God to hear their prayers. This anticipation of future salvation is related to prophetic oracles of salvation. Includes

a discussion of psalmic passages in the prophets, particularly
Habakkuk and Joel.

166 C. A. Newsom. "A Maker of Metaphors: Ezekiel's Oracles
Against Tyre." *Int* 38 (1984) 151–64. Reprinted in *Interpreting
the Prophets*, pp.188–99. Edited by J. L. Mays and P. J. Achtemeier.
Philadelphia: Fortress, 1987. Reprinted in *The Place Is Too Small
for Us: The Israelite Prophets in Recent Scholarship*, pp. 191–204.
Edited by R. P. Gordon. Sources for Biblical and Theological Study
5. Winona Lake, IN: Eisenbrauns, 1995.
Seminal essay concluding that "the analysis of the rhetoric
of metaphor is an essential part of critical exegetical method.
While it certainly does not replace traditional historical-critical
investigations, the study of literary technique and its effect on
meaning can both challenge the results of those investigations
and produce new insights into the material" (164).

167 J. L. Kugel (ed.). *Poetry and Prophecy: The Beginning of a Literary Tradition*. Ithaca, NY: Cornell University Press, 1990.
Eight essays exploring the sense(s) in which prophecy is poetry,
ranging across several literary traditions, including those of classical Greece and medieval Judaism. Essays that address biblical
prophecy are "Poets and Prophets" (J. L. Kugel); "Imagining
Prophecy" (A. Cooper); and "David the Prophet" (J. L. Kugel).

168 K. P. Darr. "Literary Perspectives on Prophetic Literature." Pp.
127–43 in *Old Testament Interpretation: Past, Present and Future: Essays in Honor of Gene M. Tucker*. Edited by J. L. Mays,
D. L. Petersen, and K. H. Richards. Nashville: Abingdon, 1995.
Reviews literary-critical work of the past, surveys contemporary scholarship, and looks ahead to future approaches.
Gives special attention to issues regarding parallelism and
metaphor. Calls for interpreting poetry in light of ancient
social and literary contexts, in combination with contemporary methods of analysis.

169 T. L. Brensinger. *Simile and Prophetic Language in the Old
Testament*. Mellen Biblical Press Series 43. Lewiston, NY:
Mellen, 1996.
Considers the use and frequency of the simile in the pro-
phetic corpus, concluding that similes occur more often in

poetry than in prose, especially in speeches and oracles of judgment and salvation. Examines the structure of prophetic similes, their sources, their functions and their description of God, concluding that similes give evidence of considerable planning before the prophets spoke, that they are not simple embellishment to the message, and that they play a key role in prophetic persuasion.

170 J. K. Kuntz. "Biblical Hebrew Poetry in Recent Research, Part I." *CurBS* 6 (1998) 31–64. "Biblical Hebrew Poetry in Recent Research, Part II." *CurBS* 7 (1999) 35–79.
Provides detailed discussions of the previous two decades of research. In part 1, basic introductions to poetry are summarized and evaluated, followed by more detailed manuals and book-length studies focusing on parallelism, linguistics, poetic theory, parallels with ANE poetry, etc. Provides an overview of the four fundamental issues in biblical poetics: poetry versus prose, parallelism, meter and rhythm, and stylistics. In part 2, the focus is on a plethora of learned essays published since 1980.

171 B. Doyle. *The Apocalypse of Isaiah Metaphorically Speaking: A Study of the Use, Function and Significance of Metaphors in Isaiah 24–27*. Bibliotheca ephemeridum theologicarum lovaniensium 151. Leuven: Leuven University Press, 2000.
Considers various theories of metaphor and their applicability to biblical texts. Concludes that "the author(s)/redactor(s) employed metaphor for pedagogical, transformational and emotive reasons" (374). The dissonance of competing metaphors for God underscores his incomparability. The relational metaphor of Yahweh as husband of his people may be considered a unifying redactional principle, suggesting that these chapters are a distinct unit of text, perhaps the work of a single redactor.

172 D. B. Sandy. *Plowshares and Pruning Hooks: Rethinking the Language of Biblical Prophecy and Apocalyptic*. Downers Grove, IL: InterVarsity, 2002.
Argues that prophetic and apocalyptic language is predominantly metaphorical, and that prophetic predictions can often only be understood after they are fulfilled. Discusses seven

distinctive traits of prophetic and apocalyptic language, as well as twelve themes of NT apocalyptic. Appendices include a compilation of various themes in the language of blessing and cursing.

173 G. Baumann. *Love and Violence: Marriage as Metaphor for the Relationship between YHWH and Israel in the Prophetic Books.* Translated by L. Maloney. Collegeville, MN: Liturgical Press, 2003. Original title: *Liebe und Gewalt: die Ehe als Metapher für das Verhältnis JHWH, Israel in den Prophetenbüchern.* Stuttgart: Verlag Katholisches Bibelwerk, 2000.
Consideration of a troubling aspect of prophetic imagery: scenes of divine degradation of God's metaphorical spouse, Israel/Jerusalem. After preliminary consideration of the research and background of the metaphor, B. considers the instances of it in Hosea, Jeremiah, Ezekiel, Isaiah, and the Book of the Twelve. The final part rejects any role for these prophetic texts in shaping modern theological sensitivity.

174 E. K. Holt (ed.). *Metaphors in Prophetic Literature. SJOT* 17 (2003) 3–88.
Includes a preface by the editor, calling for increased appreciation of the importance of metaphors. Essays include: "'From Oracles to Canon'—and the Role of Metaphor" (K. Nielsen); "Deceiving Hope: The Ironies of Metaphorical Beauty and Ideological Terror in Jeremiah" (A. R. P. Diamond); "Metaphor and Inter-textuality: 'Daughter of Zion' as a Test Case: Response to Kirsten Nielsen, 'From Oracles to Canon'—and the Role of Metaphor" (A. Labahn); "Metaphorical Shifts in the Oracle against Babylon (Jeremiah 50–51)" (P. J. P. Van Hecke).

175 S. J. Dille. *Mixing Metaphors: God as Mother and Father in Deutero-Isaiah.* JSOTSup 398. Gender, Culture, Theory 13. Sheffield: Sheffield Academic Press, 2004.
Examines five passages in Isaiah that employ parental imagery for God. Seeks to understand the mechanism and rhetorical impact of metaphor. Finds that the "images of father and mother vary greatly within Deutero-Isaiah and their implications are determined by their literary contexts and the other metaphors with which they mix" (173). These metaphors do not have consistent meanings.

3.4 Literary Interdependence

Common throughout Scripture is the use of material from other sources. It may include quotations, allusions, the reuse of themes, or a specific arrangement of material. Intertextuality and inner-biblical exegesis refer to the study of the significance of such literary interdependence within the canon and in comparison to sources outside the canon. In the prophetic books the evidence of interdependence is widespread, especially in connection with the Pentateuch, which has led some scholars to see evidence of Deuteronomistic editing of prophetic books. Others conclude that the book of Deuteronomy was the work of the prophets. Among the prophets themselves there are many examples of literary interdependence.

176 M. Fishbane. *Biblical Interpretation in Ancient Israel.* Oxford: Clarendon, 1985.
Celebrated *magnum opus* that popularized intertextual study of the Hebrew Bible. Dedicates one section to "Mantological Exegesis" (443–505), which investigates different kinds of interpretation of dreams, visions, omens, and oracles, as well as the generic transformation of oracles into nonoracles and vice versa.

177 J. Day. "Prophecy." Pp. 39–55 in *It Is Written: Scripture Citing Scripture.* Edited by D. A. Carson and H. G. M. Williamson. Cambridge: Cambridge University Press, 1988. Reprinted as "Inner-Biblical Interpretation in the Prophets" in *The Place Is Too Small for Us: The Israelite Prophets in Recent Scholarship,* pp. 230–46. Edited by R. P. Gordon. Sources for Biblical and Theological Study 5. Winona Lake, IN: Eisenbrauns, 1995.
Despite the comparatively late date of many laws preserved in the Pentateuch, preexilic prophets are indebted to early legal traditions such as those preserved in the Book of the Covenant. Deutero-Isaiah reflects and at times critiques the P version of creation in Gen. 1, while Ezek. 28 reflects a tradition similar to the J account of Gen. 2–3. Postexilic prophets, such as Joel, are especially prone to incorporating the very words of earlier prophets in their message to their own generation.

178 R. J. Coggins. "Innerbiblical Quotation in Joel." Pp. 75–84 in *After the Exile: Essays in Honour of Rex Mason.* Edited by

J. Barton and D. Reimer. Macon, GA: Mercer University Press, 1996.

Counters the identification by Nogalski (#319 and #320) of a "Joel-related layer" in the Book of the Twelve. Suggests investigation of intertextuality in Joel should proceed along three paths: scholars should study (1) how allusions integrate Joel into the Book of the Twelve; (2) Joel's creative use of earlier traditions; and (3) the setting of this process within the cult.

179 J. Jeremias. "The Interrelationship between Amos and Hosea." Pp. 171–86 in *Forming Prophetic Literature: Essays on Isaiah and the Twelve in Honor of John D. W. Watts.* Edited by J. W. Watts and P. R. House. JSOTSup 235. Sheffield: Sheffield Academic Press, 1996.

Argues, against the intent of historical-critical scholarship to isolate the singular message of each prophet, for literary interdependence in Amos and Hosea. Observes that the influence of the book of Hosea on the book of Amos can be seen in nearly every chapter. Reverse influence is also evident, but examples are fewer. Interconnections between the messages of these two prophets began in the seventh century but reached their final form in the Book of the Twelve.

180 P. T. Willey. *Remember the Former Things: The Recollection of Previous Texts in Second Isaiah.* SBLDS 161. Atlanta: Scholars Press, 1997.

After an initial summary of previous research (chap. 1) and a presentation of her theoretical reflections on intertextuality drawn from Bakhtin and Hayes (chap. 2), the main part of W.'s study discerns intertextual echoes in five passages from Second Isaiah. A final chapter concludes that the appeal to previous texts intends "to assert the message that returning to redevelop Jerusalem and YHWH's cult is the logical next chapter in Israel's sacred story" (263).

181 B. D. Sommer. *A Prophet Reads Scripture: Allusion in Isaiah 40–66.* Contraversions. Stanford, CA: Stanford University Press, 1998.

Analyzes allusion (to be distinguished from intertextuality, echo, influence, and exegesis) of earlier texts in Deutero-Isaiah (chaps. 40–66), including Jeremiah, the Psalms and other laments, fellow prophetic texts, and the Pentateuch. Allusions can be grouped thematically into confirmation, re-prediction, reversal, historical recontextualization, typology, and response. S.'s analysis leads him to argue that Isa. 40–66 was composed by a single author.

182 R. L. Schultz. *The Search for Quotation: Verbal Parallels in the Prophets*. JSOTSup 180. Sheffield: Sheffield Academic Press, 1999.

Intent on exploring the issue of inner-biblical citation, S. begins by recognizing that verbal parallels between prophets have been widely noted but not widely studied. Part 1 surveys other examinations of inner-prophetic citation and allusion. Part 2 offers an overview of nonprophetic allusions in texts from the ANE to early Judaism. Part 3 details a new approach based on S.'s study of comparative literatures, focusing mainly on Isaiah.

183 M. J. Boda and M. H. Floyd (eds.). *Bringing Out the Treasure: Inner Biblical Allusion in Zechariah 9–14* (with a major contribution by R. Mason). JSOTSup 370. London/New York: Sheffield Academic Press, 2003.

Consists of two parts: the first publishes R. Mason's influential 1973 dissertation, which examines inner-biblical exegesis in Zech. 9–14, while the second contains responses to and extensions of Mason's work. Essays in the second section include: "Deutero-Zechariah and Types of Intertextuality" (M. H. Floyd); "The Growth of the Book of Isaiah Illustrated by Allusions in Zechariah" (R. Nurmela); "Some Observations on the Relationship between Zechariah 9–11 and Jeremiah" (E. Tigchelaar); "Deuteronomic Toponyms in Second Zechariah" (R. F. Person Jr.); "Zechariah 9–14: The Capstone of the Book of the Twelve" (P. L. Redditt); "Putting the Eschatological Visions of Zechariah in Their Place: Malachi as a Hermeneutical Guide for the Last Section of the Book of the Twelve" (A. Schart).

3.5 Ideology and Theology

Ideology and theology are related concepts with some overlap in meaning—and with considerable controversy among scholars.

In a neutral sense, ideology may refer to ideas that are implicit in the worldview of prophets and their audiences, often assumed and unexpressed, such as social and political values, yet which may determine much about ways of thinking and communicating. In a more restrictive sense, ideology may carry with it the connotation of Marxism. While the ideology of prophecy is generally not explicit, the theology tends to be more self-evident. Ideological criticism is a relatively new discipline. Theology, encompassing the prophets' conscious concepts about God and how he relates to his creation and his chosen people, is not uniform among the prophets. The prophets do not have a theology in the modern sense of the word, but there is a common core, centering on the covenant and God's sovereignty over all nations. In addition to sources below, students may wish to consult: W. Brueggemann, *Theology of the Old Testament: Testimony, Dispute, Advocacy* (Minneapolis: Fortress, 1997); P. R. House, *Old Testament Theology* (Downers Grove, IL: InterVarsity, 1998); B. W. Anderson, *The Contours of Old Testament Theology* (Minneapolis: Fortress, 1999); E. S. Gerstenberger, *Theologies in the Old Testament*, trans. J. Bowden (Minneapolis: Fortress, 2002). For other OT theologies, see E. A. Martens, *Old Testament Theology*, IBR Bibliographies 13 (Grand Rapids: Baker Academic, 1997). In addition to sources below, see Gowan (#7).

184 G. von Rad. *Old Testament Theology.* Vol. 2: *The Theology of Israel's Prophetic Traditions.* Translated by D. G. M. Stalker. San Francisco: Harper & Row, 1965. Original title: *Die Theologie des prophetischen Überlieferung Israels.* Munich: Christian Kaiser, 1960.

Classic and influential theological introduction to the prophets which proceeds in chronological order from "prophecy before the classical period" through the entire history of prophecy, including the actualization of the OT in the NT, the OT's understanding of the world and man, the OT saving event in the light of NT fulfillment, and a final chapter on the Law. Vacillates between the idea that the prophets offered something completely new, and that they "were in greater or lesser degree conditioned by old traditions which they re-interpreted and applied to their own times" (4).

185 C. Stuhlmueller. *Creative Redemption in Deutero-Isaiah.* Analecta Biblica 43. Rome: Biblical Institute Press, 1970.

Finds that the redemption announced to the exiles in the Book of Consolation will be so new and amazing that it will be like creation all over again. "This idea of creation served to enhance many features of the prophet's concept of redemption, transforming it into an *exceptionally wondrous* redemptive act, performed with personal concern by Yahweh for his chosen people, bringing them *unexpectedly* out of exile, into a *new and unprecedented life of peace and abundance*, with repercussions upon the cosmos and world inhabitants" (233).

186 B. C. Ollenburger. "Isaiah's Creation Theology." *Ex Auditu* 3 (1987) 54–71.
Argues that creation is theologically implicit in First Isaiah, especially where the concern is the security of Zion. In Second Isaiah creation factors into the exaltation of Zion. "In Isaiah, creation and providence are made concrete in relation to Israel, and it is quite impossible for Isaiah to speak of God's plan or God's defeat of chaos or God's preservation and restoration of cosmic order without speaking of Zion and of Israel" (69).

187 M. Z. Brettler. *God Is King: Understanding an Israelite Metaphor.* JSOTSup 76. Sheffield: JSOT Press, 1989.
Studies the figure of God as king as a metaphorical transference from human to divine kingship, asking why certain elements of human kingship were fruitfully applied to divine rule and others were not. After an introductory chapter that delineates his understanding of metaphors, B. surveys royal appellations, qualities, trappings, the king and domestic affairs, and finally the much-studied phrase "the Lord has become King" (*yhwh mālak*).

188 R. B. Chisholm Jr. "A Theology of the Minor Prophets." Pp. 397–433 in *A Biblical Theology of the Old Testament.* Edited by R. B. Zuck. Chicago: Moody, 1991.
Investigates the theology of the eighth-, seventh-, and sixth-/fifth-century prophets, divided into two major sections for each group: "God and his people" and "God and the nations." The book of Jonah is scrutinized separately under the rubrics "God's sovereign grace" and "Jonah's response to God."

189 N. K. Gottwald. "Social Class and Ideology in Isaiah 40–55: An Eagletonian Reading." Pp. 43–57 in *Ideological Criticism of Biblical Texts*. Edited by D. Jobling and T. Pippin. Semeia 59. Atlanta: Scholars Press, 1992.

Using materialist literary criticism developed by T. Eagleton, G. suggests that Isa. 40–55 is an attempt by the ruling elite of Judah exiled in Babylon for two generations to preserve their sociocultural identity. Deutero-Isaiah seeks to motivate this elite to cast its lot with the pro-Persian political movement and so to reassign the functions of Davidic kings partly to the Persians and partly to themselves. Two responses by J. Milbank (59–71) and C. Newsom (73–78) follow G.'s paper.

190 R. Rendtorff. "The Place of Prophecy in a Theology of the Old Testament." Pp. 57–65 in *Canon and Theology: Overtures to an Old Testament Theology*. Translated and edited by M. Kohl. OBT. Minneapolis: Fortress, 1993. Original title: *Kanon und Theologie: Vorarbeiten zu einer Theologie des Alten Testaments*. Neukirchen-Vluyn: Neukirchener, 1991.

Critiques various attempts at writing a theology of the OT, from Duhm to von Rad to Blenkinsopp. Notes the differing considerations of prophecy in such theologies, whether prophets were thought to be the originators of true Israelite religion or whether they were simply perpetuating earlier traditions. Concludes: for "a canon-conscious Old Testament theology . . . we shall have to consider two fundamental elements: the tensions between the Torah and Prophets, and the final canonical relations binding them together as integral parts of the one canon" (64–65).

191 D. J. A. Clines. *Interested Parties: The Ideology of Writers and Readers of the Hebrew Bible*. JSOTSup 205. Sheffield: Sheffield Academic Press, 1995.

Decides on a definition of ideology as "the kind of large-scale ideas that influence and determine the whole outlook of groups of people" (11). Seeks to uncover various ideologies that can be detected among the Israelites and offers experimental essays regarding the clash of ideologies between authors, ancient readers, and modern readers. For example, Haggai's conception of the temple as a treasury does not match his readers' ideology.

192 N. K. Gottwald. "Ideology and Ideologies in Israelite Prophecy." Pp. 136–49 in *Prophets and Paradigms: Essays in Honor of Gene M. Tucker*. Edited by S. B. Reid. JSOT 229. Sheffield: Sheffield Academic Press, 1996.
Considers four senses of the term "ideology" and concludes that prophecy can be considered ideological in each sense: (1) prophecy is a system of ideas; (2) prophetic ideas correspond to the social setting of a particular group of people; (3) prophetic ideas may involve a false sense of reality regarding those whom the prophets condemn as well as the prophets themselves; (4) prophetic ideas may be impractical, fanatical, and utopian.

193 W. P. Griffin. *The God of the Prophets: An Analysis of Divine Action*. JSOTSup 249. Sheffield: Sheffield Academic Press, 1997.
Quantitatively classifies data from selected passages regarding the characteristics of God as an acting agent and as an object of action. Employs a method of content analysis from the social sciences, which involves coding and categorizing data. Draws conclusions regarding God's direct and indirect activity relative to humans, natural forces, etc. "God is not the 'wholly other' of some theologies, but is also not merely the personification of the average human" (249).

194 D. E. Gowan. *Theology of the Prophetic Books: The Death and Resurrection of Israel*. Louisville: Westminster/John Knox, 1998.
Summarizes the message of each of the prophetic books in light of the historical setting and the developing theology of the destruction and restoration of Israel. Observes that the prophets cluster around three events: the fall of Samaria, the fall of Jerusalem, and the return of the exiles. Provides helpful insights for interpreting the prophets.

195 W. Ma. *Until the Spirit Comes: The Spirit of God in the Book of Isaiah*. JSOTSup 271. Sheffield: Sheffield Academic Press, 1999.
Traces the ethical and eschatological development of *rûaḥ* ("spirit") in the book of Isaiah. Finds a diversity of meaning for it as applied to leaders, prophets, creation, God, wind, inauguration of a new age, the restoration of Israel, the future messiah, future prophetic roles, and the consummation of restoration.

196   P. R. House. "The Character of God in the Book of the Twelve." *Society of Biblical Literature Seminar Papers* (1998) 831–49. Reprinted in *Reading and Hearing the Book of the Twelve*, pp. 125–45. Edited by J. D. Nogalski and M. A. Sweeney. Atlanta: Scholars Press, 2000.

Since the Book of the Twelve charts a long span of history from before the Assyrian conquest of Samaria to ca. 450 BC (Malachi), a diverse portrait of God emerges from the book. God is both threatening and consoling, and is characterized as "spouse, parent, judge, healer, creator, sovereign ruler, shepherd, deliverer and refiner of a sinful world" (144).

197   K. L. Wong. *The Idea of Retribution in the Book of Ezekiel.* VTSup 87. Leiden: Brill, 2001.

Analyzes retribution in Ezekiel, finding that three principles undergird this theme: retribution might punish a breach of covenant, it may be designed to remove impurity, or it may mete out poetic justice. Thus retribution can be juridical, as in the first instance, or nonjuridical, as in the second and third. Beginning with the work of Koch, W. reviews and critiques his conclusions in the course of this study. Concludes: "The justice of Yahweh is the message of Ezekiel," and retribution forms one important component of this justice (252).

198   J. L. Crenshaw. "Theodicy and Prophetic Literature." Pp. 236–55 in *Theodicy in the World of the Bible.* Edited by A. Laato and J. C. de Moor. Leiden: Brill, 2003.

Surveys five approaches to theodicy in the prophetic literature: (1) personal affront; (2) puzzlement over the divine character; (3) the interpretation of history; (4) liturgical readings of historical events; and (5) appeal to the natural order of things. Finds that the tension between divine wrath and grace was never resolved in the Hebrew Bible.

3.6 Syncretism and Idolatry

Unlike other literature of the ANE, the Hebrew Bible is very critical of its own people, particularly regarding idolatry. Issues of insubordination are prominent in the Pentateuch. Problems in the monarchy are underscored in the Deuteronomistic History. In the prophets, idolatry is frequently decried, while social injustices are also condemned. In order to call people to repentance and away from idolatry, the prophets mock idols, refer to idolatry as sexual impurity, and chastise idolaters. Issues under discussion among scholars include the relationship between Israelite idolatry and the gods and goddesses of the ANE, the extent of syncretism, and monotheism vis-à-vis pagan deities.

199 S. Ackerman. *Under Every Green Tree: Popular Religion in Sixth-Century Judah.* HSM 46. Atlanta: Scholars Press, 1992.

Contributes to a rewriting of the religious history of the Israelites by setting aside what is normative according to the Bible and by focusing on what was common among the people. "While these alternative religious expressions do not have the approval of the biblical writers, I would insist that these popular cults are an important witness to the religion of Israel in the exile" (2). Argues that Israelite popular religion was not a syncretism of pagan influence and Yahwism, for many of the supposed foreign influences were indigenous in the worship of Yahweh.

200 W. R. Domeris. "Jeremiah and the Religion of Canaan." *Old Testament Essays* 7 (1994) 21–39.

Contends that Jeremiah was a champion of Yahwism over against the popular syncretistic form of the religion and that he engaged in "antilanguage" to further his cause, humorously reversing accepted practice in his descriptions. Jeremiah further rejected the reforms of King Josiah as tainted by popular Yahwism, despite the Deuteronomic attitude toward it.

201 M. D. Dick. "Prophetic Parodies of Making the Cult Image." Pp. 1–53 in *Born in Heaven, Made on Earth: The Making of the Cult Image in the Ancient Near East.* Edited by M. D. Dick. Winona Lake, IN: Eisenbrauns, 1999.

In light of aniconism in ancient Israel, D. examines passages in the prophets that prohibit the making of cult images. He finds parallels for the prophetic arguments against idolatry in other ancient literatures and concludes that the prophets failed to understand iconism and simply parodied it. Other essays in this volume focus on the function of cult images in Mesopotamia, Egypt, and India.

202 J. Day. *Yahweh and the Gods and Goddesses of Canaan*. JSOT-Sup 265. Sheffield: Sheffield Academic Press, 2000.
Analyzes the impact of Canaanite mythology on the religion of Israel and on the OT. Finds that the worship of other deities was frequent in preexilic Israel. Nevertheless, a monolatrous party did exist in the preexilic period and by the postexilic period—due in part to Josiah's reforms, and especially the measures of Nehemiah and Ezra—Canaanite deities were in decline.

203 Z. Zevit. *The Religions of Ancient Israel: A Synthesis of Parallactic Approaches*. London/New York: Continuum, 2001.
A comprehensive yet readable description of Israelite religion with two goals: (1) a critical determination of what may be known about Iron Age Israel; and (2) a synthesis of this knowledge within "the structure of an Israelite worldview and ethos involving kin, tribes, land, traditional ways and places of worship, and a national deity" (xiv).

204 F. E. Greenspahn. "Syncretism and Idolatry in the Bible." *VT* 54 (2004) 480–94.
Explores the question: Do the terms *syncretism* and *idolatry* accurately reflect the biblical account's assessment of the Israelites? Defines idolatry as "the practice of worshipping images" (481). Considers *syncretism* a subjective word, since borrowed motifs and practices are common in all religions. Concludes: "syncretism turns out to be our conclusion rather than something the biblical authors saw, and idolatry the prophets' interpretation of how physical objects were used" (493).

3.7 Covenant: Judgment and Blessing

Separate traditions regarding the covenant seemed to have evolved in the northern and southern kingdoms. Elijah, Hosea, and Amos hearkened back to the Mosaic covenant, which allowed for the destruction of Israel as punishment for disobedience. God's obligation to bless was dependent on the people's obligation to serve. In the southern kingdom, however, it was assumed that God had established a Davidic covenant, which guaranteed God's faithfulness and the preservation of the Davidic kingdom, regardless of the faithfulness of the chosen people. Yet the prophetic traditions are not so neat: although Jeremiah and Ezekiel speak of a new covenant based on the unconditionality of the Davidic covenant, both prophets are suffused with the realization that Israel is unable to keep the Sinai covenant although she is obligated to do so. Indeed, the failure of the people to keep the covenant seems to have provided the only rationale for understanding the exile. See also #26.

205 J. Bright. *Covenant and Promise: The Prophetic Understanding of the Future in Pre-exilic Israel*. Philadelphia: Westminster, 1976.
    Considers the promise of future salvation in the preexilic prophets, understanding eschatology in the broad sense of the term. Proceeds chronologically from early Israel down to the last days of the Judean kingdom, after discussing the divine selection of Mt. Zion and David in chap. 2.

206 E. W. Nicholson. *God and His People: Covenant Theology in the Old Testament*. Oxford: Clarendon, 1986.
    Contends that the emergence of the idea of covenant was contemporary with the rise of classical prophecy. Covenant constituted the touchstone for the change from the idea of ontological equivalence between human and divine societies to the possibility of election and human choice. Includes a helpful summary of scholarship on covenant since Wellhausen and an examination of texts thought to indicate the early date of the covenant idea (e.g., Exod. 24:1–2, 9–11; 24:3–8; 34:10–28; Josh. 24:1–28).

207 R. Rendtorff. *The Covenant Formula: An Exegetical and Theological Investigation*. Translated by M. Kohl. Edinburgh: T & T Clark, 1998. Original title: *Die "Bundesformel": eine exegetische-theologische Untersuchung*. Stuttgart: Katholisches Bibelwerk, 1995.
    Examines each of the thirty occurrences of the covenant formula, "I will be your God, you shall be my people." From the Pentateuch to the prophets, "the covenant formula is

an element of theological language which is introduced in a highly conscious manner. It expresses in an extremely pregnant way God's relationship to Israel and Israel's to God" (92).

208   D. Patrick. "Prophecy of Judgment." Pp. 119–61 in *The Rhetoric of Revelation in the Hebrew Bible.* OBT. Minneapolis: Fortress, 1999.

Based on speech-act theory, P. finds evidence throughout the biblical text for the performative nature of divine speech. In turn, there is evidence of the readers' role in shaping divine discourse and the multivalent nature of hermeneutics. Using Amos as a test case, P. demonstrates the illocutionary force of the language of divine judgment.

209   S. Hahn. "Covenant in the Old and New Testaments: Some Current Research (1994–2004)." *Currents in Biblical Research* 3.2 (April 2005) 263–92.

Reviews a decade of essays and monographs on covenant. Divides the discussion into four headings: Foundational Studies, Popular Surveys of the Covenant Theme, Studies of Particular Divine Covenants, and Synopsis of Covenant Research in the Past Ten Years. "Most scholars contributing to the field recognize that the covenant always involves mutuality and relationship . . . there seems to be the assumption of reciprocal loyalty on both sides. Covenants have not only legal but social, ethical, familial and cultic-liturgical aspects" (285).

3.8 Ethics and Social Justice

The high standards of the prophets on moral and ethical issues are evident in their criticism of societal wrongs and in their calls for reform. Two levels of ethical norms are present, one for the nations in general and one for the Israelites. Based on the oracles against the nations, the Gentiles were expected to conform to standards that may be expected of all humans, such as not committing genocide and not engaging in violence against noncombatants. For the chosen people, the standards included being other-centered rather than self-centered, expressed in terms of righteousness and justice toward the poor and disenfranchised.

210   J. L. Mays. "Justice: Perspectives from the Prophetic Tradition."
Int 37 (1983) 5–17. Reprinted in *Prophecy in Israel: Search
for an Identity*, pp. 144–58. Edited by D. L. Petersen. IRT 10.
Philadelphia: Fortress, 1987.
Analyzes justice as a central theme in the prophecies of
Amos, Micah, and Isaiah, and suggests that this part of
the prophetic message is no less relevant today. "Their
faith in justice as a value rooted in the ultimate reality
behind all social history and their calling to make it the
highest priority in a people's understanding of its common
life is an example which no subsequent era has rendered
irrelevant" (155).

211   W. Janzen. *Old Testament Ethics: A Paradigmatic Approach*.
Louisville: Westminster/John Knox, 1994.
Identifies five models for correct ethical behavior: priestly,
wisdom, royal, prophetic, and familial, with the last being
the overarching paradigm. The prophetic model is based on
the narrative of Elijah's interaction with Ahab, but extends
into the classical prophets, as illustrated by texts from Amos,
Micah, Isaiah, Jeremiah, and Ezekiel.

212   M. Weinfeld. *Social Justice in Ancient Israel*. Minneapolis:
Fortress/Jerusalem: Magnes Press, 1995.
Contends that "the concept of doing Justice and Righteousness
in the literature of ancient Israel and of the Ancient Near
East implies maintaining social justice in the society, so that
equality and freedom prevail" (5). Examines the meaning of
the phrase "justice and righteousness," its execution as the
duty of the king, privileges for temple cities, the sabbatical
year and the jubilee, and the divine role in establishing equity
and justice—among other topics.

213   C. J. Dempsey. *Hope Amid the Ruins: The Ethics of Israel's
Prophets*. St. Louis: Chalice, 2000.
Explores the ethics of the prophets thematically and herme-
neutically while critiquing the prophets' moral outlook.
Grounds the prophets' ethical vision in "right relationship"
as expressed in both covenant and creation and questions the
suitability of portrayals of God as divine warrior, as well as
abusive depictions of women for contemporary ethics. Also

emphasizes the interconnectedness of creation and envisions the restoration of all things to their proper relationships.

214 J. E. Lapsley. *Can These Bones Live? The Problem of the Moral Self in the Book of Ezekiel.* BZAW 301. New York: de Gruyter, 2000.

Argues that the book of Ezekiel combines two incompatible accounts of human morality: the language of repentance (chaps. 3, 14, 18, and 33), which presupposes an individual's ability to choose good, and the language of determinism (chaps. 16, 20, 23, and 24), which seems to preclude that ability. Ezekiel attempts to provide a new resolution in chaps. 34–48, where God's provision of a new identity ("new heart" and "new spirit") downplays the necessity of right action and instead focuses on right knowledge. In this synthesis, "character replaces action as the central component of the moral self" (186).

215 T. L. Leclerc. *Yahweh Is Exalted in Justice: Solidarity and Conflict in Isaiah.* Minneapolis: Fortress, 2001.

Investigation of the concept of justice (*mišpaṭ*) throughout the three major corpora of Isaiah (chaps. 1–39, 40–55, and 56–66) and the literary and historical context of each instance. Discovers that in chaps. 1–39, the focus of the term is primarily on issues of social justice and the righting of inequity, while in chaps. 40–55 the term has more to do with the servant/Israel's cause or the Lord's sovereignty. In the last section, justice again refers to social justice, in this case, however, enforced by the Deity.

216 J. D. Pleins. *The Social Visions of the Hebrew Bible: A Theological Introduction.* Louisville: Westminster/John Knox, 2001.

Examines the varieties of social ethics of the Israelite community through the different genres of the OT. The chapters pertaining to the prophets are: "The Ethics of Desolation and Hope: Isaiah"; "Subverting the Message: Jeremiah"; "Territory and Temple: Ezekiel"; and "The Voice of the People: Hosea–Malachi."

217 J. Barton. *Understanding Old Testament Ethics: Approaches and Explorations.* Louisville: Westminster John Knox, 2003.

Consists of nine chapters originally published from 1978 to 2001 in journals and collected essays. Those pertaining directly to the prophets are: "Amos's Oracles against the Nations"; "Ethics in Isaiah of Jerusalem"; and "Ethics in the Isaianic Tradition." A concluding chapter is entitled "The Future of Old Testament Ethics." For an annotated essay, see #515.

218   E. Nardoni. *Rise Up O Judge: A Study of Social Justice in the Biblical World.* Translated by S. C. Martin. Peabody, MA: Hendrickson, 2004. Original title: *Los que buscan la justicia: un estudio de la justicia en el mundo bíblico.* Estella: Editorial Verbo Divino, 1997.

Presents a wide-ranging consideration of social justice from its roots in the ANE through the entire Hebrew Bible and into the NT, with special attention given to the Exodus. Although only pp. 95–121 are concerned with prophecy directly, this informed study helps to situate the prophetic contribution to social justice within the larger canonical message.

3.9 Exile and Restoration

Banishment and exile are common themes throughout the OT, from the prototype of expulsion (man and woman driven out of the garden) to the Babylonians taking the Judeans captive (see ##126, 128–30, 227). It was considered the severest of consequences, especially for the covenant people who counted on the land as a permanent possession. For those involved in exile, either as participants or observers, the genre of lament expressed the depths of the emotions associated with the horror. On the other hand, concomitant with the prophets' language of judgment were promises of hope. This raises an important question: how can the prophets announce annihilation and blessing at the same time? For some scholars the solution can be found in the composite nature of prophetic books. For others, the answer is in God's sovereign restoration of a remnant. The illocution of the language of blessing was similar to the language of destruction: the criticizing terms of judgment and the energizing language of hope called the Israelites back to the covenant relationship. The restoration was generally expected to be a remnant, rather than a full-scale return. See also §2.10.

219 R. W. Klein. *Israel in Exile: A Theological Interpretation.* OBT.
Philadelphia: Fortress, 1979.
Uses a biblical theology approach to explore the implications
of exile: physical, social, economic, and theological. Examines reactions to exile in Lamentations, the Deuteronomistic
History, Jeremiah, Ezekiel, Second Isaiah, and the Priestly
source. Underscores the horrors of exile for the Israelites.
Finds application for today in light of increasingly depress-
ing experiences.

220 J. M. Scott (ed.). *Exile: Old Testament, Jewish, and Christian
Conceptions.* JSJSup 56. Leiden: Brill, 1997.
Fourteen essays pertaining to the concept of exile in the Hebrew Bible and in Jewish and Christian traditions—covering
the Babylonian and Persian periods, Greco-Roman and rabbinic literature, and the writings of early Christianity. Essays
of particular significance include: "Reassessing the Historical
and Sociological Impact of the Babylonian Exile (597/587–
539 BCE)" (D. Smith-Christopher); "The Exile and Canon
Formation" (J. A. Sanders); and "Deportation and Diasporic
Discourses in the Prophetic Literature" (R. P. Carroll). S. intends these essays to demonstrate "that a diachronic study of
the concept of exile provides a fruitful field of research that
warrants more attention" (4).

221 A. Mein. *Ezekiel and the Ethics of Exile.* Oxford Theological
Monographs. Oxford: Oxford University Press, 2001.
In light of the different moral worlds that lay behind the
biblical text, Ezekiel's oracles address moral issues that the
exiles faced, both in the spheres of family and community
and in the sphere of political and religious life. "Ezekiel's
ethical distinctiveness is seen perhaps most clearly in the
high priority the prophet places on ritual, and the way that
the language of cult dominates his analysis of past sin, present judgement, and future hope" (4).

222 J. M. Scott (ed.). *Restoration: Old Testament, Jewish and Christian Perspectives.* JSJSup 72. Leiden: Brill, 2001.
Seventeen essays concerned with restoration in the Hebrew
Bible, in the Greco-Roman period, in formative Judaism, and
in early Christianity (a companion to Scott's earlier volume

on exile [#220]). For example, see the essays "Prophetic Tradition" (O. H. Steck) and "Messianic Expectations" (J. Tromp). The essays underscore the importance of the concept of restoration in the Hebrew Bible and in Jewish and Christian traditions.

223 D. L. Smith-Christopher. *A Biblical Theology of Exile*. OBT. Minneapolis: Augsburg Fortress, 2002.
Examines the principal features and themes of diaspora theology, in light of current thinking that the canonical form of the OT originated in the exilic period and was shaped to address issues of that age. Chapter 3, "Listening to Cries from Babylon: On the Exegesis of Suffering in Ezekiel and Lamentations," is especially helpful. Argues that exilic theology has the greatest potential for impact on contemporary Christians.

3.10 Jerusalem and the Temple

The city of Jerusalem had wide-ranging symbolic and theological significance, a significance underscored by the literary reaction to its destruction, which marked the end of the Davidic dynasty, of a spiritual center, and of Yahweh's dwelling place. Centuries of religious objects and wealth accumulated in the temple were ravaged or removed. The prophets interpreted this destruction as the ultimate picture of God's rejection of his chosen people. They had criticized much of the temple cult as an affront to true worship. But they had also offered the hope of a restored temple. Hence, upon the return of the remnant from captivity, rebuilding Jerusalem and its temple became the highest priority. Expectations of the second temple exceeding the heights achieved in the first are evident in prophetic passages touting Zion theology. See also ##135, 137, and 241.

224 R. E. Clements. *God and Temple*. Philadelphia: Fortress, 1965.
Analyzes how the temple functioned as the manifestation of God's presence and how Israelite faith depended on the Jerusalem cult. Finds that the prophets were critical of the temple cult because it did not serve the interests of the covenant. Concludes: "Throughout the pages of the Old Testament

we can see that this conviction of Yahweh's dwelling in the
midst of Israel forms a unifying theme, in which we are able
to trace a certain historical development of ideas" (135).

225   J. Galambush. *Jerusalem in the Book of Ezekiel: The City as
Yahweh's Wife.* SBLDS 130. Atlanta: Scholars Press, 1992.
Analyzes the personification of Israel as Yahweh's unfaith-
ful wife, who comes under her husband's vengeance (Ezek.
16 and 23). Compares this imagery with the language and
imagery for Jerusalem appearing elsewhere in Ezekiel. Concludes that the function of the metaphor is to communicate
powerfully to the hearers that the purity of the temple and
the honor of God must be protected if they are to enjoy
God's blessing.

226   R. P. Carroll. "So What Do We Know about the Temple? The
Temple in the Prophets." Pp. 34–51 in *Second Temple Studies
2: Temple and Community in the Persian Period.* Edited by
T. C. Eskenazi and K. H. Richards. JSOTSup 117. Sheffield:
Sheffield Academic Press, 1994.
Despite elaborate accounts of the construction of earlier
temples and tabernacles, C. questions why only perfunctory
information about the building of the second temple was
furnished in the sources. Contends that the Second Temple
period may have been the focus of social conflict and that
the legitimacy of the Jerusalem temple was not recognized
by all groups.

227   R. S. Hess and G. J. Wenham (eds.). *Zion: City of Our God.*
Grand Rapids: Eerdmans, 1999.
Essays on various dimensions of the Zion tradition. R. Hess
considers the impact of Sennacherib's attack on Jerusalem
as recorded in Kings, Chronicles, and Isaiah. T. Renz traces
through the book of Ezekiel the effect of the Babylonian destruction of Jerusalem. K. Heim finds that the theology of Lamentations is a guide for dealing with grief and suffering.

228   L. J. Hoppe. *The Holy City: Jerusalem in the Theology of the
Old Testament.* Collegeville, MN: Liturgical Press, 2000.
Surveys various traditions about Jerusalem: its judgment in
the preexilic and exilic prophets, a vision of restoration in

Second Isaiah, Zion rebuilt in the postexilic period, the new Jerusalem in Isa. 56–66, Zech. 9–14, Isa. 24–27, and Daniel, and the liberated city in the Apocrypha.

229 J. Day (ed.). *Temple and Worship in Biblical Israel.* Library of Hebrew Bible/Old Testament Studies 422. London: T & T Clark, 2005.

See, for example, "The Prophets and the Cult" (J. Barton); "Temple and Worship in Isaiah 6" (H. G. M. Williamson); "Divine Reversal and the Role of the Temple in Trito-Isaiah" (J. Middlemas); "Temple and Worship in Ezekiel 40–48" (P. M. Joyce).

3.11 Eschatology and Messianism

The eschatology of prophecy is a difficult concept to define, as evidenced in the literature. Does it refer to any form of judgment or to blessing that is future, whether personal, national, or universal? Does it refer only to final forms of judgment or blessing? Do final forms of destruction and blessing entail the end of this world and the beginning of a new world? Is a messianic figure implicit in a definition of eschatology? How is biblical eschatology different from apocalyptic eschatology? With no consensus concerning these questions, individual scholars have different understandings of eschatology and how to investigate it usefully.

230 S. Mowinckel. *He That Cometh: The Messiah Concept in the Old Testament and Later Judaism.* Translated by G. W. Anderson. New York: Abingdon, 1954. Reprinted in Biblical Resource Series. Grand Rapids: Eerdmans, 2005. Original title: *Han som kommer; Messiasforventningen i det Gamle Testament og på Jesu tid.* København: G. E. C. Gad, 1951.

A classic study of the OT concept of messiah in light of ANE backgrounds, including how the concept was modified in Second Temple Judaism and in the NT. This reprint includes an important preface by J. J. Collins, reviewing scholarly insights from the DSS, etc., of the last 50 years.

231 P. E. Satterthwaite, R. Hess, and G. Wenham (eds.). *The Lord's Anointed: Interpretation of Old Testament Messianic Texts.*

Grand Rapids: Baker Academic/Carlisle, UK: Paternoster, 1995.

See these essays in particular: "Messianic Themes in Zechariah 9–11" (I. M. Duguid); "The 'Servant of the Lord' in the Servant Songs of Isaiah" (G. P. Hugenberger); "Messianic Interpretation of the Old Testament in Modern Context" (J. G. McConville); "Messianism and Messianic Prophecy in Isaiah 1–12 and 28–33" (D. Schibler); "The King in the Book of Isaiah" (R. L. Schultz).

232 H. G. Reventlow (ed.). *Eschatology in the Bible and in Jewish and Christian Tradition.* JSOTSup 243. Sheffield: Sheffield Academic Press, 1997.

Of the fourteen essays, five are of particular interest: "Eschatology in the Book of Jeremiah" (Y. Hoffman); "The Eschatologization of the Prophetic Books" (H. G. Reventlow); "Character and Function of the Divine Sayings in the Elijah and Elisha Traditions" (W. Thiel); "From Prophetic to Apocalyptic Eschatology" (B. Uffenheimer); and "Expectations of the Divine Kingdom in Biblical and Postbiblical Literature" (M. Weinfeld).

233 W. H. Bellinger Jr. and W. R. Farmer (eds.). *Jesus and the Suffering Servant: Isaiah 53 and Christian Origins.* Harrisburg, PA: Trinity, 1998.

Sixteen essays address the question of how Isa. 53 was understood, especially in relation to God's will for Israel and for the Messiah. Essays include "The World of the Servant of the Lord in Isaiah 40–55" (P. D. Hanson); "Basic Issues in the Interpretation of Isaiah 53" (H. G. Reventlow); "Isaiah 53 and the Restoration of Israel" (R. E. Clements); "On Reading Isaiah 53 as Christian Scripture" (R. F. Melugin); "Jesus and Isaiah 53" (O. Betz); "Did the Use of Isaiah 53 to Interpret His Mission Begin with Jesus?" (M. D. Hooker).

234 J. Day (ed.). *King and Messiah in Israel and the Ancient Near East.* JSOTSup 270. Sheffield: Sheffield Academic Press, 1998.

See in particular these essays: "Messianic Texts in Isaiah 1–39" (H. G. M. Williamson); "King and Messiah in Ezekiel" (P. M. Joyce); "The Messiah in the Postexilic Old Testament

Literature" (R. Mason); "Messianism in the Old Testament
Apocrypha and Pseudepigrapha" (W. Horbury).

235 H. G. M. Williamson. *Variations on a Theme: King, Messiah
and Servant in the Book of Isaiah.* The Didsbury Lectures,
1997. Carlisle, UK: Paternoster, 1998.

Defines Messianism as "the role of a human figure in establishment of God's ideal society" (203). Adopting the musical
form of theme and variations, finds that the theme of Isaiah
is king: the first variation is the "Ideal King" (Isa. 9, 11, 16,
32); second is "Immanuel" (Isa. 7); third is "Servant" (Isa.
40–55); and the fourth variation is "Messiah" (Isa. 61).

236 W. H. Rose. *Zemah and Zerubbabel: Messianic Expectations
in the Early Postexilic Period.* JSOTSup 304. Sheffield: Sheffield Academic Press, 2000.

Challenges much previous scholarship in contending that the
term usually rendered *branch* should instead be translated
vegetation, greenery and that this person is not Zerubbabel
but a future messianic figure. Hag. 2:20–23 is not necessarily
to be interpreted royally but as divine protection for Zerubbabel. Zech. 3:7; 4:14; and 6:13 should not be read as indicating
the increase in priestly power, nor is there the expectation
of an imminent restoration of the monarchy.

237 R. S. Hess and M. D. Carroll R. (eds.). *Israel's Messiah in the
Bible and the Dead Sea Scrolls.* Grand Rapids: Baker Academic,
2003.

Essays of particular interest include "My Servant David:
Ancient Israel's Vision of the Messiah" (D. I. Block); "'If He
Looks Like a Prophet and Talks Like a Prophet, Then He
Must Be . . .': A Response to Daniel I. Block" (J. D. Hays);
"New Lenses to Establish Messiah's Identity? A Response to
Daniel I. Block" (M. D. Carroll R.).

3.12 Special Studies

Numerous issues in the prophets deserve special treatment. The
sources below, discussing interpretive issues (Friebel [#240]; Geyer
[#246]), theological issues (Hugenberger [#239]), and the relationship

between prophetic books and the ANE traditions (McLaughlin [#242]), are representative. What unites these issues, aside from being difficult to locate elsewhere, is the conviction that the prophets spoke profoundly to the audiences of their own day and that their message remains relevant for their spiritual descendants.

238 W. D. Stacey. "The Function of Prophetic Drama." Pp. 260–82 in *Prophetic Drama in the Old Testament*. London: Epworth, 1990. Reprinted in *The Place Is Too Small for Us: The Israelite Prophets in Recent Scholarship*, pp. 112–32. Edited by R. P. Gordon. Sources for Biblical and Theological Study 5. Winona Lake, IN: Eisenbrauns, 1995.
Theorizes that the root of prophetic *drama* (nonverbal signs used to accompany the proclamation of the prophetic word) is the desire to render the prophetic word more powerful rather than to explain it. Further demonstrates the multi-tiered meaning resident in prophetic signs: for the prophet, for the Hebrew onlooker, for the prophet's disciples, for the editors of the prophetic work, and for the canonizing faith communities.

239 G. P. Hugenberger. *Marriage as Covenant: A Study of Biblical Law and Ethics Concerning Marriage, Developed from the Perspective of Malachi*. VTSup 52. Leiden: Brill, 1994. Reprinted Grand Rapids: Baker Academic, 1998.
Examination of Mal. 2:10–16 designed to answer the question: Is marriage a covenant for Malachi and his audience? Answering in the affirmative, H. exhaustively investigates the meaning of marriage as covenant in Mal. 2:14 and argues that the verse refers to literal, not figurative, marriage. As covenants must be ratified by an oath, H. argues that the act of marital intercourse functioned as an equivalent to swearing an oath.

240 K. G. Friebel. *Jeremiah's and Ezekiel's Sign-Acts*. JSOTSup 283. Sheffield: Sheffield Academic Press, 1999.
Analyzes eight sign-acts of each prophet for rhetorical qualities and meaning, including exegesis of relevant passages. Argues that each of the symbolic actions of Jeremiah and Ezekiel were part of the overall message designed to persuade people to repent.

241 L. L. Grabbe and R. D. Haak (eds.). *'Every City Shall Be For-saken': Urbanism and Prophecy in Ancient Israel and the Near East*. JSOTSup 330. Sheffield: Sheffield Academic Press, 2001.

Ten papers from the SBL Prophetic Texts and Their Ancient Contexts Group (1999). Essays include: "Cityscape to Landscape: The 'Back to Nature' Theme in Isaiah 1–35" (J. Blenkinsopp); "City of Chaos, City of Stone, City of Flesh: Urbanscapes in Prophetic Discourses" (R. P. Carroll); "This Land Is My Land: On Nature as Property in the Book of Ezekiel" (J. Galambush); "Sup-Urbs or Only Hyp-Urbs? Prophets and Populations in Ancient Israel and Socio-historical Method" (L. L. Grabbe); "Reconstructing Haggai's Jerusalem: Demographic and Sociological Considerations and the Search for an Adequate Methodological Point of Departure" (J. Kessler); "City as Lofty as Heaven: Arbela and Other Cities in Neo-Assyrian Prophecy" (M. Nissinen); and "Jerusalem: An Example of War in a Walled City (Isaiah 3–4)" (J. D. W. Watts).

242 J. L. McLaughlin. *The* marzēaḥ *in the Prophetic Literature: References and Allusions in Light of the Extra-Biblical Evidence*. VTSup 86. Leiden: Brill, 2001.

Finds that three elements were indicative of the *marzēaḥ* festival in all its manifestations in the ANE: (1) excessive alcohol consumption (2) by the upper class (3) in a religious context. Considers ten possible references to the *marzēaḥ* in the prophets, concluding that only four definitely allude to the practice: Amos 4:1; Hos. 4:16–19; Isa. 28:7–8 (22); and Ezek. 39:17–20. Although many consider the *marzēaḥ* tied to funerary practices, Isa. 28:7–8 (22) is the earliest biblical or extra-biblical passage to make such a connection.

243 A. Fitzgerald. *The Lord of the East Wind*. Catholic Biblical Quarterly Monograph Series 34. Washington, DC: Catholic Biblical Association of America, 2002.

A study of storm theophanies, focusing primarily on the metereological context of the sirocco, referred to in Scripture as the *east wind*. Analyzes eighteen OT texts, all but three being prophetic. Argues that the extreme language of storm theophanies can be adequately interpreted only by understanding the weather patterns of Palestine.

244 J. Stiebert. *The Construction of Shame in the Hebrew Bible: The Prophetic Contribution.* JSOTSup 346. London: Sheffield Academic Press, 2002.

Explores the concept of shame in Isaiah, Jeremiah, and Ezekiel using recent psychological research. Discussion of Isaiah discloses the inadequacy of the honor/shame model, while analysis of Jeremiah considers the use of shame in ideological discourses. Scrutiny of Ezekiel concentrates on the relationship of shame and impurity especially in the female imagery in chaps. 16 and 23. Rejects a rigid differentiation of shame from guilt.

245 S. Paas. *Creation and Judgement: Creation Texts in Some Eighth Century Prophets.* Old Testament Studies 47. Leiden: Brill, 2003.

Thoroughly examines the use of creation imagery in Isaiah, Amos, and Hosea. Questions von Rad's subordination of creation faith to salvation faith, arguing that creation, especially procreation imagery, was theologically important from the earliest history of Israel. In Amos, creation thought is separate from historical considerations, although both themes function with a similar purpose. For Hosea, creation and history are much more closely linked. Isaiah uses creation imagery primarily to emphasize divine kingship.

246 J. B. Geyer. *Mythology and Lament: Studies in the Oracles about the Nations.* Society for Old Testament Studies Monograph Series. Aldershot, UK: Ashgate, 2004.

Inquires into the origins of the oracles about the foreign nations in Isaiah, Jeremiah, and Ezekiel, concluding that they are indebted to a temple liturgy which had its own roots in Sumerian laments. Delineates five elements of the form of the oracles: (1) the superscription; (2) destruction; (3) lament; (4) flight; and (5) Yahweh. Argues that the oracles are to be interpreted mythologically, not politically, by exegeting Isa. 14:4–23 and Ezek. 27 and 31.

247 L.-S. Tiemeyer. "Prophecy as a Way of Canceling Prophecy—The Strategic Uses of Foreknowledge." *ZAW* 117 (2005) 329–50.

Employs predictions in 1–2 Sam. and 1–2 Kings to demonstrate that the foretold future does not need to come to pass in order for the prediction to accomplish its purpose. Predictions may simply evoke repentance, which nullifies the prediction. Or when David learns that the inhabitants of Keilah will turn him over to Saul, he departs from the city, resulting in the prediction accomplishing its purpose of protecting David (1 Sam. 23:9–13). The foreknowledge provided by the prophecy was the intent.

4

Composition and Compilation

4.1 Isaiah

For much of the twentieth century the consensus of critical scholarship considered the book of Isaiah to be two if not three independent compositions originating in different historical settings. Most
scholars concurred that portions of Isa. 1–39 contained the oracles
of Isaiah of Jerusalem (late eighth century); that Isa. 40–55 originated in the Babylonian exile (sixth century BC); and that Isa. 56–66
took shape in postexilic Palestine (late sixth to fifth century BC).
A fresh presentation of this theory can be found in J. Blenkinsopp's
three volumes on Isaiah in the Anchor Bible series. Meanwhile, the
traditional approach assuming single authorship for Isaiah was represented among a few scholars, who placed its date of composition
from the eighth century (e.g., J. A. Motyer) to the late fifth century
(e.g., J. D. W. Watts). More recently, alternative proposals to the
theory of independent compositions have been under consideration:
(1) an Isaianic school of disciples expanded what Isaiah wrote to the
present shape of the book; (2) the composition and redaction of the
book are closely aligned, with a corollary of the three sections being

interdependent; (3) consistent themes appearing throughout the book suggest overarching redactional activity or a common underlying tradition; (4) structural unity points toward redactional efforts at tying the book together; and (5) the interpretation of the book does not depend on historical-critical research but on the meaning of Isaiah within the faith community (in line with canonical criticism or reader-response criticism). The paradigm shift to reading Isaiah holistically encompasses many different viewpoints, from theories about sophisticated redactors structuring the book to be read as a whole, to reading Isaiah synchronically through the eyes of implied readers. The diversity of views results in numerous possibilities of interpretation. See also ##19, 21–22, 26, 79, 82, 110–11, 127, 154, 171, 175, 180–81, 185, 189, 195, 215–17, 233, 235, 244–46, 323, 406–8, 413–18, 420, 432, 437, 439–40, 452, and *Review and Expositor* 88.2 (1991).

248 B. Duhm. *Das Buch Jesaia.* Fifth edition. Göttingen: Vandenhoeck & Ruprecht, 1968.
    Classic work that provided the twentieth-century scholarly impetus for seeing Isaiah as divisible into three separate books: "The Older Book of Isaiah" (chaps. 1–39) and the "Appendix to the Book of Isaiah," further subdivided into chaps. 40–55 and 56–66. D.'s major contribution in this commentary is the separation of chaps. 56–66 (Trito-Isaiah) from chaps. 40–55 (Deutero-Isaiah).

249 J. Blenkinsopp. "The 'Servants of the Lord' in Third Isaiah: Profile of a Pietistic Group in the Persian Epoch." *Proceedings of the Irish Biblical Association* 7 (1983) 1–23. Reprinted in *The Place Is Too Small for Us: The Israelite Prophets in Recent Scholarship*, pp. 392–412. Edited by R. P. Gordon. Sources for Biblical and Theological Study 5. Winona Lake, IN: Eisenbrauns, 1995.
    Profiles the "prophetic-eschatological" movement that he finds to have been inspired by the nameless sufferer of the Servant Songs in Deutero-Isaiah. This pietistic group regarded the sufferer as its founder and was active in the Persian era, though it is unknown how long the group outlasted Ezra and Nehemiah. Suggests that the Christian sect, in claiming to be founded by a martyred prophetic leader, could have been following a "pattern" previously set by members of this group.

250 R. Whybray. *The Second Isaiah.* OTG. Sheffield: Sheffield Academic Press, 1983. Reprinted 1997.
Concise summary of the major issues attendant to the interpretation of Isa. 40–55, acknowledging that "its redactional history may be more complex than that of any other prophetical book of the Old Testament" (ix). Considers the relationship of Second Isaiah to the rest of the book, to the historical background of the prophecy, to the prophetic mission of Deutero-Isaiah, to the literary unity and forms of the book, and to the message of the corpus.

251 M. A. Sweeney. *Isaiah 1–4 and the Post-Exilic Understanding of the Isaianic Tradition.* BZAW 171. Berlin: de Gruyter, 1987.
Combines historical criticism with criticism of Isaiah as a whole, arguing that chaps. 1–39 are presented in such a way as to anticipate the concerns of chaps. 40–66 and that analysis of the redaction of the first chapters must take the whole book into account. Two major blocks of redactional material are identified, chap. 1 and chaps. 2–4, with each exhibiting a long process of editing and adaptation.

252 E. W. Conrad. *Reading Isaiah.* OBT 27. Minneapolis: Fortress, 1991.
Reader-response and holistic interpretation of the book of Isaiah concerned "with the text's aesthetic momentum, not its historical development" (29). Repetition in vocabulary, motifs, themes, and rhetorical devices creates continuity in the book, although these repetitions always occur with a difference. The audience encoded in the text consisted of survivors with minority status. Chapters 1–5 and 40–66 serve as a framework for the sixth-century audience's reading of the book of Isaiah's vision (chaps. 6–39).

253 C. R. Seitz. *Zion's Final Destiny: The Development of the Book of Isaiah: A Reassessment of Isaiah 36–39.* Minneapolis: Fortress, 1991.
Working from previous research and the conclusion that definite literary, chronological, and geographical boundaries do not exist between First, Second, and Third Isaiah, S. explores the interrelationships of portions of Isaiah. While finding the redaction history of the book very complex, S. identifies

a variety of evidence in Isa. 36–39 that the parallel account in 2 Kings was dependent on Isaiah. Concludes that these chapters focus especially on the destiny of Zion and are transitional in the growth of the book.

254 G. I. Emmerson. *Isaiah 56–66.* OTG. Sheffield: Sheffield Academic Press, 1992. Reprinted 1996.
Introduction to the most prominent issues in interpreting Trito-Isaiah, including date, authorship, structure, provenance, and relationship to the rest of the book. A final chapter considers the significance of Isa. 56–66, highlighting the strong demand for ethical action, its universality, and democratization.

255 M. A. Sweeney. "The Book of Isaiah in Recent Research." *CurBS* 1 (1993) 141–62.
Reviews research on the book of Isaiah as a whole, investigating the character and role of Trito-Isaiah in the formation of the book, suggesting that it is necessary to abandon traditional concepts of First and Second Isaiahs. Focuses on the "inner hermeneutical dynamics" of the book. Finds that the last fifteen years have seen a revolution in Isaianic studies that "opens a whole new range of possibilities for considering the process by which Isaiah was produced and the interpretation of its final form" (158).

256 D. M. Carr. "Reaching for Unity in Isaiah." *JSOT* 57 (1993) 61–80. Reprinted in *The Prophets: A Sheffield Reader,* pp. 164–83. Edited by P. R. Davies. Biblical Seminar 42. Sheffield: Sheffield Academic Press, 1996.
Critically assesses the various studies that assert that any of several passages (Isa. 1; 35:1–40:8; 65–66) imply an organizational macrostructure for the book of Isaiah. Determines that none of these passages adequately explains the structure of the book. Postulates that several redactors have left their organizational stamp on the book, and these attempts to mold Isaiah into a cohesive unit embody parallel attempts to "reach for unity" in Isaiah.

257 H. G. M. Williamson. *The Book Called Isaiah: Deutero-Isaiah's Role in Composition and Redaction.* Oxford: Clarendon, 1994.

Applies historical-critical methods to the question of the unity
of Isaiah. Concludes that Deutero-Isaiah was influenced by
First Isaiah, that Deutero-Isaiah believed himself to be her-
alding things that had been sealed up in First Isaiah, and that
Deutero-Isaiah adapted prophecies from First Isaiah and edited
them into his own work in order to bind the two parts together.
Includes a review and critique of previous scholarship.

258 J. Barton. *Isaiah 1–39*. OTG. Sheffield: Sheffield Academic
Press, 1995.
Concise introduction to the major issues concerning Isa.
1–39, treating its composition and editing, Isaiah's politics,
his relationship to social morality, and his view of the future. B.'s last chapter, "After Isaiah," considers inauthentic
oracles and their role in the shaping and structure of the book,
concluding that despite multiplicity of authorship, Isa. 1–39
remains readable.

259 P. A. Smith. *Rhetoric and Redaction in Third Isaiah: The
Structure, Growth, and Authorship of Isaiah 56–66*. VTSup
62. Leiden: Brill, 1995.
Analyzes the redaction and growth of Trito-Isaiah, finding
that he was responsible for most of 60:1–63:6 and that a later
editor is responsible for the organization and composition of
the rest of these chapters, with the exception of 66:18–24.
Apart from this appendix, most of Trito-Isaiah can be dated
within 538–515 BC and not against the sectarian background
of the mid-fifth century BC.

260 R. F. Melugin and M. A. Sweeney (eds.). *New Visions of Isaiah.*
JSOTSup 214. Sheffield: Sheffield Academic Press, 1996.
Twelve essays from the Formation of the Book of Isaiah Semi-
nar (SBL) with the common objective of interpreting Isaiah
holistically. For an annotated essay, see Rendtorff (#440). Other
essays include: "The Book of Isaiah as Prophetic Torah" (M. A.
Sweeney); "Reading Isaiah from the Beginning (Isaiah 1) to End
(Isaiah 65–66): Multiple Modern Possibilities" (D. M. Carr); "The
'Scope' of Isaiah as a Book of Jewish and Christian Scriptures"
(G. T. Sheppard); "Figurative Speech and the Reading of Isaiah 1
as Scripture" (R. F. Melugin); "Prophet, Redactor and Audience:
Reforming the Notion of Isaiah's Formation" (E. W. Conrad).

261 M. A. Sweeney. "Reevaluating Isaiah 1–39 in Recent Critical Research." *CurBS* 4 (1996) 79–113.
Comes to three conclusions after surveying recent research on Isa. 1–39: (1) that the short form-critical unit may no longer be studied in isolation from the surrounding literary structures and rhetoric; (2) that the historical Isaiah cannot be described exclusively as preaching judgment, but must be considered informed by current events and Zion/Jerusalem theology; and (3) that First Isaiah must be studied in connection with the rest of the book as well as the traditions of Jeremiah.

262 M. E. Tate. "The Book of Isaiah in Recent Study." Pp. 22–56 in *Forming Prophetic Literature: Essays on Isaiah and the Twelve in Honor of John D. W. Watts.* Edited by J. W. Watts and P. R. House. JSOTSup 235. Sheffield: Sheffield Academic Press, 1996.
Focuses on the authorship of Isaiah: one-prophet interpretation, three-book interpretation, and the more recent one-book interpretation. Offers suggestions for future research on unfinished work in the study of Isaiah, regarding the nature of the unity of the book, the unlikelihood of scribal prophecy, and the social context of exilic and postexilic Judeans.

263 H. M. Barstad. *The Babylonian Captivity of the Book of Isaiah: "Exilic" Judah and the Provenance of Isaiah 40–55.* Oslo: Novus, 1997.
Investigates the history of research that led modern scholarship to the conclusion that Isa. 40–55 was composed in the Babylonian exile and questions this consensus. Since the conclusion that Deutero-Isaiah was composed in Babylon rests on late nineteenth-century and early twentieth-century methods of argumentation that are no longer regarded as valid, B. argues that Babylonian provenance must be abandoned. See also his *The Servant of YHWH and Cyrus: A Reinterpretation of the Exilic Messianic Programme in Isaiah 40–55.* Stockholm: Almqvist & Wiksell, 1992.

264 C. C. Broyles and C. A. Evans (eds.). *Writing and Reading the Scroll of Isaiah: Studies of an Interpretive Tradition.* 2 vols. VTSup 70. Leiden/New York: Brill, 1997. [Also annotated at #405 and #412.]

A two-volume collection of thirty-six articles investigating the book of Isaiah's formation and leitmotifs, oracles and passages, and interpretation in late antiquity. Includes essays on a wide range of topics: authorship, unity, canon, ethics, righteousness, metaphors, rhetorical questions, Zion theology, Qumran, LXX, Josephus, rabbinic interpretation, etc. The work aims "to combine recent approaches that treat the formation of the final form of the book of Isaiah with the more conventional historical-critical approaches that treat the use of traditions by the book's authors and editors" (ix). See, for example, "Reading Isaiah and the Twelve as Prophetic Books" (E. W. Conrad); "The Book of Isaiah and the Construction of Meaning" (R. F. Melugin); "Bibliography of Isaiah" (C. C. Broyles and C. A. Evans).

265 J. Van Ruiten and M. Vervenne (eds.). *Studies in the Book of Isaiah: Festschrift Willem A. M. Beuken.* Bibliotheca ephemeridum theologicarum lovaniensium 132. Leuven: Leuven University Press, 1997.
Twenty-eight essays including "Zion as Symbol and Political Reality: A Central Isaianic Quest" (R. E. Clements); "The Reconceptualization of the Davidic Covenant in Isaiah" (M. A. Sweeney); "Back to Historical Isaiah: Reflections on the Act of Reading" (Y. Gitay); "Historical Information in Isaiah 1–39" (A. Schoors); "Who Was Second Isaiah?" (S. McEvenue); "History and Eschatology in Deutero-Isaiah" (H. Leene); "Lawsuit, Debate and Wisdom Discourse in Second Isaiah" (M. Dijkstra); "'His Master's Voice?' The Supposed Influence of the Book of Isaiah in the Book of Habakkuk" (J. Van Ruiten); "Wisdom of Solomon 3,1–4,19 and the Book of Isaiah" (P. C. Beentjes); "The Language of Suffering in Job 16–19 and in the Suffering Servant Passages of Deutero-Isaiah" (J. C. Bastiaens); "Quotations from Isaiah and Matthew's Christology (Matt. 1,23 and 4,15–16)" (W. Weren); "The Phraseology of 'Knowing Yahweh' in the Hebrew Bible: A Preliminary Study of Its Syntax and Function" (M. Vervenne).

266 A. Laato. *"About Zion I will not be silent": The Book of Isaiah as an Ideological Unity.* Coniectanea Biblica: Old Testament Series 44. Stockholm: Almqvist and Wiksell, 1998.
"Our aim is to examine how the present form of the whole book of Isaiah was interpreted at the time when it was

composed. Why was the Book of Isaiah written? What was its message to the Jews living in the Persian (if not the Hellenistic) period?" (viii). Concludes that the important themes of the book are as follows: the defeat of the Assyrian invasion demonstrated that promise of salvation for Israel is real; chaps. 55–66 explain that the promises of 40–55 have not been fulfilled because of disobedience; if readers will be obedient to Yahweh, they will receive the promise of salvation; and the promise of salvation applies to all nations.

267 H. J. Bosman and H. van Grol (eds.). *Studies in Isaiah 24–27: The Isaiah Workshop*. Leiden: Brill, 2000.
Representative essays include: "Annotated Translation of Isaiah 24–27 (H. J. Bosman and H. W. M. van Grol); "Isaiah 24–27: Text-Critical Notes" (A. van der Kooij); "Syntactic Cohesion in Isaiah 24–27" (H. J. Bosman); "An Analysis of the Verse Structure of Isaiah 24–27" (H. W. M. van Grol); "Petucha and Setuma: Tools for Interpretation or Simply a Matter of Lay-Out?" (K. D. Jenner); "The Prophet Leads the Readers into Praise: Isaiah 25:1–10 in Connection with Isaiah 24:14–23" (W. A. M. Beuken).

268 D. C. Polaski. *Authorizing an End: The Isaiah Apocalypse and Intertextuality*. Leiden: Brill, 2001.
Thorough investigation of the "Isaiah Apocalypse" as a means to consider early postexilic culture, which entails "reading Isaiah 24–27 closely, attempting to catch glimpses of the way it participates in the textual universe of that time" (46). Threads of connection between these chapters are examined thoroughly for their contribution toward the early postexilic culture which P. argues can be approached through textual means.

269 P. D. Quinn-Miscall. *Reading Isaiah: Poetry and Vision*. Louisville: Westminster/John Knox, 2001.
A literary introduction, reading Isaiah's sweeping vision "as a single work, a vision expressed in poetic language, with a focus on both what is said and how it is said" (169). Offers ways to assess the diversity within the book, rather than assuming that the book is a composite work. Applies a methodology of reading Isaiah from the standpoint of themes, imagery, and characters.

270   M. Goulder. *Isaiah as Liturgy*. Aldershot, UK: Ashgate, 2004.
Argues that Isaiah is a liturgical, not literary, work. "Isaiah was
a *preaching* prophet, who delivered his messages principally
when all Israel came together for the Feast" (2). The expansion
and development of the book occurred as it was adapted and
proclaimed in various festivals. Finds that the book of Isaiah
breaks down into eight sections for the eight days of the Feast,
each with a theme and new vision (or announcement of a
vision). Matches the sequence of themes in Isaiah with the
sequence of themes for the Feast in the Psalter.

271   P. Höffken. *Jesaja: Der Stand der theologischen Diskussion*.
Darmstadt: Wissenschaftliche Buchgesellschaft, 2005.
A survey of scholarship on Isaiah since 1975. Considers the
witnesses to the text of Isaiah (MT, LXX, and Qumran), the
themes and structures evident in the book, the movement in
scholarship toward recognizing the unity and artistic merits
of the book, the history of the formation of the book, and the
book's impact. Includes extensive bibliography.

4.2 Jeremiah

Compositional analysis, especially source criticism, dominated
Jeremiah studies during most of the twentieth century. S. Mowinckel
proposed several major sources for Jeremiah: a Deuteronomic redaction, a postexilic addition called the Book of Consolation (chaps.
30–31), authentic oracles from the prophet himself, and narrative
materials that describe the prophet's career. While some scholars
(e.g., W. L. Holladay) continue to use the text of Jeremiah in an ef-
fort to determine the circumstances to which certain oracles were
directed, others (e.g., R. P. Carroll) represent a much more skeptical
viewpoint, arguing that little or nothing can be learned about a historical prophet from study of the book. Those who assume at least
some historical reliability for the book investigate it for clues as to
what can be learned about power struggles of the time, theological
responses to the exile, how archaeology can better explain the book,
and the succession of the prophet's ministry.

In recent decades scholars have been attuned to the polyphony
of voices in Jeremiah and approach sections of the book using literary criticism and redaction history. The relationship of Jeremiah to

the Deuteronomistic school continues to intrigue those who try to quantify its precise nature. For the relationship between the shorter LXX version of Jeremiah and the longer traditional Hebrew version, see §5.1. See also ##21, 22, 24, 26, 68, 71, 91, 105, 110, 112, 127, 150, 200, 216, 240, 244, 246, 403, 406, 409, 445–46, 449, and *Review and Expositor* 101.2 (2004).

272 E. W. Nicholson. *Preaching to the Exiles: A Study of the Prose Tradition in the Book of Jeremiah*. Oxford: Basil Blackwell, 1970. Reprinted New York: Shocken, 1971.

Suggests that both the prose sermons and the prose narratives in Jeremiah should be attributed to the Deuteronomistic school because of theological similarities (such as the authority of the prophetic word and false prophecy) and literary considerations. Maintains that the intent of the prose narratives is not to provide a biography of Jeremiah but to "present a theological interpretation of the prophetic teaching and ministry of Jeremiah" (36).

273 R. P. Carroll. *From Chaos to Covenant: Prophecy in the Book of Jeremiah*. New York: Crossroad, 1981.

Argues that Jeremiah was unknown, except by those who produced the book in his name: "the Jeremiah tradition was constructed out of the poetry of Jeremiah, worked on by many redactional circles, including a major deuteronomic redaction, and produced over a lengthy period of time" (11). In the light of the external and internal chaos facing the community, the redactors of Jeremiah held out various visions of hope and restoration of the community. Two appendices furnish a list of books on Jeremiah in English and suggestions for "using" Jeremiah today.

274 J. L. Crenshaw. "A Living Tradition: The Book of Jeremiah in Current Research." *Int* 37 (1983) 117–29. Reprinted in *Interpreting the Prophets*, pp. 100–12. Edited by J. L. Mays and P. J. Achtemeier. Philadelphia: Fortress, 1987.

Asks five questions designed to give organization to research on Jeremiah: (1) Which texts were written by Jeremiah? (2) Is it possible that the prophet borrowed the speech or diction of another source, toward which he felt ambivalent? (3) Does the book of Jeremiah reflect the prophet's words or those of a

later group of disciples? (4) Do Jeremiah's confessions reflect
the authentic experience of the prophet? (5) How isolated
was Jeremiah with respect to other contemporary prophets?
After surveying the responses of various scholars to these
questions, C. finds that they still await resolution.

275   L. Stulman. *The Prose Sermons of the Book of Jeremiah*. SBLDS
      83. Atlanta: Scholars Press, 1986.
      Compares the prose sermons of Jeremiah with Deuteronomis-
      tic literature using four criteria: words/phrases attested more
      than once in the Deuteronomistic history; words/phrases at-
      tested once; words/phrases present in Deut. 4:44–29:1 but not
      in the Deuteronomistic history; and words/phrases that are
      purportedly Deuteronomic but not present in Deuteronomy
      or the Deuteronomistic history. Finds that Deuteronomistic
      language in MT Jeremiah's prose sermons is derivative of that
      in the *Vorlage* of Old Greek Jeremiah.

276   A. R. P. Diamond. *The Confessions of Jeremiah in Context:
      Scenes of Prophetic Drama*. JSOTSup 45. Sheffield: JSOT Press,
      1987.
      Considers the confessions of Jeremiah in three respects: in
      terms of genre, setting, and purpose; in their relationship to
      each other; and in their literary contexts. Analyzes each la-
      ment, with the goal of seeing how these chapters function as
      a whole. Finds that the Deuteronomic redaction of Jeremiah
      incorporated the confessions into its own interpretive frame-
      work, serving a "distinctly apologetic purpose of constructing
      a theodicy of Yahweh's judgment upon Judah" (189).

277   W. Baumgartner. *Jeremiah's Poems of Lament*. Translated by
      D. E. Orton. Historic Texts and Interpreters in Biblical Scholar-
      ship 7. Sheffield: Almond, 1988. Original title: *Die Klagedichte
      des Jeremia*. BZAW 32. Giessen: Töpelmann, 1917.
      Classic work that assesses the relationship of Jeremiah's
      poems of lament to the lament psalms, concluding that gen-
      erally the psalms are older than the prophet and constituted
      an important source for him. Jeremiah's laments may be dis-
      tinguished from those in the Psalter based primarily on their
      content. The five full laments and four partial laments may
      generally be attributed to Jeremiah.

278 K. M. O'Connor. *The Confessions of Jeremiah: Their Interpretation and Role in Chapters 1–25.* SBLDS 94. Atlanta: Scholars Press, 1988.

Examination of Jeremiah's "confessions" (11:18–12:6; 15:10–21; 17:14–18; 18:18–23; 20:7–13 [18]), including a thorough exegesis of each passage and a consideration of the poems as a collection and their immediate contexts. Considers how these five poems function in Jer. 1–25, finding that the poems had a public function in legitimating Jeremiah as a prophet.

279 R. P. Carroll. *Jeremiah.* OTG. Sheffield: JSOT Press, 1989. Reprinted 1997.

Suggesting that "argument is the essence of reading Jeremiah," C. provides an introduction to the prophetic book which mirrors his conclusions in earlier studies, namely that the book reflects a complex of traditions built up around a largely fictional character under unclear and irretrievable circumstances. Valuable for its questioning of traditional assumptions about reading the prophetic book.

280 C. R. Seitz. *Theology in Conflict: Reactions to the Exile in the Book of Jeremiah.* Berlin: de Gruyter, 1989.

Through a detailed sociohistorical analysis of the situation in Judah just before and after the exile, S. argues that divergent interpretations of the exile accounted for the primary and secondary traditions of Jeremiah as well as the fifty-two chapters (MT) of the book. Examines Ezekiel and 2 Kings 24, the latter of which offers an account of the 597 BC exile independent of 2 Kings 25, for their contributions toward a knowledgeable historicist reading of Jeremiah.

281 W. L. Holladay. *Jeremiah: A Fresh Reading.* New York: Pilgrim, 1990.

Makes the conclusions of H.'s two volumes on Jeremiah in the Hermeneia commentary series accessible to laypersons and beginning students through a less technical but valuable articulation of H.'s view of the chronological development of the book. A final chapter situates Jeremiah within the context of OT prophecy and suggests ways to understand the significance of the prophet for contemporary readers.

282 P. J. King. *Jeremiah: An Archaeological Companion.* Louisville: Westminster/John Knox, 1993.
Provides archaeological background for interpreting Jeremiah, while recognizing the difficulties in describing the historical prophet. Includes diverse aspects of life that inform Jeremiah's prophecy, such as geography, inscriptions, literature, cultic practices, agriculture, and funerary customs. Includes helpful photos, diagrams, maps, charts, and indices.

283 J. G. McConville. *Judgment and Promise: An Interpretation of the Book of Jeremiah.* Winona Lake, IN: Eisenbrauns/Leicester: Apollos, 1993.
Attributes the book of Jeremiah to the prophet himself, not the Deuteronomic school, since significant differences between Jeremiah and the Deuteronomistic works can be discerned (e.g., the definition of Israel's future hope). Since Jeremiah is "substantially the work . . . of one mind," M. is concerned to define the way sections of the book relate to each other and to elucidate Jeremiah's contextual meaning (23). A final chapter explores Jeremiah's fundamental congruity with northern and southern prophecy.

284 H. O. Thompson. *The Book of Jeremiah: An Annotated Bibliography.* American Theological Library Association Bibliographies 41. Lanham, MD: Scarecrow, 1996.
Alphabetical arrangement of 2,777 entries, mostly in English. Provides comprehensive coverage of the previous fifty years, with greater selectivity prior to that. Annotations vary from a word or two to a paragraph. Includes a separate listing of the specific volumes of journals that are cited in the bibliography (keyed to authors' names). Dissertations are listed separately. Indices include author/editor, Scripture references, and subject.

285 A. H. W. Curtis and T. Römer (eds.). *The Book of Jeremiah and Its Reception/Le livre de Jérémie et sa reception.* Bibliotheca ephemeridum theologicarum lovaniensium 128. Leuven: Peeters/University Press, 1997.
Comprised of thirteen essays presented at a seminar on Jeremiah conducted jointly between the biblical studies faculty at the Universities of Manchester and Lausanne, Switzerland

(1995). In place of the quest for the authentic oracles of Jeremiah, these essays instead "focus on a literary entity, its redaction and reception" (11). Six essays appear in French; seven in English.

286 L. Stulman. *Order Amid Chaos: Jeremiah as Symbolic Tapestry*. Biblical Seminar 57. Sheffield: Sheffield Academic Press, 1998.
Presents four theses regarding Jeremiah: it displays a discernable literary intention as discerned from its structure; Jeremiah contains macro-structural units strategically placed throughout the book; Jeremiah's prose sermons are "the most important interpretive guides for reading Jeremiah" (18); and the book comprises a two-part drama (chaps. 1–25 and 26–52) that is marked by a theological and social shift from a national entity to a diaspora community. Concludes that Jeremiah "succeeds in sculpting new shapes and fresh possibilities out of the rubble of exile and dislocation" (187).

287 A. R. P. Diamond, K. O'Connor, and L. Stulman (eds.). *Troubling Jeremiah*. JSOTSup 260. Sheffield: Sheffield Academic Press, 1999.
Collection of twenty-four articles presented at the Composition of the Book of Jeremiah Group at SBL. The articles are organized under four headings: "Text-Centered Readings of Jeremiah"; "Reader-Centered Readings of Jeremiah"; "Theological Construction"; and "Response." D. provides an introduction to the collection, which is intended to "press for an end to 'innocent' readings of Jeremiah" and to illustrate the diversity of interpretations Jeremiah has evoked (32).

288 R. P. Carroll. "Century's End: Jeremiah Studies at the Beginning of the Third Millennium." *CurBS* 8 (2000) 18–58.
Summarizes the major developments in Jeremianic studies, especially the major commentaries of W. McKane (ICC) and W. L. Holladay (Hermeneia). Complement to C.'s earlier article "Surplus Meaning and the Conflict of Interpretations: A Dodecade of Jeremiah Studies." *CurBS* 4 (1996): 115–59; compare also his article, "Radical Clashes of Will and Style: Recent Commentary Writing on the Book of Jeremiah." *JSOT* 45 (1989): 99–114.

289   G. H. Parke-Taylor. *The Formation of the Book of Jeremiah: Doublets and Recurring Phrases.* Society of Biblical Literature Monograph Series 51. Atlanta: SBL, 2000.
Probes the extensive occurrences of repeated words, phrases, and passages in Jeremiah in both prose and poetry in order to unravel the complicated editorial formation of the book. Finds that a large proportion of the doublets parallel Deuteronomistic literature, allowing for a tentative reconstruction of the process of Jeremiah's formation, while acknowledging that further work needs to be done.

290   C. J. Sharp. *Prophecy and Ideology in Jeremiah: Struggles for Authority in the Deutero-Jeremianic Prose.* London: T & T Clark, 2003.
Analyzes the conflict after 597 BC between a group in Judah and a competing group in Babylon over cultic and political legitimacy. Demonstrates that both groups use the tradition of Jeremiah's call as a prophet to the nations, the prophetic succession, and other motifs to further their own interests. Illustrates substantial differences between prophetic roles in the Deuteronomistic corpus and in Jeremiah. Concludes that Jeremiah's multivocality is "the heart and substance of that message itself" (169).

291   B. Becking. *Between Fear and Freedom: Essays on the Interpretation of Jeremiah 30–31.* Old Testament Studies 51. Leiden: Brill, 2004.
Aims to "offer . . . a coherent set of essays on the interpretation of Jer. 30–31," paying careful attention to methodology (1). Focusing on whether the two chapters can be read as a coherent whole, B. begins with text-critical issues, finding that the MT is a reliable basis for interpretation. He proceeds to examine five of the ten "sub-cantos" of these chapters (30:5–11, 12–17; 31:15–22, 31–34, 35–37). Concludes with a theological reading of the chapters as a way to interpret them coherently.

4.3 Lamentations

Most scholars understand the present form of Lamentations to consist of five poems composed between the fall of Jerusalem and

the return of the exiles. The view that the poems were written by
Jeremiah has largely been abandoned, though some think it was a
literary unit written by a single author, as indicated by similar patterns in the poems. Others conclude that the poems were composed
by several authors and then edited into a single text. The poems
likely represent a variety of oral traditions lamenting the worst
event in the history of Judah, then woven together in an acrostic
form. Chapters 2 and 4 may be eyewitness accounts of the fall of
Jerusalem. Except for chap. 5, the poems were composed in elegiac
3/2 meter (the so-called *qînâ* meter). Regarding genre, the consensus
is that chaps. 1, 2, and 4 are dirges, while chap. 5 is a communal
lament. Chapter 3 is considered the key to the book, but opinions
vary on the nature of the chapter.

292 N. K. Gottwald. *Studies in the Book of Lamentations.* SBT
37. Chicago: Allenson, 1954. Reprinted London: SCM, 1962.
Classic work that contends that Lamentations is "a primary
source for an understanding of the Hebrew religion." Finds
that the book possessed a significant communal role and illustrates an adaptable faith in the face of ruin. Discusses the
acrostic form of Lamentations, its forms (esp. the national
lament), its theology with similarities to and differences from
the lament for the dead, and the influence of Lamentations
on Deutero- and Trito-Isaiah.

293 R. B. Salters. *Jonah and Lamentations.* OTG. Sheffield: Sheffield Academic Press, 1994.
Basic introduction to the historical and interpretive issues
surrounding the interpretation of Lamentations, including
its historical setting, connection to Jeremiah, place in the
canon, structure, poetry, genre, and theology.

294 C. Westermann. *Lamentations: Issues and Interpretation.*
Translated by C. Muenchow. Minneapolis: Fortress, 1994.
Original title: *Die Klagelieder: Forschungsgeschichte und
Auslegung.* Neukirchen-Vluyn: Neukirchener, 1990.
Carefully examines the genre of lament, the history of inter-
pretation, and Lamentations's five songs of lament. Argues
that Lamentations is not "literature," but a record of the
reaction of eyewitnesses to the destruction of Jerusalem.
The reactions became venerable words for the descendants

of the eyewitnesses to contemplate. From the standpoint of the book as a whole, W. concludes that by its accusations against God, the book of Lamentations is claiming that God brought about the collapse and humiliation of the chosen, but not without legitimate reason. Concurrent with lament is admission of the people's guilt.

295   T. Linafelt. *Surviving Lamentations: Catastrophes, Lament, and Protest in the Afterlife of a Biblical Book*. Chicago: University of Chicago Press, 2000.
Reading Lamentations after the Holocaust, L. understands the book as survival literature. Asserts that the key to the book is found not in the patient sufferer of Lam. 3 but in the suffering of maternal Zion in chaps. 1–2, and that the absence of divine response to the laments in these chapters generated wide-ranging responses, from Second Isaiah to modern Jewish literature. Concludes: "Text after text has answered Lamentations, but none have replaced it" (143).

296   N. C. Lee. *The Singers of Lamentations: Cities under Siege, from Ur to Jerusalem to Sarajevo*. Biblical Interpretation Series 60. Leiden: Brill, 2002.
Study of biblical lament literature—primarily the book of Lamentations—in comparison with lament in the ANE and former Yugoslavia. Applies an oral-poetic method from folklore and anthropology, noting that "repetition of formula and themes is a main feature of oral poetry" (5). Explores "how each poet casts traditional forms in his or her unique style" (7). Concludes that Jeremiah is not the sole poet of Lamentations but is one poetic singer. "Poets and prophets often personify their towns to render their community's suffering . . . for where the city or village is felt to be a *persona*, a living entity, there is genuine community" (195).

297   C. W. Miller. "The Book of Lamentations in Recent Research." *CurBS* 1 (2002) 9–29.
Reviews important research on Lamentations since 1990, including approaches to date, authorship, genres, and patterns in the individual poems, poetic patterns in the book, the speakers' voices in the poems, and the importance of reading against the grain of the text. Notes the explosion of

popularity of studying Lamentations and the emergence of
new perspectives in reading the book.

298 K. M. O'Connor. *Lamentations and the Tears of the World.*
Maryknoll, NY: Orbis, 2002.
Concise and incisive commentary on Lamentations with a
second section ("Reflections: A Theology of Witness") ex-
positing the theology of Lamentations. Discusses a hermeneutical struggle over language portraying God as abusive.
An epilogue compares the character of God as portrayed in
Lamentations with that in Second Isaiah, which provides a
portrayal of a God concerned with his people's suffering.

299 B. Morse. "The Lamentations Project: Biblical Mourning
through Modern Montage." *JSOT* 28 (2003) 113–27.
Against the conclusion that Lamentations is "a corrupt con-
catenation of verses that have been pieced together according
to an awkward and unpredictable conceptual plan" (114), M.
argues that the fragmentary thematic development is deliberate, offering jarring images and sentiments in order to shock
the reader into various stages of belief and disbelief. Comparison is made with modern photomontages, in which photos
are dismembered and reassembled for graphic effect.

4.4 Ezekiel

The book of Ezekiel has proven to be as elusive and enigmatic as
it is important. Bizarre imagery, extended allegories, and elevated
language make it one of the most difficult of the prophetic works to
interpret. Yet it is at least as important as it is difficult, as seen in its
wide influence. Its language shares close affinities with the Holiness
Code of Lev. 17–26, on which basis some scholars have tried to date
the Priestly source. Little agreement exists, however, on how much
of the book goes back to the prophet himself. Some see extensive
redactional activity by disciples, while others attribute the main
part to the prophet. The book is noteworthy for its explicit dating
(from ca. 593 to 571 BC), which illustrates the general chronological progression of the book. Other questions under consideration
are: How was Ezekiel's prophetic role influenced by also being a
priest? What can be learned from Ezekiel about how the priesthood

functioned during the exile, once the system of rituals had been terminated? What explains the unusual intellect and literary gifts of Ezekiel? What is the significance of certain topics: cherubim, Torah, the land, creation, wild and domesticated animals, shame, the Tyre oracle? What gave rise to the levels of sacred authority in Ezekiel? Were chaps. 40–48 an extended metaphor designed to energize the exiles with the hope of restoration, or a description of a particular entity in the future? See also ##21, 68, 85, 92, 127, 197, 214, 216, 221, 223, 225, 240, 244, 246, 410, 419, 439, and 445.

300 J. D. Levenson. *Theology of the Program of Restoration of Ezekiel 40–48.* HSM 10. Missoula, MT: Scholars Press, 1976.
Elucidates the theological traditions of Ezek. 40–48 by examining the "very high mountain" of Ezek. 40:2 as Mount Zion, the Garden of Eden, Sinai, and Abarim. Considers the role of the *nāśî'*, concluding that it represents a Davidic figure stripped of autocratic imperium. Deals with priesthood in a liturgical kingdom.

301 M. Greenberg. "The Design and Themes of Ezekiel's Program of Restoration." *Int* 38 (1984) 181–208. Reprinted in *Interpreting the Prophets*, pp. 215–36. Edited by J. L. Mays and P. J. Achtemeier. Philadelphia: Fortress, 1987.
Attributes Ezek. 40–48 to the prophet credited with the rest of the book, since it is organized according to principles known from comparative literature and since its themes serve an organized literary function. Finds three themes: (1) the vision of the future temple, through which Ezekiel can guide those who officiate in it; (2) the description of detailed method of behavior in the temple; (3) an accounting of the division of the land. These three themes were modeled on the priestly sources in the Pentateuch. However, Ezekiel's vision failed to determine behavior in the postexilic period.

302 J. Lust (ed.). *Ezekiel and His Book: Textual and Literary Criticism and Their Interrelation.* Bibliotheca ephemeridum theologicarum lovaniensium 74. Leuven: Leuven University Press, 1986.
Thirty-one essays given at the thirty-fifth Colloquium Biblicum Lovaniense (August 27–29, 1985). The first section, "Textual Criticism and Its Relation with Literary Criticism,"

includes nine essays especially exploring the relationship of
the MT and LXX texts of Ezekiel. The second section, "Literary
Criticism, Its Methods and Its Relation to Other Approaches,"
concerns itself with a variety of perspectives on the literary and
rhetorical character of the book. The final section, "The Message
of the Book and Its Relation with Other Biblical and Nonbiblical Literature," examines diverse literary tropes, themes,
and connections within Ezekiel and with other texts.

303 E. F. Davis. *Swallowing the Scroll: Textuality and the Dynamics of Discourse in Ezekiel's Prophecy.* Bible and Literature
Series 21. Sheffield: Almond, 1989.
Seeks to remedy one common failure of studies on Ezekiel,
namely, "that [scholars] do not treat the functional aspects
of Ezekiel's status as a writer" by recourse to a thorough examination of the book as a text (23). Prophecy underwent a
transition in the exile from a form of preaching to textuality, a
change to which D. finds that Ezekiel contributed. Considers
Ezekiel's inability to speak, his narrative, his sign actions,
and his engaging an audience, especially as these impact the
notion of textuality in Ezekiel.

304 P. Joyce. *Divine Initiative and Human Response in Ezekiel.*
JSOTSup 51. Sheffield: JSOT Press, 1989.
Treats the two "poles" of Ezekiel's message, divine initiative
and human responsibility. Analyzes portions of Ezekiel concerning the culpability of the generation of the exile (chaps. 9,
14, and 18) and investigates collective and individual responsibility in the OT. Considers Ezekiel's "radical theocentricity" and the promise of divine transformation for the nation
(e.g., 11:19–20 and 36:26–27). Ultimately, the pole of human
responsibility fades in importance before Ezekiel's concern
for God and his mysterious nature.

305 M. F. Rooker. *Biblical Hebrew in Transition: The Language of
the Book of Ezekiel.* JSOTSup 90. Sheffield: JSOT Press, 1990.
Given the existence of early (preexilic) biblical Hebrew
and late (postexilic) biblical Hebrew, R. argues that "Ezekiel appears to be the best representative of the mediating
link between preexilic and postexilic Hebrew and hence the
exemplar of Biblical Hebrew in transition" (186). Twenty

grammatical forms and seventeen lexemes demonstrate correspondence between Ezekiel and late biblical Hebrew. Of these thirty-seven innovations, R. attributes fifteen to Aramaic influence.

306 D. Bodi. *The Book of Ezekiel and the Poem of Erra*. Orbis biblicus et orientalis 104. Fribourg: Universitätsverlag Fribourg, 1991.
Argues that Ezekiel consciously appropriated an Akkadian work, the Poem of Erra, as indicated by twelve probative characteristics, which can be divided into two groups: (1) features unique to the two works; and (2) features Ezekiel has in common with other OT passages but that seem to have been changed in light of Erra.

307 S. S. Tuell. *The Law of the Temple in Ezekiel 40–48*. HSM 49. Atlanta: Scholars Press, 1992.
Approaches the Law of the Temple (Ezek. 43:10–46:24) as based on an authentic vision of Ezekiel but updated by a redactor in the Persian period. The Law of the Temple is an Israelite analogue to the Demotic Chronicle, which established Persian religious expectations in Egypt; so the *nāśî'* of Ezek. 40–48 is the Persian governor, not a Davidic monarch. The Law of the Temple thus reflects the actual situation in Judah during the Persian period.

308 D. J. Halperin. *Seeking Ezekiel: Text and Psychology*. University Park, PA: Pennsylvania State University, 1993.
Grounds the study of the book of Ezekiel in the study of the prophet's dream and vision language rather than in outside historical events. Postulates that Ezekiel's outrageous imagery can be traced to unresolved psychic trauma, including sexual abuse at the hands of an older male and rage at his mother and Oedipal desire for her. Concludes that Ezekiel's behavior violated normal standards for a prophetic intermediary and veered into pathology. Recognizing this pathology in Ezekiel should compel the prophet's readers to find healing for their own injuries.

309 H. McKeating. *Ezekiel*. OTG. Sheffield: JSOT Press, 1993. Reprinted 1995.

Provides a concise overview of the main issues encountered in studying Ezekiel, including a relatively extended sketch of the history of Ezekiel research. Discusses the specific dates present in Ezekiel, followed by a treatment of the book's theology (including a section on the book's reshaping of history), the other prophetic traditions, the *nāśîʾ* in Ezekiel, and the book's Messianism.

310 K. P. Darr. "Ezekiel among the Critics." *CurBS* 2 (1994) 9–24.

Traces the ebb and flow of scholarship on the critical questions regarding Ezekiel: date of composition; Ezekiel's location(s) at the time of his ministry; Ezekiel's intelligence and sophistication; whether Ezekiel made pronouncements that were converted to written forms or whether he himself was the author; the book as a unified work of art or a multiple-piece puzzle; redactional history; priestly elements in Ezekiel; and the reliability of the MT. Encourages rapprochement between scholars presently mining the Ezekiel scroll for insights into Israel's history and the literary critics who are less interested in the historical setting.

311 K. R. Stevenson. *The Vision of Transformation: The Territorial Rhetoric of Ezekiel 40–48*. SBLDS 154. Atlanta: Scholars Press, 1996.

Demonstrates that Ezekiel 40–48 is not intended as a blueprint for postexilic Jerusalem, but is "territorial rhetoric" that describes "the control of space for social purposes." In this case, the territorial rhetoric constitutes a reimagining of Jerusalem's temple area that reflects a new political structure (79). More basically, however, "the rhetoric claims that YHWH is the only power holder; all others are power subjects in YHWH's territory" (164).

312 T. Renz. *The Rhetorical Function of the Book of Ezekiel*. VTSup 76. Leiden: Brill, 1999.

Defining rhetoric as "the art of persuasion," R. holds that the entire book of Ezekiel functions as a single rhetorical structure designed for readership in the late exilic period. The main genre of the book is epideictic, which is "aimed at establishing a specific kind of community by promoting certain values" (59) that are distinct from idealized versions of Jerusalem's past and from the temptation to accommodate to Babylonian culture. Rhetorical features of Ezekiel include the creation of a theocentric narrative, use of legal traditions, use of emotive language, and the use of deliberate terms for the community.

313 J. F. Kutsko. *Between Heaven and Earth: Divine Presence and Absence in the Book of Ezekiel.* Biblical and Judaic Studies from the University of California, San Diego 7. Winona Lake, IN: Eisenbrauns, 2000.

Considers the exiles' dilemma of how to explain God's apparent absence in the face of the competing deities in foreign cults, especially in statuary. Although Ezekiel never uses the phrase "image of God," K. argues that he was aware of such priestly traditions, which promoted God's presence and deterred idolatry, thus reinforcing monotheism in the face of alluring alternatives.

314 M. S. Odell and J. T. Strong (eds.). *The Book of Ezekiel: Theological and Anthropological Perspectives.* SBLSymS 9. Atlanta: SBL, 2000.

Assembles nine essays, drawn mainly from the Seminar on Theological Perspectives on the Book of Ezekiel (SBL), organized under the categories of theology and anthropology. Theological topics investigated include divine absence (D. Block), Ezekiel's dim view of Israel's restoration (B. Schwartz), the *kābôd* in Ezekiel (J. Strong), and divine presence and absence (S. Tuell). Anthropological essays include the ethical implications of the prophet's anthropology (J. Kutsko), the positive role of shame (J. Lapsley), the primal human and the image of God (D. Callender Jr.), genre and persona in Ezek. 24:15–24 (M. Odell), and a response to feminist critiques of Ezek. 23 (C. Patton).

315 M. A. Corral. *Ezekiel's Oracles against Tyre: Historical Reality and Motivations.* Biblica et Orientalia 46. Rome: Editrice Pontificio Istituto Biblico, 2002.

Suggests that the reason for the puzzling presence of Ezekiel's oracles against Tyre (26:1–28:19) is that city's unfair economic policies toward Judah, including strategic metals, travel, and the slave trade, among other factors. Through consideration of the historical and literary evidence, C. dates these oracles between 599 and 573 BC, or within Ezekiel's lifetime.

316 R. L. Kohn. "Ezekiel at the Turn of the Century." *CurBS* 2 (2003) 9–31.
Discusses the status of Ezekiel studies, especially in regard to advances in understanding the time of the exile. Treats recent commentaries, the relative date of Ezekiel's language, intertextuality between Ezekiel and the rest of the Hebrew Bible, psychological evaluations of Ezekiel, his sign-acts, the explicit imagery of Ezek. 16 and 23, the notion of responsibility in chap. 18, and the nature of the final section (chaps. 40–48).

317 S. L. Cook and C. L. Patton (eds.). *Ezekiel's Hierarchical World: Wrestling with a Tiered Reality.* SBLSymS 31. Atlanta: SBL, 2004.
Consists of twelve essays and two responses concerned with the levels of authority held by priests and heavenly beings according to Ezekiel. For trends in Ezekiel studies, see in particular: "Introduction: Hierarchical Thinking and Theology in Ezekiel's Book" (S. L. Cook and C. L. Patton); "In Search of Theological Meaning: Ezekiel Scholarship at the Turn of the Millennium" (D. I. Block); and "Contemporary Studies of Ezekiel: A New Tide Rising" (S. S. Tuell).

4.5 Book of the Twelve

Until the last couple of decades, the individual books comprising the Book of the Twelve (also somewhat infelicitously known as the Minor Prophets) were studied on their own with little consideration of their connections to each other. However, these books were connected from ancient times, as is evident from Sir. 49:10 and from Josephus's comments concerning the canon. The twelve books are arranged in approximate chronological order (except, perhaps Joel; see §4.7, especially Sweeney [#342]), but the presence of literary catchwords seems to be the most important organizing principle. Nogalski (#319, #320) has provided a thorough investigation of the redaction-history of the book, which serves as a starting place for discussion, whether or not all agree with his conclusions. Some scholars have traced specific themes (e.g., the Day of the Lord) throughout the entire corpus, while others have examined the changing perception of prophecy in the book and its relationship to angelic mediation. The redaction of the Book of the Twelve was apparently part of the larger movement toward canon. Not every scholar agrees that the Book of the Twelve should be read as a unity, for example Ben Zvi (#322). See also ##88–89, 109, 161, 196, 216, 404, and 450.

318 P. R. House. *The Unity of the Twelve*. JSOTSup 97. Bible and Literature Series 27. Sheffield: Almond, 1990.

Argues that the Minor Prophets are a unified literary work, arranged in a sequence matching the prophetic message as a whole: sin—Hosea through Micah; punishment—Nahum, Habakkuk, Zephaniah; and restoration—Haggai, Zechariah, and Malachi. Concludes that unity is also evident in genre, plot, and characterization.

319 J. D. Nogalski. *The Literary Precursors of the Book of the Twelve*. BZAW 217. Berlin: de Gruyter, 1993.

Seeks to uncover the "origin, purpose and nature" of the unity of the Book of the Twelve. Finds the key to unity in the "catchword phenomenon," in which the beginning of one book takes up important words or phrases from the conclusion of the previous book. Offers literary observations on Hos. 14:2–10, Amos, Micah, Zephaniah, Haggai, and Zech. 1–8. Discerns two preexisting corpora: Zech. 1–8 and Haggai; and a Deuteronomistic corpus consisting of Micah, Amos, and Zephaniah. These arguments are continued in Nogalski (#320).

320 J. D. Nogalski. *Redactional Processes in the Book of the Twelve*. BZAW 218. Berlin: de Gruyter, 1993.

A companion to the author's *Literary Precursors* (#319), this volume treats the macrostructure, intertextuality, and literary nature of Joel, Obadiah, Nahum, Habakkuk, Malachi, Zech. 9–14, and Jonah. Finds evidence of a "Joel-related layer" that resulted when preexisting prophetic corpora (Zech. 1–8 and Haggai; the Deuteronomistic corpus) were combined, and suggests that the "majority of the editorial work related to the production of the Book of the Twelve occurs" in this layer (275). Finally, Jonah and Zech. 9–14 were added to the Book of the Twelve.

321 B. A. Jones. *The Formation of the Book of the Twelve: A Study in Text and Canon*. SBLDS 149. Atlanta: Scholars Press, 1995.
Contends that "at least three versions of the Hebrew text of the Book of the Twelve were in circulation in antiquity" (x). Suggests that the evidence of these divergent versions provides a reliable basis upon which to begin a study of the literary history of the collection. Further argues that textual evidence for the formation of the Book of the Twelve can provide insight into the process of canonization.

322 E. Ben Zvi. "Twelve Prophetic Books or 'The Twelve': A Few Preliminary Considerations." Pp. 125–56 in *Forming Prophetic Literature: Essays on Isaiah and the Twelve in Honor of John D. W. Watts*. Edited by J. W. Watts and P. R. House. JSOTSup 235. Sheffield: Sheffield Academic Press, 1996.
Challenges the thesis that the twelve Minor Prophets should be read as a unity. Argues, for example, that the evidence for a single book is much later than the date of composition and that there was not a fixed order for the twelve prophets. "None of the arguments supporting the validity of the claim . . . withstood scrutiny. Moreover, clear, textually inscribed pieces of evidence seem to invalidate such a claim" (154).

323 J. W. Watts and P. R. House. *Forming Prophetic Literature: Essays on Isaiah and the Twelve in Honor of John D. W. Watts*. JSOTSup 235. Sheffield: Sheffield Academic Press, 1996.
Fourteen essays, most presented to the Consultation on the Formation of the Book of the Twelve (SBL) in 1994–95. For essay annotations, see Tate (#262); Ben Zvi (#322); Jeremias (#179). Fuller and Nogalski present evidence in favor of the unity of the Twelve, but Ben Zvi challenges that thesis. Odell analyzes Hosea's references to other prophets. Jeremias argues for literary interdependence in Amos and Hosea. Christensen (#375) surveys research on the book of Nahum. House argues for coherence in Nahum, Habakkuk, and Zephaniah based on dramatic similarities. Watts analyzes the hymn in Hab. 3. Craig examines the interrogatives in Haggai and Zech.

1–8. Berry (#401) considers Malachi's role at the end of the Twelve and the end of the canon.

324　D. L. Petersen. "The Book of the Twelve/The Minor Prophets." Pp. 95–126 in *The Hebrew Bible Today: An Introduction to Critical Issues*. Edited by S. L. McKenzie and M. P. Graham. Louisville: Westminster John Knox, 1998.
Provides an introduction to the Book of the Twelve, its formation, and ways of reading the Minor Prophets as one book. Surveys the significant issues surrounding each of the twelve Minor Prophets, incorporating recent scholarship.

325　R. Fuller. "The Text of the Twelve Minor Prophets." *CurBS* 7 (1999) 81–95.
Elucidates the present state of scholarly activity on the transmission of the text of the Book of the Twelve and its relevance for studying the redactional history of the Minor Prophets. Descriptions of major manuscripts from the Judean desert are included. A classified bibliography gives general resources, resources for studying Hebrew manuscripts, Greek manuscripts, and manuscripts of the various versions.

326　J. D. Nogalski and M. A. Sweeney (eds.). *Reading and Hearing the Book of the Twelve*. SBLSymS 15. Atlanta: SBL, 2000.
Assembles thirteen essays that "present a wide array of perspectives with which to consider the scroll of the Twelve as a single, albeit complexly unified, corpus" (xv). The first section contemplates the Twelve as a unity, while the second is concerned with the treatment of major themes, including the character of God (P. R. House) and Joel as a "literary anchor" for the Twelve (J. Nogalski).

327　P. L. Redditt. "Recent Research on the Book of the Twelve as One Book." *CurBS* 9 (2001) 47–80.
Surveys research that reads the book of the twelve Minor Prophets as a single composition. Questions that frame the discussion include (1) the nature of the redaction, the phases of redaction, and the order of individual prophets; (2) the kinds of intertextuality and how that assists in reading the book as a unity; (3) the possibility of coherence within the book;

and (4) how the Book of the Twelve is related to the rest of the canon.

328 P. L. Redditt and A. Schart (eds.). *Thematic Threads in the Book of the Twelve.* BZAW 325. Berlin: de Gruyter, 2003. Collection of seventeen papers given at the SBL "Formation of the Book of the Twelve" Seminar (1999–2002). Representative essays include: "The Formation of the Book of the Twelve: A Review of Research" (P. L. Redditt); "The Ties that Bind: Intertextuality, the Identification of Verbal Parallels, and Reading Strategies in the Book of the Twelve" (R. L. Schultz); "Forming the Twelve and Forming Canon" (E. W. Conrad); "The Place and Function of Joel in the Book of the Twelve" (M. A. Sweeney); "Theodicy in the Book of the Twelve" (J. L. Crenshaw); "The Day(s) of the Lord in the Book of the Twelve" (J. D. Nogalski); and "Endings as New Beginnings: Returning to the Lord, the Day of the Lord, and Renewal in the Book of the Twelve" (P. R. House).

4.6 Hosea

Central to the study of Hosea is whether the book can be used as a source for information about the man whose name is attached to the book. In what sense was he a prophet, what did he speak or write, and what was his theology? In the last quarter century the trend (though not a consensus) has been away from confidence in the book as a source for historical data. Attention for many scholars has shifted to the final redaction of the book. But were the Hosean materials taken to Jerusalem after the fall of Samaria and redacted there, or did the final work of redaction occur after the fall of Jerusalem? As with most of the OT, later rather than earlier dating of the final redacted form of the book is in vogue. Prominent issues for the study of Hosea include the extensive use of metaphors throughout the book, especially the marriage metaphor that dominates chaps. 1–3 (cf. ##444–45, 448) and the use of tradition in the book. Questions common to the study of other prophetic literature are also germane, such as how the redaction of Hosea proceeded, the historical context of his prophetic activity, and the possibility of reading the book as a unified composition. In addition to sources below, see ##23, 110, 154, 179, 245, 453, *Review and Expositor* 90.2 (1993), and *Biblical Viewpoint* 30.2 (1996).

329 G. A. Yee. *Composition and Tradition in the Book of Hosea: A Redaction Critical Investigation.* Atlanta: Scholars Press, 1987.

Offers a redaction-critical theory of the development of Hosea by beginning with the final form of the book and working backward. Suggests four stages in the book's growth: the work of the prophet himself to which very little of chaps. 1–3 is assigned; a collector who created the figure of Yahweh's marriage to Israel; a Deuteronomistic redactor who worked during Josiah's reformation; and a final redactor who contributed several chapters (3, 11, 14) that lend a final shape to the book.

330 P. J. King. *Amos, Hosea, Micah: An Archaeological Companion.* Philadelphia: Westminster, 1988.

Accepting Albright's definition of biblical archaeology as "the systematic analysis or synthesis of any phase of biblical scholarship which can be clarified by archaeological discovery," K. treats the relationship between archaeological finds and the eighth-century prophets, helping to situate them in their historical setting (13). Pertinent excavations illuminate aspects of life in ancient Israel, including warfare, the cult, and celebratory occasions (e.g., the *marzēaḥ*). Extensive charts, diagrams, and indices are included.

331 D. R. Daniels. *Hosea and Salvation History: The Early Traditions of Israel in the Prophecy of Hosea.* Berlin: de Gruyter, 1990.

Examines Hosea's use of earlier historical traditions with regard to "a proper evaluation of history as a mode of revelation and within the context of Old Testament Theology" (1). After laying out his understanding of the shape and growth of the book of Hosea, D. analyzes a series of passages that refer to earlier historical traditions (9:10–13; 11:1–7; 12:13–15; 13:4–8), concluding that the historical traditions known to Hosea differed from those recorded in the Pentateuch.

332 G. I. Davies. *Hosea.* OTG. Sheffield: Sheffield Academic Press, 1993.

A brief introduction to many of the topics involved in the study of Hosea, including an overview of Hosea and his time,

Hosea's teaching and its development, and the religious situation in Hosea's time. Delays treatment of Hosea's marriage until later in the book, and so gives a fairer representation of Hos. 4–14 than some more detailed studies. Concludes by considering various literary approaches to Hosea.

333 E. K. Holt. *Prophesying the Past: The Use of Israel's History in the Book of Hosea.* JSOTSup 194. Sheffield: Sheffield Academic Press, 1995. Reprinted 1998.
Examines the traditions of Israel's past as they are used in the book of Hosea, on the assumption that the book of Hosea provides the earliest fixed, written version of those traditions. Focuses on the Jacob material in Hosea, on the election of Israel, and on the significance of the prophets for the faith of Israel. Concludes that the two central concepts of Hosea are the knowledge of God and his demand for exclusivity.

334 G. Eidevall. *Grapes in the Desert: Metaphors, Models and Themes in Hosea 4–14.* Stockholm: Almqvist & Wiksell, 1996.
After a brief definition of terminology and an investigation of modern metaphor theory and a methodological discussion, E. analyzes the metaphors in each discourse unit in Hos. 4–14. In his assessment of the results, E. finds judicial, covenantal, and monarchical models to be dominant, although those of farmer and parent are also significant.

335 G. Morris. *Prophecy, Poetry and Hosea.* JSOTSup 219. Sheffield: Sheffield Academic Press, 1996.
Focuses on the literary qualities of Hosea, specifically verbal repetition and wordplay. Argues that the foundational genres of poetry and rhetoric are distinct and nearly mutually exclusive and that Hosea is primarily poetic. "My brief poetic reading uncovered much meaning in the book, meaning that generations of rhetorical analysis have missed or ignored" (133).

336 Y. Sherwood. *The Prostitute and the Prophet: Hosea's Marriage in Literary-Theological Perspective.* JSOTSup 212. Sheffield: Sheffield Academic Press, 1996.
Scrutinizes Hos. 1–3 using four interpretive methods—metacommentary, semiotics, Derridean deconstructionism, and

feminist interpretation—based on the methods fitting together in a "methodological continuum" (17). Demonstrates that tensions between the apparent ethical dilemmas in these chapters have been customarily downplayed, but an analogy with Shakespeare's "problem plays" helps to provide a literary method for dealing with this fragmented text.

337 J.-G. Heintz and L. Millot. *Le livre prophétique d'Osee: Texto-Bibliographie du XXème siècle*. Wiesbaden: Harrassowitz, 1999.
Citations of approximately 1,900 books and articles on Hosea. Of those, about 300 are general monographs and articles (arranged alphabetically). The remainder are listed by verse and arranged chronologically.

338 B. E. Kelle. *Hosea 2: Metaphor and Rhetoric in Historical Perspective*. Atlanta: SBL/Leiden: Brill, 2005.
Offers a rhetorical-critical reading of Hos. 2, focusing on investigation of the text's major metaphors in light of biblical and ANE traditions and comparative texts on the meaning of marriage and divorce. Analyzes Hos. 2 as a single rhetorical unit and understands the historical situation addressed by the text's rhetoric to be the close of the Syro-Ephraimite War (731–730 BC).

4.7 Joel

The canonical position of Joel as the second prophet in the Book of the Twelve (in the MT, not the LXX) has suggested to some that it is one of the oldest prophetic books. However, this placement may reflect the literary parallels between Joel 1 and Amos 3, not the date of composition. Several factors suggest a postexilic date for the book: the reference to the Greek slave trade (3:6) and the frequent citation and allusion to earlier prophetic books (e.g., 3:4–8 [MT 4:4–8] reflecting Amos 1:6–10, and the similarities between Joel 2:1–11 and Isa. 13). These frequent allusions make intertextuality a significant issue for contemporary study of the book. One of the most debated issues in interpreting Joel is the question whether the locust plague described in the first half of the book should be understood as a metaphor for an armed invasion or some other form

of judgment. Some recent research on Joel has focused on its conceptual unity (e.g., Prinsloo [#340]) and redaction. Other significant
issues in research include the difference between the conception of
prophecy in Joel compared with other prophetic books, the nature
of the deity in the book, and the significance of the Day of the Lord.
In addition to sources below, see ##24, 82, 165, 178, and *Biblical
Viewpoint* 29.2 (1995).

339 W. S. Prinsloo. *The Theology of the Book of Joel*. BZAW 163.
Berlin: de Gruyter, 1985.
Rather than developing a comprehensive account of the
theology of Joel, P. examines "what the book of Joel tells us
about Yahweh" (2). Divides Joel into ten pericopes, gives a
brief commentary on each section, and briefly discusses the
theological contribution of that section. Concludes: "It seems
as if a crisis situation (a plague of locusts) occurring after the
exile was interpreted theologically and then used in these
grim times to kindle fresh hope for the future" (127).

340 W. S. Prinsloo. "The Unity of the Book of Joel." *ZAW* 104
(1992) 68–81.
Each pericope of the book of Joel is integrated in a "step-by-
step progression" and builds on the themes of its predecessor
through repetitions of key words and phrases (81). Joel begins
with trouble, but ends on a note of triumph: "Judah can find
a secure refuge with Yahweh, their God, who lives in Jerusalem" (81). The coherence in the book, while not necessarily
indicative of a single author, indicates a conceptual unity.

341 R. A. Mason. *Zephaniah, Habakkuk, Joel*. OTG. Sheffield:
JSOT Press, 1994.
Examines the contents, historical background, and theological
significance of Zephaniah, Habakkuk, and Joel. Conversant
with both historical and literary approaches to interpretation and the secondary literature surrounding each book,
M. provides ample bibliography. Concludes that these three
books exude "a hope that God will establish his right order
of 'justice' throughout the kingdoms of the world" (126).

342 M. A. Sweeney. "The Place and Function of Joel in the Book
of the Twelve." *Society of Biblical Literature Seminar Papers*

(1999) 570–95. Reprinted in *Thematic Threads in the Book of the Twelve*, pp. 133–54. Edited by P. L. Redditt and A. Schart. BZAW 325. Berlin: de Gruyter, 2003.

Considers the literary structure and genre of Joel, its intertextual relationships to the Exodus tradition (locusts, darkness, desert wind), the Day of the Lord, 2 Chron. 20, and the Book of the Twelve. Argues that the placement of Joel in the LXX was original, as it reflects Judean concerns of exilic and early postexilic times, not those of the later Persian period as does the MT. The LXX placement of Joel also makes sense thematically, treating the northern kingdom first before considering Judah.

343   R. J. Coggins. "Joel." *CurBS* 2 (2003) 85–103.

Evaluates recent research on Joel, considering recent work on the position of Joel within the Book of the Twelve, a consideration of the unity of Joel, how best to explain prophetic traits of Joel which are at variance with other types of prophecy in the Book of the Twelve, themes within Joel (especially the locusts and the Day of the Lord), and later interpretations of Joel. Throughout, C. notes the difficulties of interpretation.

4.8 Amos

Amos is generally considered the earliest collection of oracles under a prophet's name, and the book gives clear evidence why such an innovation likely occurred. It bears a spirited literary creativity, especially in the ironic use of forms (e.g., see Dell [#348] and Möller [#353]). Like other prophetic books, issues of composition and redaction have figured into Amos studies. A unique problem is the determination of whether Amos originated from the Judean south or the Israelite north, and scholars continue to argue over both options, which bears on Amos's relationship to the Davidic monarchy.

Amos is noteworthy for his polemics against religious abuses and for his oracles against foreign nations, which in the past were usually assigned to a later redactor but now are sometimes ascribed to the prophet himself. Amos's strident denunciation of unjust social structures has provided the basis for modern polemics against similar unjust structures (e.g., Carroll [#352], which also provides a treatment of research on Amos through 2002). In addition to sources below see ##19, 21, 23, 106–7, 110, 161, 179, 208, 217, 245, 330, 443, 453, and *Biblical Viewpoint* 27.2 (1993).

344 H. M. Barstad. *The Religious Polemics of Am 2,7B–8; 4,1–13; 5,1–27; 6,4–7; 8,14.* VTSup 34. Leiden: Brill, 1984.
Examination of five topics: a son and father going to the same girl (2:7b–8), the interpretation of the cows of Bashan (4:1–13), religious polemics (chap. 5), the *marzēah* institution (6:4–7), and the deities of Amos 8:14. Throughout B. argues that Amos helped give Yahwism its distinctive shape.

345 A. G. Auld. *Amos.* OTG. Sheffield: JSOT Press, 1986. Reprinted 1999. Reprinted in T & T Clark Study Guides. London: T & T Clark, 2004.
Basic guide to the introductory issues surrounding the interpretation of Amos, beginning with Amos's five visions (concluding it is likely they can be traced back to Amos) and then considering if Amos can be understood as a prophet. Inquires into his occupation, his oracles against the nations, literary issues surrounding the book, and Amos's social and religious criticism. Concludes by treating Amos's message.

346 M. E. Polley. *Amos and the Davidic Empire.* Oxford: Oxford University Press, 1989.
Discussion of Amos from a sociohistorical perspective that portrays Amos as a proponent of the legitimacy of the state religion of Judah rather than of ethical monotheism and of the reunification of the northern kingdom with the southern kingdom. The failure of the northern kingdom to do so resulted in Amos's proclamation of the exile and destruction of the north.

347 S. N. Rosenbaum. *Amos of Israel: A New Interpretation.* Macon, GA: Mercer University Press, 1990.
Contends that "Amos was not simple, was not a shepherd, and was not even a Judean" (3). Rather, Amos was a relatively wealthy functionary of Jeroboam's kingdom who was expelled for his treasonous prophecies against the monarch. As a consequence, R. holds that the vast majority of the book, with the exception of a few minor passages (e.g., 1:1, 3:7), was delivered in one continuous performance.

348   K. J. Dell. "The Misuse of Forms in Amos." *VT* 45 (1995) 45–61.

Argues that when Amos intentionally "misuses" an existing form in a new context he intentionally subverts the audience's expectation of the form's meaning for rhetorical effect. This ironic use of forms emphasizes the inventiveness of Amos's message, suggesting that most of the book derives from the prophet. Perhaps this explains why Amos is the first to have his oracles collected and passed on to future generations.

349   H. O. Thompson. *The Book of Amos: An Annotated Bibliography.* American Theological Library Association Bibliographies 42. Lanham, MD: Scarecrow, 1997.

Alphabetical arrangement of 1,729 entries, mostly in English. Provides comprehensive coverage since World War II, with greater selectivity for earlier years. Annotations vary from a word or two to a paragraph. Dissertations are listed separately. Includes a separate listing of the specific volumes of journals that are cited in the bibliography (keyed to authors' names). Indices include author/editor, Scripture references, and subject.

350   R. F. Melugin. "Amos in Recent Research." *CurBS* 6 (1998) 65–101.

Examines recent research on Amos, including the following topics: analysis of three commentaries that presume most of the book goes back to Amos himself; whether the origins of Amos were southern or northern; redaction-critical studies of the book; synchronic and aesthetic investigations of the book; and reader-response and postmodern interpretations of the book.

351   A. W. Park. *The Book of Amos as Composed and Read in Antiquity.* Studies in Biblical Literature 37. New York: Peter Lang, 2001.

Explains Amos 9:11–15 as "a later redaction during the seventh century BCE, which is characterized by its positive portrayal of Judah, and which revised a theme of exile that culminated in Amos 5:25–27 in the earlier edition" (1). Uses synchronic analysis to establish the form, structure, genre, and setting of Amos, as well as diachronic analysis to distinguish earlier and later levels. The second major section examines the appropriation of Amos by later tradents until the closing of the canon.

352 M. D. Carroll R. *Amos—The Prophet and His Oracles: Research on the Book of Amos.* Louisville: Westminster/John Knox, 2002.
Introduction to major currents of thought on the book of Amos. Part 1 addresses "What Lies Behind, Within, and in Front of the Text." The first two chapters survey approaches to Amos from Wellhausen to 1990 and then from 1990 to the present. The third chapter lends attention to treatments of Amos "from the margins," or those studies that apply Amos to contemporary situations of injustice and marginalization. Part 2 includes an extensive annotated bibliography.

353 K. Möller. *A Prophet in Debate: The Rhetoric of Persuasion in the Book of Amos.* JSOTSup 372. Sheffield: JSOT Press, 2002.
Scrutinizes the rhetoric of Amos through a two-part analysis. The first provides the work's theoretical basis by examining Amos's rhetorical structure, rhetorical situation and strategy, while the second part proceeds with a rhetorical analysis of Amos 1–4. Argues that the book comprises a debate in which Amos fails to convince his Israelite listeners of the need for repentance, serving as a warning to the Judeans who finished redacting his book.

4.9 Obadiah

The shortest book in the Hebrew Bible, Obadiah has often suffered from neglect due to its predominantly negative character. In view of the few clues in the book, the most natural date is one after Jerusalem's destruction in 587 BC, especially in light of vv. 11–14, but it is impossible to be certain. Striking similarities exist between Obad. 1–9 and Jer. 49:7–16, but no consensus has emerged as to how this correspondence is best explained. In its present form, the book falls into two major sections: indictments and denunciations of Edom (vv. 1–14), and oracles of salvation for Israel and judgment for foreign nations (vv. 15–21). Significant questions for the study of Obadiah include its relationship to Jeremiah, its literary cohesiveness and history of redaction, and the function of judgment language against one of the Israelites' neighbors. In addition to sources below, see #369 and *Biblical Viewpoint* 29.2 (1995).

354 S. D. Snyman. "Cohesion in the Book of Obadiah." *ZAW* 101 (1989) 59–71.

Despite the literary disunity (*Uneinheitlichkeit*) of Obadiah, S. finds a circular structure in the book which lends Obadiah a sense of cohesion. Even though judgment is coming on Edom (vv. 2–9), salvation is in store for Judah (vv. 19–21); and Edom's behavior toward Judah (vv. 10–14, 15b) will be reversed on the Day of Yahweh (v. 18).

355 E. Ben Zvi. *A Historical-Critical Study of the Book of Obadiah.* BZAW 242. Berlin: de Gruyter, 1996.

Posits that the original audience of Obadiah was a group of educated (re)readers who would have required repeated readings to discern the minute textual clues to its unity and development, and who were probably situated within Achaemenid Judah. Addresses the relationship between Obad. 1–7 and Jer. 49:7–22, finding evidence of a common source and concluding that the reason for focusing hostility on Edom was the latter's perceived status as the brother of Jacob.

356 T. Lescow. "Die Komposition des Buches Obadja." *ZAW* 111 (1999) 380–98.

Sees Obadiah as divisible into three layers. The first, the core text (vv. 10–14, 15b) derives from the early exilic period and denounces Edom for advocating Jerusalem's destruction. The second, a gloating sermon (vv. 1a, 1b–9), with its center in v. 6, was prefaced to the core text late in the exile. In the late postexilic period, the third section (vv. 15a, 16–18, 21) was added, derived from prophecy against Edom and an eschatological vision of judgment, and was itself supplemented with two very late prose insertions (vv. 19–20).

357 P. J. Botha. "Social Values in the Book of Obadiah." *Old Testament Essays*, n.s., 16 (2003) 581–97.

Applies social scientific criticism to Obadiah and finds that the specific social and theological situation behind the book was Edom's betrayal, which was interpreted as an act of arrogance against Yahweh. "The proof that Israel had been punished, that Yahweh had forgiven them, that he was still interested in them as his special people and Jerusalem as his special dwelling, would begin when Edom (and the nations) would be shamed and reduced to nothing" (598).

4.10 Jonah

The book of Jonah has presented a crux in interpretation due to its almost exclusively narrative content that renders it highly distinctive in the prophetic corpus. Since it is a story independent of a larger narrative and includes only one extremely brief "oracle" (3:4b), its form has more in common with books such as Ruth and Esther than with other prophetic writings. In view of the mention of Jonah ben Amittai in 2 Kings 14:25, some scholars have proposed dates for the book from the time of Jeroboam II, but the most common date is generally held to be in the Persian or even the Hellenistic period, although the date continues to be a point of contention. Determining the genre of the book has been a particularly thorny issue, causing some (c.g., Bolin #360) to dismiss the problem as insoluble. While the psalm of thanksgiving in 2:2b–9 (MT 2:3b–10) was routinely dismissed as secondary by interpreters in the previous century, the more recent trend has seen it as integral to the book. Given the difficulty with more historically-oriented methods of interpretation, literary criticism has proven especially fruitful in interpreting Jonah, both in its more traditional methods such as reader-response (e.g., Ben Zvi [#364]) and in innovative ones like conversation analysis (e.g., Person [#359]) and psychological analysis. In addition to sources below, see ## 26, 293, and 435.

358 J. Magonet. *Form and Meaning: Studies in Literary Techniques in the Book of Jonah.* Sheffield: Almond, 1983.
A literary study of Jonah, beginning with an analysis of divine names and verbs and verbal roots. Focuses on the psalm of Jon. 2, arguing for its authenticity and demonstrating that the psalm should be interpreted ironically. It serves to link both halves of the book together. Concludes that one theme of Jonah is "the freedom of God to be beyond any definition by which man would limit him" (112).

359 R. F. Person. *In Conversation with Jonah: Conversation Analysis, Literary Criticism and the Book of Jonah.* JSOTSup 220. Sheffield: Sheffield Academic Press, 1996.

Seeking to apply conversation analysis to the book of Jonah, P. first provides an introduction to the discipline, especially highlighting "adjacency pairs." Through analysis of explicit and omitted dialogue, P. analyzes how conversations function and how his analysis is related to literary elements such as plot, characters, and atmosphere. Discusses the idea of the implied reader and explores principles that guide the interaction between text and reader. Underscores misreadings that result from discrepancies between the implied reader and actual readers.

360 T. M. Bolin. *Freedom Beyond Forgiveness: The Book of Jonah Re-Examined.* JSOTSup 236. Copenhagen International Seminar 3. Sheffield: Sheffield Academic Press, 1997.

Critiques various methods of the interpretation of Jonah, finding that the issues of genre and the date of Jonah cannot be ascertained given the present state of knowledge (although opting tentatively for a Hellenistic date). Offers a commentary on the book, throughout which B. finds that "the fundamental issue is the affirmation of the absolute freedom, power and sovereignty of Yahweh over all creation" (183).

361 P. A. Trible. "Divine Incongruities in the Book of Jonah." Pp. 198–208 in *God in the Fray: A Tribute to Walter Brueggemann.* Edited by T. Linafelt and T. K. Beal. Minneapolis: Fortress, 1998.

Tests W. Brueggemann's claim of an irreconcilable tension between sovereignty and solidarity at the core of Yahweh's character by examining the portrayal of God in Jonah. Finds that the tension between divine threat and divine salvation is not resolved in Jonah. Concludes: "Within this single text, sovereignty, freedom, retribution, vindictiveness, violence, repentance, mercy and pity sound the disjunctions that Brueggemann perceives at the core of Israel's God" (208).

362 K. M. Craig Jr. *A Poetics of Jonah: Art in Service of Ideology.* Second edition. Macon, GA: Mercer University Press, 1999.

Presents a literary approach to Jonah that does not avoid historical issues but instead is governed by the principles of ideology, prophecy, and historiography. After a discussion of the change in translation of Jonah from the RSV to the NRSV, C. investigates Jonah's narrator and characters and the process of reading. An exposition of poetic prayer and poetry follows. Concluding this study is an account of Jonah's inner life and the ideology of the book.

363 K. M. Craig Jr. "Jonah in Recent Research." *CurBS* 7 (1999) 97–118.
Investigates recent research on Jonah since Sasson's Anchor Bible commentary on Jonah (1990). After reviewing books and commentaries, C. summarizes research on Jonah's literary aspects, intertextual dimensions, genre studies, canon, Jonah as a theological book, isolated passages, prophecy and the prophet, and concludes with other research. Finds that not everything recent is new, but new perspectives do exist and are likely to continue.

364 E. Ben Zvi. *Signs of Jonah: Reading and Rereading in Ancient Yehud.* JSOTSup 367. Sheffield: Sheffield Academic Press, 2003.
Approaches Jonah through the lens of how Jerusalemite literati would have read it. Examines selected issues, including the tension between the destruction of the historical Nineveh and the salvation of its literary representative, the ambiguity between the change of prepositions in the divine commands in 1:2 and 3:2, the status of the book as meta-prophecy, and the self-criticism of the intelligentsia who produced it. Argues that these literary ambiguities reflect in part the literati's recognition of God's freedom and their own incomplete understanding. A final chapter offers a theoretical basis for the many divergent readings of Jonah in different interpretive communities.

365 J. H. Gaines. *Forgiveness in a Wounded World: Jonah's Dilemma.* SBL Studies in Biblical Literature 5. Atlanta: SBL, 2003.
Examines Jonah as a paradigm of forgiveness with attention to a wide array of input outside the normal library of academic biblical criticism (e.g., teachings of Martin Luther King Jr.). Reviews issues surrounding the interpretation of the book,

such as date and genre (no genre is felt to be sufficient by itself), after which she devotes each chapter of her book to an examination of how each chapter of Jonah advances her theme of forgiveness. A final chapter surveys significant modern attitudes toward forgiveness.

366 A. Kamp. *Inner Worlds: A Cognitive Linguistic Approach to the Book of Jonah.* Translated by D. Orton. Leiden: Brill, 2004. Original title: "Innerlijke werelden: een cognitief taalkundige benadering van het Bijbelboek Jona." PhD diss., Theologische Faculteit Tilburg, 2002.
Reexamines the text in light of cognitive linguistics, text-syntactic, and text-semantic analysis, aiming "to provide an insight into the conceptual structure called into mind by the book of Jonah, which comes into being in interaction with the reader" (4). Concludes that "the narrative world of Jonah offers an insight into an entirely new reality in word and picture. . . . Left behind after the reading is a structurally altered view of God and the world" (234).

4.11 Micah

Recent studies on Micah treat its redaction history (Wagenaar [#371]), both in the context of the Book of the Twelve (Zapff [#370]) and in consideration of whether Micah is capable of being read as a coherent unit (Hagstrom [#367]). Micah apparently began prophesying before the destruction of Samaria, warning Israel of the impending destruction. The language of judgment against Jerusalem can be associated with the Assyrian siege in 701. The book is noteworthy for the variety of literary forms within the book, including prayers, hymns, lawsuits, laments, etc. The sudden shifts in content and form leave scholars puzzling over a unifying principle and major structural divisions. Reasoning that oracles of judgment are more likely to be attributed to Micah—and promises of blessing less likely—many scholars ascribe most of chaps. 1–3 to Micah but little of chaps. 4–7, positing the gradual growth of the book and redactional process. In addition to sources below, see #330 and #453.

367 D. G. Hagstrom. *The Coherence of the Book of Micah: A Literary Analysis.* SBLDS 89. Atlanta: Scholars Press, 1988.

Seeks to answer the question, "Does the book of Micah display a certain significant type of coherence which renders it capable of meaningful construal as a unit?" (4). Answers this question in the affirmative, finding that the summons to "hear" is significant in 1:2 and 6:1, and thus the book consists of two major sections (chaps. 1–5, chaps. 6–7). Throughout, H. argues that while the final form is not the only object of legitimate interest, it remains an important element of a book's meaning.

368 A. van der Wal. *Micah: A Classified Bibliography*. Amsterdam: Free University Press, 1990.
     Citations of approximately 1,220 books and articles published between 1800 and 1989. One-third of the entries are listed in twenty-two classifications based on key words (versions, stylistic features, commentaries, etc.). The remainder are listed by verse. Citations are arranged alphabetically. Includes author index.

369 R. A. Mason. *Micah, Nahum, Obadiah*. OTG. Sheffield: Sheffield Academic Press, 1991.
     Intended for those with little familiarity with biblical criticism, this brief guide provides an outline of Micah, Nahum, and Obadiah, a consideration of the historical circumstances of each, and a history of research on each prophet. Investigates the theology of each book. Includes bibliography.

370 B. M. Zapff. *Redaktionsgeschichtliche Studien zum Michabuch im Kontext des Dodekapropheton*. BZAW 256. Berlin: de Gruyter, 1997.
     Asks whether the book of Micah was redacted in the context of the Book of the Twelve or independently. Argues that the core of Micah (1–3, 6) was expanded by *Fortschreibung*, the redactional addition of passages with an eye for their contextual suitability and congruence with earlier traditions, whose *Sitz im Leben* Z. locates in Jerusalem in the third century. Provides a close consideration of 2:12–13; 4:6–7; 5:6–7; and chap. 7 to validate his thesis.

371 A. Wagenaar. *Judgment and Salvation: The Composition and Redaction of Micah 2–5*. VTSup 85. Leiden: Brill, 2001.

Contributes to the discussion of the formation of Mic. 2–5
by analyzing three models of its origins: (1) as a purposeful
composition; (2) as a dialogue; and (3) as the product of a process of redaction. W. accepts the third option and proceeds to
argue that a late preexilic layer, recorded by Micah's disciples,
was augmented by early exilic (Jeremiah), late exilic (Ezekiel),
early postexilic (Isaianic), and late postexilic layers. Valuable
for its close reading of Mic. 2–5.

4.12 Nahum

Nahum is almost exclusively concerned not with Israel or Judah
but with the enemy, Assyria. Due to the association of oracles against
foreign nations with the temple cult, some have suggested that Nahum
was a cult prophet. Nahum seems to reflect the period between the
fall of Thebes and the fall of Nineveh and likely dates to the earlier
portion of this period (ca. 650–630 BC), although some (e.g., Sweeney
[#374]) have argued for a date much closer to 612 BC. A partial acrostic
poem appears in 1:2–8, representing the first half of the alphabet, and
lauds the Lord using holy warrior imagery, although scholars debate
its coherence and meaning. Nahum presents an interesting problem in
intertextuality, since in the context of the Book of the Twelve Jonah
can be read as a critical reaction to it. Moreover, the close relationship between Nah. 1:15 [MT 2:1] and Isa. 40:9 and 52:7, coupled with
Nahum's relationship to Isaiah's predictions of Assyria's impending
demise (e.g., Isa. 10:5–19), raise additional problems of textual relationship. In addition to sources below, see #369.

372   A. van der Wal. *Nahum, Habakkuk: A Classified Bibliography:*
With a Special Paragraph Concerning Literature on the Qum-
ran Commentaries on Nahum and Habakkuk. Amsterdam:
Free University Press, 1988.
Citations of approximately 1,250 books and articles published between 1800 and 1987. One-third of the entries on
Nahum are listed according to key words (introductions,
aspects of the MT, history of exegesis, etc.). The remainder
are listed by verse. The third section of the bibliography includes citations of approximately 400 books and articles on
Qumran commentaries on Nahum and Habakkuk listed in
seven classifications.

373 D. L. Christensen. "The Book of Nahum as a Liturgical Composition: A Prosodic Analysis." *JETS* 32 (1989) 159–69.
Provides an analysis of the poetic structure of the book of
Nahum, focusing on its nature as a musical composition.
Suggests that the MT of Nahum is well preserved and that
its musical nature argues for an original setting in the cultic
life of ancient Israel. Like many oracles against foreign nations, Nahum belongs to a holy war tradition.

374 M. A. Sweeney. "Concerning the Structure and Generic Character of the Book of Nahum." *ZAW* 104 (1992) 364–77.
Examines the term *belîyā'al* and the forms of address in Nah.
1:9–2:1 in order to elucidate the structure and genre of the
book, finding that the final form constitutes a refutation
speech with roots in the genre of disputation. Defines three
major structural elements in the book (1:2–10; 1:11–2:1; and
2:2–3:19), and concludes that the final form dates around the
fall of Nineveh in 612 BC. An appendix includes a structural
diagram of Nahum.

375 D. L. Christensen. "The Book of Nahum: A History of Interpre-
tation." Pp. 187–94 in *Forming Prophetic Literature: Essays on
Isaiah and the Twelve in Honor of John D. W. Watts.* Edited by
J. W. Watts and P. R. House. JSOTSup 235. Sheffield: Sheffield
Academic Press, 1996.
Summarizes how the book of Nahum has been understood
from biblical times to the present. The book calls for trust in
God in the presence of tyranny. Though closely related to the
books of Jonah and Habakkuk, Nahum focuses on the dark
side of God. The book is noted for its aesthetic brilliance, the
best example of poetry in the prophetic corpus.

376 M. Weigl. "Current Research on the Book of Nahum: Exegetical Methodologies in Turmoil?" *CurBS* 9 (2001) 81–130.
Surveys research on Nahum within the past fifteen years,
including the validity of the acrostic in 1:2–8, synchronic
vs. diachronic approaches to the book, the authenticity of
1:2–8 and 1:9–2:3 and the book's unity, its relationship to
the Book of the Twelve, the theology of the book, and its history of interpretation. Nahum is found to be an example of
bifurcation between the synchronic and diachronic methods,

which should serve to emphasize the need for their inter-dependence since "neither of these methodologies is self-sufficient" (123).

4.13 Habakkuk

Habakkuk is not a typical prophetic book. It has often been ex-plained as a dialogue, in which Habakkuk makes two complaints (1:2–4; 1:12–2:1), which are followed by two responses from Yahweh (1:5–11; 2:2–5). Current scholarship, however, debates many aspects of the book, particularly whether it was written by one person or is a haphazard collection of sources. The psalm in chap. 3 has been assessed variously as both authentic and a later addition, but in the present form of the book it serves as a theological reflection on the events narrated in the first section of the book. One of the most important verses for both Judaism and Christianity occurs in Habak-kuk 2:4b: "The righteous will live by faith." The text of Habakkuk served as the vehicle for an important *pesher* commentary found at Qumran (1QpHab) in which the book was interpreted as a guide to the enigmatic events in contemporary community experience. Significant issues for understanding Habakkuk include deciphering its sometimes difficult text, the authenticity and interpretation of the psalm in the book, and the issue of theodicy. In addition to sources below, see ##165, 341, 372, and 411.

377 T. Hiebert. *God of My Victory: The Ancient Hymn in Habak-kuk 3*. HSM 38. Atlanta: Scholars Press, 1986.
Examines Hab. 3 in order "to clarify the nature of the poem itself as well as its relationship to the prophecy of Habak-kuk" (1). The text of the poem is established through tex-tual considerations, poetic structure is described as a literary unity in four stanzas, and the setting is discerned as the pre-monarchic Israelite league. This ancient poem, originally an ancient hymn of triumph, was only secondarily linked with Hab. 1–2 and subsequently reinterpreted as Habakkuk's eschatological vision.

378 M. A. Sweeney. "Structure, Genre and Intent in the Book of Habakkuk." *VT* 41 (1991) 63–83. Reprinted in *Prophecy in the Hebrew Bible: Selected Studies from Vetus Testamentum*, pp.

224–44. Compiled by D. E. Orton. Brill's Readers in Biblical Studies 5. Leiden: Brill, 2000.
After giving reasons for discontent with the present consensus about Habakkuk's structure, genre, and intent, S. finds that the book has a coherent and unified structure, based on the prophetic announcement (*maśśā'*) and the petition (*tepilâ*). It seeks to explain the emergence of the Neo-Babylonian Empire in a way that does not compromise divine support for Judah, which is maintaining its loyalty throughout the present crisis.

379 R. D. Haak. *Habakkuk*. VTSup 44. Leiden: Brill, 1992.
Consists of three main chapters that consider text-critical issues, followed by translation and notes on the book. Concludes by consideration of the historical setting of the book. Argues that the wicked king should be identified as one who opposes the Babylonians (Jehoiakim), whereas the righteous one (Jehoahaz) will be returned to power by the Babylonians.

380 O. Dangl. "Habakkuk in Recent Research." *CurBS* 9 (2001) 131–68.
Focuses on research on Habakkuk in the 1990s, especially methodological disagreements, discussing text-critical tendencies, the literary development of the book, the historical circumstances behind the book, special studies of the psalm in Hab. 3, form- and genre-critical considerations, contextualization and intertextuality, and its influence and reception. Notes the increase in influence of synchronic studies in interpretation of the book.

381 D. Cleaver-Bartholomew. "An Alternative Approach to Hab 1,2–2,20." *SJOT* 17 (2003) 206–25.
Notes numerous problems with the traditional approach to reading Hab. 1:2–2:20, which sees these chapters as a dialogue between God and Habakkuk. Suggests instead that the *maśśā'* genre indicated in 1:1 incorporates a previous divine oracle (1:5–11) whose fulfillment remains unclear (1:2–4, 12–17), and so Habakkuk seeks clarification (2:1). This clarification comes in the second divine oracle (2:2–20). A literary-critical reading seconds this impression, since the techniques of in medias res, flashbacks, and inclusions are evident.

4.14 Zephaniah

The unusual superscription to Zephaniah (1:1), going back four generations to a person named Hezekiah, may suggest a royal background for the prophet, although it is uncertain whether the superscription refers to the famous king. According to the superscription, Zephaniah was active during the time of King Josiah (640–609 BC). Many scholars see Zephaniah as prophesying before Josiah's reforms (ca. 621 BC), since they see little evidence in the book of the reforms described in 2 Kings 22–23. The Day of the Lord is an especially prominent theme. Based on references to worship (1:7b–8 and 3:11, 14–18), some scholars have hypothesized that Zephaniah was a cult prophet. Issues significant for the study of Zephaniah include its compositional history, the possibility of reading it in dramatic terms, and the tension between synchronic and diachronic readings of the book. In addition to sources below, see #341.

382 P. R. House. *Zephaniah: A Prophetic Drama*. JSOTSup 69. Sheffield: JSOT Press, 1988.

With the conviction that "Zephaniah definitely deserves more attention than it has received," H. proceeds to give an overview of genre criticism, including a review of the three classical genres and an analysis of biblical prose and poetry (21). A close reading of Zephaniah leads to three conclusions: Zephaniah is structured as an alternating set of speeches; the plot includes a definite crisis and resolution; and the plot is marked by the presence of the Day of the Lord. Concludes that the genre of Zephaniah is best described as prophetic drama.

383 E. Ben Zvi. *A Historical-Critical Study of the Book of Zephaniah*. BZAW 198. Giessen: Töpelmann, 1991.

Defends the historical-critical method in studying the prophets, despite the rise of literary approaches. Separate sections are devoted to textual, linguistic, and comparative notes and to commentary proper on Zephaniah. Finds that Zephaniah was composed "later than the early post-monarchic period and earlier than the Hellenistic period" (356), and that it underwent three stages of redaction.

384 D. H. Ryou. *Zephaniah's Oracles against the Nations: A Synchronic and Diachronic Study of Zephaniah 2:1–3:8.* Leiden: Brill, 1995.

Argues that synchronic and diachronic methods of textual analysis are not incompatible but complementary. Reads Zeph. 2:1–3:8 first as a unity, asking how different units of the text contribute to the meaning of the whole, noting three different textual units (2:1–4; 2:5–3:5; and 3:6–8). The diachronic section of the work finds traces of three layers: oracles of the prophet himself dating to the reign of Josiah; a revision toward the end of Josiah's rule that holds out hope of salvation for the faithful; and an exilic redaction intended "to open the eyes of the postexilic community to grace" (354).

385 M. A. Sweeney. "Zephaniah: A Paradigm for the Study of the Prophetic Books." *CurBS* 7 (1999) 119–45.

Asserting that Zephaniah "was and is a paradigmatic prophetic book," S. surveys form- and redaction-critical approaches and then examines treatments of Zephaniah from a literary and social-science perspective (121). A final section interacts with approaches that are concerned with Zephaniah's place in and contributions to the Book of the Twelve.

386 W. L. Holladay. "Reading Zephaniah with a Concordance: Suggestions for a Redaction History." *JBL* 120 (2001) 671–84.

Suggests that comparisons in terminology and phrasing between Zephaniah and other prophetic books can provide a clue to the book's redactional history. Based on comparisons with Isaiah and Jeremiah, H. identifies which portions of Zephaniah are authentic and secondary and suggests the origins of secondary passages.

4.15 Haggai and Zechariah

Both Haggai and Zechariah date themselves to two years in the early postexilic period (520–518 BC; Zech. 1:1, 1:7, 7:1; cf. Hag. 1:1, 2:1, 2:10). Consequently, Zech. 1–8 is often considered in conjunction with Haggai. Haggai used kingly language of a Davidic heir named Zerubbabel (2:21–23), although any messianic hopes for him seem to have gone unfulfilled, raising an interpretive problem.

The book of Zechariah falls into two (or three) different collections. Chapters 1–8 (Proto-Zechariah) are usually attributed to the prophet Zechariah, while chaps. 9–14 (Deutero-Zechariah) are assigned by many critical scholars to later anonymous prophets (some see chaps. 9–11 and 12–14 as distinct units). Proto-Zechariah includes a startling and unconventional composite of visions, images, and oracles, so oddly joined that some have denied the possibility of reading the book coherently. Ezra 5:1 mentions the prophets Zechariah and Haggai as ministering during the period after the exile, but the books do not fit together neatly in every respect. Haggai and Zechariah suggest that the construction of the temple had not yet begun, though Ezra-Nehemiah suggests it had. Among other significant facets of Zechariah is the picture it provides of the development of the genre of apocalyptic (see Tigchelaar [#492]). See also ##79, 86, 183, 236, 430–31, *Biblical Viewpoint* 32.2 (1998), and §2.12.

387 R. A. Mason. "The Purpose of the 'Editorial Framework' of the Book of Haggai." *VT* 27 (1977) 413–21. Reprinted in *Prophecy in the Hebrew Bible: Selected Studies from Vetus Testamentum*, pp. 115–23. Compiled by D. E. Orton. Brill's Readers in Biblical Studies 5. Leiden: Brill, 2000.
Contends that the purpose of the editorial framework of Haggai is to attempt to reconcile some of Haggai's prophecies, which apparently had failed to materialize, with confident anticipation in the future based on those promises which had been fulfilled. Such an understanding of Haggai's editorial framework does not necessarily imply a late date for the final form of the book.

388 R. J. Coggins. *Haggai, Zechariah, Malachi.* OTG. Sheffield: Sheffield Academic Press, 1987.
Includes a brief discussion of the historical context of each of the three prophetic books and a treatment of the editorial framework of Haggai and Zech. 1–8. Other chapters treat Haggai, Zech. 1–8, Zech. 9–14, and Malachi, concluding with an assessment of these books as contributing to our knowledge of the Second Temple period and the "literary process of drawing together in final form the sacred traditions" of that period (86).

389 M. Butterworth. *Structure of the Book of Zechariah.* JSOTSup 130. Sheffield: JSOT Press, 1992.

Examines earlier approaches to discerning structure in biblical literature, finding that such approaches suffer from a lack of an objectively defined method. B. provides six guidelines on how a more rigorous investigation of literary structure should proceed. Defines the division of sections in Zechariah, and then considers the literary structure of the smaller and larger sections. Finds that while evidence for rhetorical structuring of Zech. 1–8 is very strong, the structuring of Zech. 9–14 is less clear and does not support a single editing of the entire book.

390 J. E. Tollington. *Tradition and Innovation in Haggai and Zechariah 1–8.* JSOTSup 150. Sheffield: JSOT Press, 1993.
Theorizes that Haggai and Zech. 1–8 represent both continuity with preexilic prophecy and significant new developments in response to the postexilic period. After discussing the literary composition of these two prophetic corpora, T. investigates the authority of Haggai and Zechariah, finding that both prophets fulfilled roles similar to preexilic prophets. Suggests that the rise in literacy in postexilic Israel resulted both in Zechariah's recording much of his own prophecy and in drawing on earlier prophecies.

391 H. O. Thompson. *Haggai: A Bibliography.* Delhi: Indian Society for Promoting Christian Knowledge, 1995.
Citations of 609 books and articles (arranged alphabetically). Includes an author/editor index, a brief subject index, and a Scripture index.

392 J. Kessler. *The Book of Haggai: Prophecy and Society in Early Persian Yehud.* VTSup 91. Leiden: Brill, 2002.
Examines the portrayal of prophecy and society against the background of the context of Judean society, arguing that the book was written and redacted before 500 BC, and that Haggai should be interpreted without reference to Zech. 1–8. K. lays stress on the effectiveness of the divine message entrusted to Haggai and finds that the prophetic role was vibrant in reconstructing the temple and in the society of the Yehud. Haggai was a complex prophet, creatively using earlier traditions to address both the returnees and those who had never been exiled.

393 M. J. Boda and M. H. Floyd (eds.). *Bringing Out the Treasure: Inner Biblical Allusion in Zechariah 9–14* (with a major contribution by R. Mason). JSOTSup 370. London/New York: Sheffield Academic Press, 2003.

Consists of two parts: the first part publishes R. Mason's influential 1973 dissertation, which examines inner-biblical exegesis in Zech. 9–14, while the second contains responses to and extensions of Mason's work. Essays in the second section include "Zechariah 9–14: Methodological Reflections" (D. L. Petersen); "Deutero-Zechariah and Types of Intertextuality" (M. H. Floyd); "The Growth of the Book of Isaiah Illustrated by Allusions in Zechariah" (R. Nurmela); "Some Observations on the Relationship between Zech. 9–11 and Jeremiah" (E. Tigchelaar); "Deuteronomic Toponyms in Second Zechariah" (R. F. Person Jr.); "Reading Between the Lines: Zechariah 11.4–16 in Its Literary Contexts" (M. J. Boda); "Zechariah 13.7–9 as a Transitional Text: An Appreciation and Re-evaluation of the Work of Rex Mason" (J. D. Nogalski); "Zechariah 9–14: The Capstone of the Book of the Twelve" (P. L. Redditt); "Putting the Eschatological Visions of Zechariah in Their Place: Malachi as a Hermeneutical Guide for the Last Section of the Book of the Twelve" (A. Schart); and "A Response" (R. Mason).

394 M. J. Boda. "Majoring on the Minors: Recent Research on Haggai and Zechariah." *CurBS* 2 (2003) 33–68.

Focuses on research within the prior fifteen years, especially commentaries' portraits of history, redaction and unity, history and sociology, form, tradition and intertextuality, and rhetorical and canonical criticism. Concludes that "the way ahead will involve deeper reflection on the ability of these texts to shape modern readers and their world" (56).

395 C. Tuckett (ed.). *The Book of Zechariah and Its Influence.* Aldershot: Ashgate, 2003.

Includes the following essays given at a joint colloquium between the Faculties of Theology of Oxford and the University of Leiden at Oxford (2002): "The Guilty Priesthood (Zech 3)" (L.-S. Tiemeyer); "Why Is Second Zechariah So Full of Quotations?" (R. Mason); "The Literary Contexts of Zechariah 9:9" (T. Collins); "Bad Divination in Zechariah 10:1–2" (J. Tromp); "The Septuagint of Zechariah as Witness to an Early Interpretation of the Book" (A. van der Kooij); "The Use of Zechariah in Matthew's Gospel" (P. Foster); "The Cleansing of the Temple in Mark 11:15 and Zechariah 14:21" (H. J. de Jonge); "Zechariah 13:7 and Mark's Account of the Arrest in Gethsemane" (J. Muddiman); "Zechariah 12:10 and the New Testament" (C. M. Tuckett); "The Attitude towards Christians Who Are Doubting: Jude 22–3 and the Text of Zechariah 3" (H. W. Hollander); and "Why Would a Pagan Read Zechariah? Apologetics and Exegesis in the Second Century Apologists" (J. S. Boccabello).

396 M. J. Boda. *Haggai and Zechariah Research: A Bibliographic Survey.* Leiden: Deo, 2004.
Beginning with an essay on the state of research of Zechariah and Haggai, the bibliography includes the following sections: History of Persia and Persian Period Yehud, Haggai, Zech. 1–8, and Zech. 9–14. No annotations given beyond bibliographic information.

4.16 Malachi

As the final installment of both the Book of the Twelve and the prophetic corpus, Malachi possesses an importance far out of proportion to its size. In the Christian canon, it concludes the OT and serves as a transition to Jesus through its prediction of Elijah's return and the promise to restore family ties. Like the Pentateuch (Deut. 34:10–12), Malachi ends with an affirmation of the primacy of the revelation to Moses (Mal. 4:4–6 [MT 3:22–24]), although it is more optimistic about the status of prophecy, as shown in the predicted return of Elijah the prophet. The connections between Malachi and the Pentateuch make consideration of the book vital for theories of canonical development (see §3.1). Malachi also factors into discussions concerning the nature of the Book of the Twelve, especially in its relation to Zech. 9–14. Major questions involved in the study of Malachi include the precise nature of its relationship to Deuteronomy, the interpretation of the figure of Edom (archetypical enemy or historical remembrance?), the nature of its critique of the priesthood, the social setting of the book, and its redactional history. In addition to sources below, see ##97, 239, 338, 430–31, *Biblical Viewpoint* 32.2 (1998), and §2.12.

397 B. Glazier-McDonald. *Malachi: The Divine Messenger.* SBLDS 98. Atlanta: Scholars Press, 1987.
Provides a detailed commentary on Malachi. Argues for the poetic nature of Malachi, provides evidence for the coherence of Malachi, and discovers insight into the postexilic period through a close exegesis of the book.

398 P. L. Redditt. "The Book of Malachi in Its Social Setting." *Catholic Biblical Quarterly* 56 (1994) 240–55.
Isolates "two series of written messages . . . that condemned interpersonal and cultic sins" (241). Given in question and answer format, the messages were integrated and supplemented by a redactor to form the book of Malachi. Hypothesizes that the redactor belonged to an opposition (perhaps Levitical) community that envisioned the protection and eventual vindication of its own status and privileges.

399 H. O. Thompson. *A Bibliography on Malachi.* Delhi: Indian Society for Promoting Christian Knowledge, 1994.
Citations of 640 books and articles (arranged alphabetically). Includes Scripture index, a brief subject index, and an author/editor index.

400 J. M. O'Brien. "Malachi in Recent Research." *CurBS* 3 (1995) 81–94.
Observes that the surge in interest in the Persian period since the 1970s and in the formation of the canon has invigorated the study of Malachi. Commentaries, dissertations, and studies of the past fifteen years are surveyed, focusing on various areas of research: textual matters, Malachi as disputation speech, source-critical questions and redaction, the consensus of dating the book in the postexilic period, social conflict, and messianism.

401 D. K. Berry. "Malachi's Dual Design: The Close of the Canon and What Comes Afterward." Pp. 269–302 in *Forming Prophetic Literature: Essays on Isaiah and the Twelve in Honor of John D. W. Watts.* Edited by J. W. Watts and P. R. House. JSOTSup 235. Sheffield: Sheffield Academic Press, 1996.
Considers Malachi's role at the end of the Book of the Twelve and at the end of the canon. Offers a list of comparisons

between Malachi and the rest of the canon, which indicate Malachi's awareness of and dependence on Scripture. Concludes that Malachi was intentionally designed as a fitting closure to the development of the canon. Malachi sums up the message of the canon and of the Twelve and prepares for the future.

402 L.-S. Tiemeyer. "Giving Voice to Malachi's Interlocutors." *SJOT* 19 (2005) 173–92.

Examines the perspective of Malachi's opponents vis-à-vis the prophetic voice, on the assumption that the prophet accurately reports the sayings of the priests and people. Concludes that the interlocutors were sincerely seeking to fulfill their religious duties and were expressing honest bewilderment about God's judgment.

5

Transmission and Interpretation

5.1 Textual History: MT, LXX, DSS, Targums, Peshitta

Establishing the ancient text of a prophetic book is a complex endeavor, one which often cannot be separated fully from exegesis. The most important witnesses for the OT are the traditional Hebrew version (the MT), the early Greek translations/adaptations (the Old Greek or LXX), the Dead Sea Scrolls, the Syriac translation (Peshitta), and the Aramaic (Targum) translations/adaptations. The task is greater than simply deciding which of several readings is most likely original. For example, the book of Jeremiah is about one-seventh longer in its Hebrew version than in the LXX, and the order of passages is sometimes very different. Some have argued that these different versions indicate that no "original" version of a text was intended, but different literary versions circulated freely in early Judaism without concern for maintaining exact wording. Nevertheless, relationships between different versions can often be determined, as shown by studies below. For a general introduction to textual criticism of the Hebrew Bible, see E. Tov, *Textual Criticism of the Hebrew Bible*, 2nd ed. (Minneapolis: Augsburg Fortress, 2001). For the LXX see, for example, K. Jobes and M. Silva, *Invitation* to the *Septuagint* (Grand Rapids: Baker Academic, 2000). The volumes of *A Bilingual Concordance to the Targum of the Prophets* are particularly useful in studying the Targums. In addition to sources below, see essays in Lust (#302).

403 E. Tov. *The Septuagint Translation of Jeremiah and Baruch: A Discussion of an Early Revision of the LXX of Jeremiah 2–52 and Baruch 1:1–3:8.* HSM 8. Missoula, MT: Scholars Press, 1976.

Argues that an unknown translator revised the Old Greek translation of Jeremiah and Bar. 1:1–3:8, but that the work of this reviser is extant only for Jer. 29–52, while the unrevised Old Greek version survived for chaps. 1–28. Since this theory explains both the similarities and dissimilarities between the two halves of LXX Jeremiah, T. rejects Thackeray's theory of two translators for the book.

404 R. P. Gordon. *Studies in the Targum to the Twelve Prophets, from Nahum to Malachi.* VTSup 51. Leiden: Brill, 1994.

Addresses questions of the Targum's origin and development in nine essays prefaced by an introduction that surveys the history of scholarship and frames the questions pursued in the rest of the book. Subsequent chapters address historical allusions in the Targum, its Hebrew *Vorlage*, the relationship of the Targum on Habakkuk to 1QpHab, the relationship of the Targum and the Peshitta, and the concepts of the land and the *Shekinah* in the Targum.

405 C. C. Broyles and C. A. Evans (eds.). *Writing and Reading the Scroll of Isaiah: Studies of an Interpretive Tradition.* 2 vols. VTSup 70. Leiden/New York: Brill, 1997. [Also annotated at #264 and #412.]

Contains essays pertinent to the textual criticism of Isaiah, including, "An Index to the Contents of the Isaiah Manuscripts from the Judean Desert" (E. Ulrich); "The Isaiah Scrolls from the Judean Desert" (P. W. Flint); "The Text of Isaiah at Qumran" (E. Tov); "Isaiah in the Septuagint" (A. van der Kooij); "Isaiah through Greek Eyes: The Septuagint of Isaiah" (S. E. Porter and B. W. R. Pearson); "Two in One: Renderings of the Book of Jonathan in Targum Jonathan" (B. Chilton); and "Was the Peshitta of Isaiah of Christian Origin?" (A. Gelston).

406 J. De Waard. *A Handbook on Isaiah. Textual Criticism and the Translator 1*. Winona Lake, IN: Eisenbrauns, 1997. *A Handbook on Jeremiah. Textual Criticism and the Translator 2*. Winona Lake, IN: Eisenbrauns, 2003.

Two volumes designed to make the results of the United Bible Societies' Hebrew Old Testament Text Project, which analyzes textually difficult passages in the Hebrew Bible, accessible for translators and other scholars. Only includes passages that raise translational difficulties, following a threefold format: a description of the textual problem, an evaluation of it, and suggestions for potential translation.

407 D. A. Baer. *When We All Go Home: Translation and Theology in LXX Isaiah 56–66*. JSOTSup 318. Sheffield: Sheffield Academic Press, 2001.

"Explores matters of translation technique and theology as these are to be glimpsed in the Greek translation of the Hebrew biblical book of Isaiah" (11). While recognizing that divergences between the Hebrew and Greek texts are not explicable through a single process, B. elucidates the homiletical, political, and theological tendencies of the translator of LXX Isa. 56–66.

408 P. Pulikottil. *Transmission of Biblical Texts in Qumran: The Case of the Large Isaiah Scroll 1QIsaᵃ*. JSPSup 34. Sheffield: Sheffield Academic Press, 2001.

Considered one of the most important of biblical DSS, *1QIsaᵃ* provides the basis for reevaluation of scribal activity in copying biblical manuscripts. Concludes that scribes were more than mere copyists; that they introduced interpretive readings, in part to prevent readers from misunderstanding their view of God; and that they considered the biblical text flexible and its literary growth ongoing.

409 A. G. Shead. *The Open Book and the Sealed Book: Jeremiah 32 in Its Hebrew and Greek Recensions*. JSOTSup 347. The Hebrew Bible and Its Versions 3. London: Sheffield Academic Press, 2002.

Limiting himself to a consideration of only one chapter so as to avoid producing only the best examples for his case, S. examines the discourse analysis of each version, concluding that the literary goals of the MT and LXX result in different macrostructures. After a detailed textual study of the different subunits (vv. 1–15, 16–25, 36–44), S. concludes that the LXX is not necessarily earlier than the MT but that each version represents an attempt to deal with an enigmatic *Vorlage* which is beyond recovery of textual criticism.

410 J. Lust. "Major Divergencies between LXX and MT in Ezekiel." Pp. 83–92 in *The Earliest Text of the Hebrew Bible: The Relationship between the Masoretic Text and the Hebrew Base of the Septuagint Reconsidered.* Edited by A. Schenker. Society of Biblical Literature Septuagint and Cognate Studies 52. Atlanta: SBL, 2003.

Examines four instances in which the Masoretic Text is longer than the best manuscripts of the LXX (Ezek. 12:26–28; 32:25–26; 26:23b–38; and 7:1–11) and argues that the Greek manuscripts translate an earlier "canonical" Hebrew text of Ezekiel than that preserved in the MT. The longer MT is expanded according to its own theological emphases, including eschatology and apocalyptic.

5.2 Prophecy in Jewish and Christian Traditions

The prophetic corpus has extensively influenced Judaism and Christianity, even though in Jewish tradition prophecy was accorded a role subservient to the Torah. However, Moses' being named the greatest prophet (Deut. 34:10) ensured the importance of the prophetic writings. According to the Talmud, there were hundreds of thousands of prophets in the history of Israel, while only about fifty-five had relevance beyond their own generation and were recorded in Scripture. The prophetic books, especially Isaiah, were important for the fledgling Christian community and proved essential for its self-understanding in its first centuries and beyond. Nevertheless, ways that early Jewish and Christian communities appropriated the prophetic writings are extraordinarily diverse, though almost without exception being governed by the assumption that the prophets contained a message of great significance. One innovative appropriation of prophecy was called *pesher* interpretation. Appearing especially in the Qumran scrolls, *pesher* interpretation saw the prophetic writings as a kind of code to which an authoritative teacher had been given the key by God. According to this method of interpretation, the prophets have eschatological significance mainly for the present generation. Another major focus of appropriating prophecy is the use of the LXX in the NT, which is addressed in many of the sources listed below. See also §2.13.

411 W. H. Brownlee. *The Midrash Pesher of Habakkuk*. Missoula, MT: Scholars Press, 1979.

A foundational study of 1QpHab by one of the early pioneers of research into the Dead Sea Scrolls. Significant for its discussion of a paradigmatic Qumran text. Includes a pointed Hebrew text with translation followed by exposition. The introduction is important for its discussion of *pesher* as a kind of commentary that is related to the process of reinterpretation in postexilic prophecy. A companion to B.'s *Text of Habakkuk in the Ancient Commentary from Qumran* (Society of Biblical Literature Monograph Series 11 [Missoula, MT: Scholars Press, 1959; reprinted 1978]).

412 C. C. Broyles and C. A. Evans (eds.). *Writing and Reading the Scroll of Isaiah: Studies of an Interpretive Tradition*. 2 vols. VTSup 70. Leiden/New York: Brill, 1997. [Also annotated at #264 and #405.]

Contains essays pertinent to the appropriation of Isaiah by Jews and Christians, including "Josephus' Portrait of Isaiah" (L. H. Feldman); "Isaiah in the Pesharim and Other Qumran Texts" (G. J. Brooke); "Isaianic Traditions in the Apocrypha and Pseudepigrapha" (M. A. Knibb); "From Gospel to Gospel: The Function of Isaiah in the New Testament" (C. A. Evans); and "Isaiah and the Kings: The Rabbis on the Prophet Isaiah" (G. G. Porton).

413 R. I. Denova. *The Things Accomplished among Us: Prophetic Tradition in the Structural Pattern of Luke-Acts*. JSOTSup 141. Sheffield: Sheffield Academic Press, 1997.

Contends that Luke-Acts is controlled by the idea of prophetic fulfillment of Scripture, particularly of Isaiah. Isolates five themes from Isaiah that are constitutive for the narrative of Luke-Acts: (1) formation of a remnant; (2) release of the exiles; (3) inclusion of the nations; (4) punishment of those who do not repent; and (5) the restoration of Zion.

414 F. Wilk. *Die Bedeutung des Jesajabuches für Paulus*. Forschungen zur Religion und Literatur des Alten und Neuen Testaments 179. Göttingen: Vandenhoeck & Ruprecht, 1998.
Surveys allusions to and citations of Isaiah in Paul's seven undisputed letters and concludes that Paul saw Isaiah as a thematic unity and was aware of the Isaianic context of his citations. In addition, W. develops a four-stage process of Paul's appropriation of Isaiah and considers the effect of the book on his theology as a whole.

415 J. R. Wagner. *Heralds of the Good News: Isaiah and Paul in Concert in the Letter to the Romans*. Leiden: Brill, 2003.
A thorough investigation of the citations of and allusions to Isaiah in Romans, examining the *Vorlage* of the texts Paul cited, his interpretive strategies, and the Isaianic themes that recur in Romans. Finds that these citations "are the product of sustained and careful attention to the rhythms and cadences of individual passages as well as to larger themes and motifs that run throughout the prophet's oracles" (356).

416 B. S. Childs. *The Struggle to Understand Isaiah as Christian Scripture*. Grand Rapids: Eerdmans, 2004.
Surveys the range of appropriation of Isaiah as part of the Christian canon, from Justin Martyr through the twentieth century, preceded by a treatment of Isaiah in the LXX and the NT. Throughout his survey, the interplay of literal and spiritual meanings of the OT is a major focus.

417 C. A. Evans (ed.). *From Prophecy to Testament: The Function of the Old Testament in the New*. Peabody, MA: Hendrickson, 2004.
An introduction to and reader on the use of the OT in the New. Note in particular: "The Aramaic Psalter and the New Testament: Praising the Lord in History and Prophecy" (C. A. Evans); "Immanuel: Virgin Birth Proof Text or Programmatic Warning of Things to Come" (R. E. Watts); and "The Significance of Signs in Luke 7:22–23 in the Light of Isaiah 61 and the *Messianic Apocalypse*" (M. Labahn).

418 B. Janowski and P. Stuhlmacher (eds.). *The Suffering Servant: Isaiah 53 in Jewish and Christian Sources*. Translated by D. P.

Bailey. Grand Rapids: Eerdmans, 2004. Original title: *Der leidende Gottesknecht*. Tübingen: Mohr Siebeck, 1996.
A collection of ten essays pertinent to the interpretation of Isa. 52:13–53:12 within its OT context as well as its appropriation in Judaism and Christianity. Contributions include: "The Effective History of Isaiah 53 in the Pre-Christian Period" (M. Hengel with D. P. Bailey); "Isaiah 53 in the Gospels and Acts" (P. Stuhlmacher); "The Fourth Servant Song in the NT Letters" (O. Hofius); "The Servant of Isaiah 53 as Triumphant and Interceding Messiah: The Reception of Isaiah 52:13–53:12 in the Targum of Isaiah with Special Attention to the Concept of the Messiah" (J. Ådna); "Jesus Christ as Man before God: Two Interpretive Models for Isaiah 53 in the Patristic Literature and Their Development" (C. Markschies). Includes a classified bibliography.

419 G. T. Manning Jr. *Echoes of a Prophet: The Use of Ezekiel in the Gospel of John and in the Literature of the Second Temple Period*. Journal for the Study of the New Testament: Supplement Series 270. London: T & T Clark, 2004.
An intertextual study that focuses on John's allusions to specific passages in Ezekiel in the wider context of Second Temple usage—especially in the Dead Sea Scrolls. Concludes that "most of John's allusions to Ezekiel are intended to show how Ezekiel's restoration oracles . . . are fulfilled through Jesus to his followers. . . . John's allusions strongly focus on Ezekiel's themes of life and the giving of the Spirit" (199). "The fact that John uses all of Ezekiel's restoration metaphors suggests an aspect of his Christology which is otherwise muted: John saw Jesus as the fulfillment of the promises of restoration in the OT" (212).

420 S. Moyise and M. J. J. Menken (eds.). *Isaiah in the New Testament*. The New Testament and the Scriptures of Israel. New York: Continuum, 2005.
Following an introduction by the editors, the volume consists of eleven essays: "Isaiah within Judaism of the Second Temple Period" (D. D. Hannah); "Isaiah in Mark's Gospel" (M. D. Hooker); "Isaiah in Q" (C. Tuckett); "Isaiah in Matthew's Gospel" (R. Beaton); "Isaiah in Luke-Acts" (B. J. Koet); "Isaiah in John's Gospel" (C. H. Williams); "Isaiah in Romans and Galatians" (J. R. Wagner); "Isaiah in 1 and

2 Corinthians" (F. Wilk); "Isaiah in Hebrews" (J. C. Mc-
Cullough); "Isaiah in 1 Peter" (S. Moyise); and "Isaiah in
Revelation" (D. Mathewson).

5.3 Interpretive Issues

The hermeneutics of the Hebrew Bible has become increasingly
complex. Instead of focusing primarily on form-critical considerations, the modern interpreter is confronted by a diversity of methods, each of which is based on different sets of presuppositions
and goals. This wide range of interpretive approaches flows in two
broad streams: diachronic, which investigates the development of a
text over time, and synchronic, which focuses on the final form of
the text. In the past, interpretation of the prophets was consumed
with discovering the exact words of the prophets, but confidence in
the methods used to determine original oracles has faltered, as has
faith in the ability to recover historical information from prophetic
writings. The proliferation of new interpretive methods such as canonical, rhetorical, and literary criticism (see §5.4–6) has rendered
the notion of a single approach to the text obsolete. This section
focuses on general hermeneutical questions including historicity,
the synchronic versus diachronic debate, and proposals for new
methodologies (e.g., semiotic theory).

421 J. L. Mays and P. J. Achtemeier (eds.). *Interpreting the Prophets.*
Philadelphia: Fortress, 1987.
  Originally appearing in five issues of *Interpretation* (1978–85),
  these twenty-one essays "offer students and interpreters a
  resource and companion to the study of the prophets that is
  somewhat different from the usual historical-critical introduction" (ix). Should be one of the first stops in investigating
  any biblical prophet.

422 W. Houston. "What Did the Prophets Think They Were Doing?
Speech Acts and Prophetic Discourse in the Old Testament."
Biblical Interpretation 1 (1993) 167–88. Reprinted in *The Place
Is Too Small for Us: The Israelite Prophets in Recent Scholarship*, pp. 133–53. Edited by R. P. Gordon. Sources for Biblical and Theological Study 5. Winona Lake, IN: Eisenbrauns,
1995.

Examines the oracle of doom in terms of the theory of
"speech acts" pioneered by J. L. Austin and his successors.
H. concludes that oracles of doom hold out the possibility of
repentance while still maintaining the "response of mourn-
ing-humiliation" which the prophet called for (151).

423 J. C. de Moor (ed.). *Synchronic or Diachronic? A Debate on
Method in Old Testament Exegesis.* Leiden: Brill, 1995.
Papers from the joint meeting of the Oudtestamentisch Werkgezelschap in Nederland en België and the Society for Old Testament Study (1994). Five essays pertain to prophecy: "Isaiah
28: Is It Only Schismatics That Drink Heavily? Beyond the
Synchronic Versus Diachronic Controversy" (W. A. M. Beuken); "Synchronic Deconstructions of Jeremiah: Diachrony
to the Rescue?" (R. P. Carroll); "Synchronic and Diachronic
Perspectives on Ezekiel" (P. M. Joyce); "Synchronic and Diachronic Approaches to the Book of Nahum" (K. Spronk);
"Synchronic and Diachronic in Isaian Perspective" (H. G. M.
Williamson).

424 B. S. Childs. "Retrospective Reading of the OT Prophets."
ZAW 108 (1996) 362–77.
Examines and critiques various proposed methods for reading the prophetic corpus retrospectively, including adaptation, *Fortschreibung*, editorial redaction, etiology, and
prophecy after the event. Offers four critical hermeneutical
issues in interpreting edited prophetic literature: temporal
sequence and prophetic dialectic, criteria of present truth,
the text as the tradent of authority, and the final form of
the text.

425 A. Laato. *History and Ideology in the Old Testament Prophetic
Literature: A Semiotic Approach to the Reconstruction of the
Proclamation of the Historical Prophets.* Coniectanea biblica:
Old Testament Series 41. Stockholm: Almqvist and Wiksell,
1996.
Responding to the lack of consensus of portraits of the prophets
from books that bear their name, L. uses C. Pierce's theory of
semiotics to resolve the dilemma. In the book's first part, L.
evaluates literary, redaction, and form criticism, religious and
tradition history, and socio-rhetorical criticism through the

use of "empirical models," concluding that normal methods of OT criticism are inadequate. The second part of the book presents a theoretical model for reading the prophets, distinguishing the exegete's twin roles as both a modern ideological reader ("I-reader") who reads primarily synchronically, and a modern reader ("M-reader") who depends on the I-reader and reads diachronically.

426 R. F. Melugin. "Prophetic Books and the Problem of Historical Reconstruction." Pp. 62–78 in *Prophets and Paradigms: Essays in Honor of Gene M. Tucker*. Edited by S. B. Reid. JSOTSup 229. Sheffield: Sheffield Academic Press, 1996.
Questions the value of historical criticism along three lines: ambiguity of language, insufficient historical evidence, and lack of objectivity in interpreting data. Explores examples from the prophets in each case. Concludes that historical criticism must play a modest role, while putting greater focus on Israel's story, "which functions as revealing word" (78).

427 G. M. Tucker. "The Futile Quest for the Historical Prophet." Pp. 144–52 in *A Biblical Itinerary: In Search of Method, Form and Content: Essays in Honor of George W. Coats*. Edited by E. E. Carpenter. JSOTSup 240. Sheffield: Sheffield Academic Press, 1997.
Despite the larger question facing biblical studies—i.e., whether a paradigm shift is occurring from historical-critical methods to literary and other methods—Tucker argues that the historical enterprise is still tenable for studying the prophets. But it is the work of historical reconstruction rather than a positivistic view of "real facts."

428 T. J. Sandoval and C. Mandolfo (eds.). *Relating to the Text: Interdisciplinary and Form-Critical Insights on the Bible* (M. J. Buss Festschrift). JSOTSup 384. London: T & T Clark, 2003.
Includes four essays pertaining to prophecy: "Metaphor and Rhetorical Strategy in Zephaniah" (M. A. Sweeney); "Isaiah and Micah: Two Modes of Prophetic Presentation" (Y. Gitay); "A Deconstructive Reading of Hosea 1–3" (D. Jobling); and "Honor Restored: Honor, Shame and God as Redeeming Kinsman in Second Isaiah" (S. J. Dille).

5.4 Literary and Rhetorical Criticism

Though there is some ambiguity as to what "literary criticism" denotes, it basically functions as an umbrella category for many methods of interpretation. In common with form criticism, it considers identification of genre essential. Fundamental to the approach is taking the final form of the text as the point of departure. While practitioners differ in their estimations of the value of investigating the historical development of the text, they are in general agreement on identifying its literary features, such as plot, character, structure, and poetic devices. With respect to a given text, when identifying these features, critics will draw on parallel material elsewhere in the OT as well as from other ANE literature.

Rhetorical criticism received its impetus from J. Muilenburg's programmatic presidential address to the Society of Biblical Literature in 1968, which pointed out the limitations of form criticism and named *rhetorical* criticism as a supplementary interpretive discipline (see annotation below #429). Muilenburg's definition of rhetoric has not been without critics, some of whom disapprove of his focus on literary and artistic features of the text as not paying enough attention to its persuasive force. Nevertheless, the development of rhetorical criticism by scholars like Trible (#435) and others testifies to the growing influence of this method of biblical criticism. For form, redaction, and genre criticism, see §3.2.

429 J. Muilenburg. "Form Criticism and Beyond." *JBL* 88 (1969) 1–18.
Points out the limitations of form criticism by emphasizing the uniqueness of individual texts. Names rhetorical criticism as a supplementary interpretive discipline, to which are assigned two tasks: to delimit the boundaries of a pericope by analyzing its structure, and to determine how the individual statements, rhetorical devices, and structure contribute to the meaning of the whole.

430 R. Pierce. "Literary Connectors and a Haggai/Zechariah/Malachi Corpus." *JETS* 27 (1984) 277–89.
Examines five literary connectors between Haggai, Zechariah, and Malachi suggesting that when read together these books are useful sources of information about postexilic Judaism, which in turn serves to clarify the messages of the books

themselves. The literary connectors include the historical framework of Haggai/Zech. 1–8, the literary/thematic unity of Zechariah, the oracle titles of Zech. 9–11, 12–14, and Malachi, the interrogative element in the books, and their narrative genre.

431 R. Pierce. "A Thematic Development of the Haggai/Zechariah/Malachi Corpus." *JETS* 27 (1984) 401–11.
Treating Haggai, Zechariah, and Malachi as a unified literary work, P. analyzes the theme of the whole by examining narrative interludes that interrupt interrogative material, especially Zech. 9–14, which proves central. Finds that the theme of the collections of sermons and oracles is quite negative compared to the positive eschatology of the individual sermons.

432 Y. Gitay. *Isaiah and His Audience: The Structure and Meaning of Isaiah 1–12*. Studia semitica neerlandica 30. Assen: Van Gorcum, 1991.
Analyzes the text of Isa. 1–12 in terms of rhetoric and audience response. "Rhetoric is concerned with the mutual relationships existing between the three dimensions of a discourse: the author (speaker), the audience, and the text itself" (6). G. divides the first twelve chapters of Isaiah into thirteen units of discourse and subjects them to rhetorical analysis. Use of this rhetorical analysis enables G. to attribute the entirety of Isa. 1–12 to Isaiah of Jerusalem, specifically in the context of the Syro-Ephraimite conflict. See also his *Prophecy and Persuasion: A Study of Isaiah 40–48*. Forum Theologicae Linguisticae 14. Bonn: Linguistica Biblica, 1981.

433 T. Jemielity. *Satire and the Hebrew Prophets*. Louisville: Westminster/John Knox, 1992.
Reflects on the similarities between prophecy and satire, in that they both point fingers of searing insight at the stifling, myopic present and at the same time point fingers toward a vision of a more desirable future (11). Examines how prophecy and satire function in a society, how they employ rhetorical techniques, how they use a variety of parodies, and how prophets and satirists present themselves and their mission in similar ways.

434 D. F. Watson and A. J. Hauser. *Rhetorical Criticism of the Bible: A Comprehensive Bibliography with Notes on History and Method.* Leiden: Brill, 1993.
In addition to bibliographic information on rhetorical criticism as a method and in relation to source and form criticism, section five contains bibliography on each of the prophets (approximately 250 sources total).

435 P. A. Trible. *Rhetorical Criticism: Context, Method and the Book of Jonah.* OTG. Minneapolis: Fortress, 1994.
Combines an introduction to rhetorical criticism with an application of that interpretive method to the book of Jonah. Sketches the development of rhetorical criticism, arguing that texts should be understood in part as a picture of their authors but also as a mirror pointing back to the reader. In her investigation of Jonah, P. examines the book's external structure (in chap. 5) and investigates the internal structure of four scenes (1:1–16; 2:1–11; 3:1–10; 4:1–11). The final chapter, "Guidelines for Continuing," discusses authorial intention and the perceived subjectivity of rhetorical criticism.

436 A. L. H. M. Van Wieringen. *The Implied Reader in Isaiah 6–12.* Biblical Interpretation Series 34. Leiden: Brill, 1998.
Subjects the text of Isa. 6–12 to three methods of analysis in order to describe the implied reader of these chapters: (1) text-linguistic analysis; (2) subjective domain analysis, which is concerned with who thinks or perceives in a textual unit; and (3) communication analysis, which describes the interrelationships between the implied author, the characters and the implied reader. Interprets the characters in Isa. 7 against the paradigm of holiness discovered in chap. 6.

437 R. R. Lessing. *Interpreting Discontinuity: Isaiah's Tyre Oracle.* Winona Lake, IN: Eisenbrauns, 2004.
Analyzes the discontinuities in Isa. 23 in light of redaction and rhetorical criticism. Against redaction criticism, which sees discontinuities in a text as evidence of editorial layers, L. concludes in favor of rhetorical criticism, which sees those same discontinuities as intentional acts designed to persuade. It "accounts for more of the data that actually exist, makes

a coherent sense of the whole, accounts for the historical setting of the text and is holistic" (270).

5.5 Canonical Criticism

Due to dissatisfaction with a perceived overemphasis on historical-critical exegesis, some interpreters began to read the biblical text deliberately as Scripture. Canonical criticism emerged as primarily a theological mode of interpreting Scripture within the context both of the community that gave it birth and of the present community which now interprets it. Childs (#438) and J. Sanders are particularly associated with the origin of canonical criticism. Unlike diachronic methods that seek to explain the complicated history that led to the present form of the text, canonical criticism focuses on its final form. More than interpreting single verses or units of text in isolation, canonical criticism is concerned with larger issues—studying the entire shape of the biblical corpus and reading particular texts in light of the whole. The thesis is that texts will exhibit increased significance when read in the context of the entire canon versus being read only on their own. Rather than pursuing interpretation for exclusively academic reasons, canonical critics are concerned to discern the import of a specific text for a specific community of faith.

438 B. S. Childs. "The Canonical Shape of the Prophetic Literature." *Int* 32 (1978) 46–55. Reprinted in *Interpreting the Prophets*, pp. 41–49. Edited by J. L. Mays and P. J. Achtemeier. Philadelphia: Fortress, 1987. Reprinted in *The Place Is Too Small for Us: The Israelite Prophets in Recent Scholarship*, pp. 513–22. Edited by R. P. Gordon. Sources for Biblical and Theological Study 5. Winona Lake, IN: Eisenbrauns, 1995.
   Criticizes historical-critical methodology on the basis of three weaknesses: (1) the distinction between authentic and inauthentic passages creates suspicion of those texts deemed inauthentic; (2) form criticism results in a severely disjointed text based largely on the biases of the interpreter; and (3) critical scholars have unduly emphasized the political overtones of prophetic literature. On the other hand, canonical criticism places due weight on the final form of the text which "alone bears witness to the full history of revelation" (514–15).

C. then exemplifies eight different methods by which prophetic literature became canonical literature. C. concludes
that the interpreter must resist the urge to run every prophetic
text "through an established historical-critical mesh before
one can even start the task of interpretation" (522).

439 R. Rendtorff. *Canon and Theology: Overtures to an Old Testament Theology.* Translated and edited by M. Kohl. OBT.
Minneapolis: Fortress, 1993. Original title: *Kanon and Theologie: Vorarbeiten zu einer Theologie des Alten Testaments.*
Neukirchen-Vluyn: Neukirchener, 1991.
Lays the groundwork for a new approach to the theology
of the OT, with special focus on canonical readings and on
Jewish-Christian readings. Includes a chapter on the place of
prophecy in OT theology, three chapters on the composition
of Isaiah, and one on the composition of Ezekiel.

440 R. Rendtorff. "The Book of Isaiah: A Complex Unity: Synchronic and Diachronic Reading." Pp. 32–49 in *New Visions
of Isaiah.* Edited by R. F. Melugin and M. A. Sweeney. Sheffield: Sheffield Academic Press, 1996. Revised and updated in
*Prophecy and Prophets: The Diversity of Contemporary Issues
in Scholarship*, pp. 109–28. Edited by Y. Gitay. SBL Semeia
Studies. Atlanta: Scholars Press, 1997.
Surveys a variety of approaches for reading Isaiah as a unity,
focusing on editorial shape and canonical design. "The position which reads the book of Isaiah mainly in its given
'canonical' shape, though in full awareness of its (diachronic)
complexity provides, in my view, the great advantage of such
a sophisticated synchronic reading—that the interpreter is
able to read the text in its given continuity" (123).

441 E. W. Conrad. *Reading the Latter Prophets: Toward a New
Canonical Criticism.* JSOTSup 376. London: T & T Clark,
2003.
Against other approaches to prophetic literature, C. seeks
to understand the prophets synchronically as compilational
wholes. Uses semiotic theory to identify "coded information,
which scribal authors expected their readers to possess in
order to read the texts" (2). His reading of prophecy is illustrated with examples from various prophetic texts.

5.6 Feminist and Liberation Criticism

Feminist theology and hermeneutics are intended to critique the male-dominated (patriarchal) societal structures and methods of interpretation. Rather than denoting a single approach to the text, feminist criticism represents a diversity of female perspectives and approaches to interpretation. At least three modes of feminist hermeneutics exist, none of which is practiced on its own without reference to the others. The deconstructive mode breaks down the patriarchal assumptions of narratives, translations, and interpretations, exposing their androcentric tendencies and assumptions with the goal of liberating females from male oppression. The reconstructive mode seeks to recover the lives and contributions of women in all areas of life where the narratives either remember their legacy fragmentarily or pass over it in silence. The constructive mode consists of scholarly contributions of all sorts to feminist interpretation. Especially significant for feminist study of the prophets is the relationship of the deity to Israel using the imagery of husband and wife, e.g., Hosea's marriage to Gomer in Hos. 1–3. (See ##336, 338, and §4.6.)

Liberation theology, which originated in Latin American contexts in the 1960s, is concerned to interpret the Bible with special attention to narratives of deliverance, especially the Exodus, that serve to assist in the present-day liberation of oppressed people groups from unjust social structures. Proponents of liberation theology are often skeptical of traditional hermeneutics, since these tend to reinforce existing social structures rather than subverting them into more equitable arrangements. Foundational to liberation theology is the preferential option for the poor, which means that God acts on the side of the marginalized and impoverished, against the interests of the wealthy. Much of the prophetic corpus is of interest to liberation theologians, since it often critiques the wealthy and their unjust treatment of the poor.

442 P. A. Trible. *Texts of Terror: Literary-Feminist Readings of Biblical Narratives*. OBT. Philadelphia: Fortress, 1984.
Using sophisticated literary criticism, T. analyzes four narratives from a feminist perspective, including two from the former prophets (about the nameless concubine in Judg. 19 and Jephthah's daughter). T.'s purpose is to call to mind "tales of terror with women as victims" (1) and to urge readers to identify with both the oppressed and the oppressor.

443 M. D. Carroll R. *Contexts for Amos: Prophetic Poetics in Latin American Perspective*. JSOTSup 132. Sheffield: JSOT Press, 1992.

Discerns a method for reading Amos in ethical thought specifically within a Latin-American context. Offers an alternative to existing liberation theologies through an extensive poetic reading of Amos 1–6 that shows how the prophet dismantles popular Yahwism in favor of an encounter with Yahweh himself. The final chapter uses Amos as a roadmap for understanding contemporary Latin American popular religion.

444 A. Brenner (ed.). *A Feminist Companion to the Latter Prophets*. The Feminist Companion to the Bible 8. Sheffield: Sheffield Academic Press, 1995.

Eighteen essays on female images in the prophets, largely focusing on Hosea. B.'s preface considers the meaning of the prophets, concluding that it is better to regard the prophetic books as "a collection of related literary genres than as depictions of historical phenomena" (19). B. also contributes an introduction to the volume in which she considers prophetic images of women and femaleness, the "pornoprophetics of sexual violence," and whether the God of the prophets is trustworthy.

445 R. J. Weems. *Battered Love: Marriage, Sex, and Violence in the Hebrew Prophets*. OBT. Minneapolis: Fortress, 1995.

Inquiry into the language of sexual violence in Hosea, Jeremiah, and Ezekiel. W. finds that the marriage metaphor's androcentrism is not one that a modern reader must uncritically accept, but that contemporary interpreters "have the right to reject living in worlds which in the end diminish their humanity" (104).

446 A. Bauer. *Gender in the Book of Jeremiah: A Feminist-Literary Reading*. Studies in Biblical Literature 5. Bern: Peter Lang, 1999.

Examines representations of the female in Jeremiah through the use of rhetorical criticism. Intends to show that "traces of the female lead from call to repentance in the face of impending death and destruction, through remembrance in mourning to an eschatological vision of redemption in exile" (2–3).

447 C. J. Dempsey. *The Prophets: A Liberation-Critical Reading.* A Liberation-Critical Reading of the Old Testament. Minneapolis: Fortress, 2000.
A reading of the prophets in light of the patriarchal society in which they originated and in light of contemporary ideological concerns such as gender and classism. Examines the prophetic corpus according to how power can be used "to dominate, liberate, and to engender harmonious relations" (1). Highlights God's intolerance of injustice and the role of eschatological vision in transforming society from a worldview of domination to mutuality.

448 A. A. Keefe. *Woman's Body and the Social Body in Hosea.* JSOTSup 338. Gender, Culture, Theory 10. Sheffield: Sheffield Academic Press, 2001.
Seeks to show that the traditional interpretation of female imagery to denote cultic apostasy in Hosea is inadequate. Rather, such imagery "bespeaks [the author's] contemporary situation in which the realities of intra-societal violence and the transgression of traditional communal values had irreparably ruptured the order of the world as known by these people" (221).

5.7 Homiletics and Contemporary Application

The prophetic corpus was preserved as an object of faith among the Jewish and Christian communities, and both groups continue to discover contemporary significance from these writings. Following are resources that consider how best to communicate the prophets and the significance they continue to enjoy in modern culture. See also the journal issues on Isaiah (*Word and World* 19.2 [1999]) and Jeremiah (*Word and World* 22.4 [2002]).

449 W. Brueggemann. "Prophetic Ministry: A Sustainable Alternative Community." *Horizons in Biblical Theology* 11.1 (1989) 1–33.
Discerns four realities that shape Jeremiah's prophetic faith: normative covenantal faith; a mythic, metaphorical claim of

authority; the concrete pain of his situation; and a powerful
vision of an alternative future. Elaborates on the prophet's
ancient and contemporary role in the face of societal rejection: imaginative rereading and re-signifying of social reality,
reinterpretation, and a push beyond certain judgment toward
redemption. Throughout, B. finds the prophetic sequence of
"risky prayer–grief–new possibility" helpful in sustaining
the alternative prophetic community.

450 E. Achtemeier. *Preaching from the Minor Prophets: Texts and
Sermon Suggestions.* Grand Rapids: Eerdmans, 1998.
Against the common neglect of the Minor Prophets as suitable sermon material, A. provides useful insights on how
the Minor Prophets can serve as a basis for transformative
preaching. Provides a short list of suggested commentaries, a
sketch of the historical and theological contexts of each book,
as well as selected texts from each of the Minor Prophets.
For each selected text, A. includes "Features to Note in the
Text" and "Sermon Possibilities," which provide options for
further homiletical development of each passage.

451 W. Brueggemann. *Texts that Linger, Words that Explode: Listening to Prophetic Voices.* Edited by P. D. Miller. Minneapolis:
Fortress, 2000.
Includes seven essays, one previously unpublished, all with
a focus on the prophets. Concerns of these essays include
rhetoric in rereading the prophets, the impact of politics on
community, and the interplay of human speech and the divine. Despite the wide range of the essays, there is still a
marked unity in this collection, and B.'s trademark integra-
tion of the Hebrew Bible with contemporary experience finds
full expression here.

452 L. D. Bierma (ed.). *Calvin Theological Journal* 39.1–2 (2004).
Papers from a conference entitled, "Reading and Preaching
the Gospel of Isaiah in the Twenty-first Century" (Calvin
Theological Seminary, 2003). Representative essays include:
"The Challenges of Reading the 'Gospel' of Isaiah for Preach-
ing" (C. J. Bosma); "The Book of Isaiah: A Short Course on
Biblical Theology" (J. N. Oswalt); "Can Zion Do without
the Servant in Isaiah 40–55?" (A. van der Woude); "'You Are

My Servant, You Are the Israel in Whom I Will Be Glorified':
The Servant Songs and the Effect of Literary Context in Isa-
iah" (C. R. Seitz); "Isaiah in Christian Liturgy: Recovering
Textual Contrasts and Correcting Theological Astigmatism"
(J. D. Witvliet).

453 C. L. Aaron Jr. *Preaching Hosea, Amos, and Micah*. St. Louis:
Chalice, 2005.
Includes brief introductions to Hosea, Amos, and Micah
intended for preachers. Following each introduction, passages from each prophetic book are chosen (Hos. 2:14–23;
11:1–11; Amos 5:18–24; 7:10–17; Mic. 4:1–7; 5:1–5a; 6:1–8),
for which brief exegesis of the verses is given followed by
two or three illustrative sermons on each passage. A. contributes the exegesis and first sermon to each passage, and
the remaining sermons are provided by pastors and professors
of homiletics (A. C. Shelley, A. I. Hoch, W. C. Turner, V. P.
Howard, D. S. Jacobsen, P. L. D. Creach, T. K. Bruster, and
A. M. McKenzie).

Part 2

APOCALYPTIC

6

Information and Orientation

6.1 Introductions

The resurgence of interest in apocalyptic beginning in the second half of the twentieth century renewed debate about one of the most fundamental problems involved in its study: defining what it is. Scholars' common approach to the problem had been to take Daniel or Revelation, the two biblical apocalypses, as the starting point and to compile lists of characteristics that defined the genre as a whole. The problem with this approach is that no apocalypse—no matter how universally acknowledged as belonging to the genre—meets all the criteria. Scholarly research into the problem of definition now takes its impetus from the definition of the Society of Biblical Literature seminar devoted to apocalyptic (Collins [#466]), which distinguished historical apocalypses and those with otherworldly journeys, which display different characteristics. Many scholars now focus their understanding of apocalyptic on revising or adding to this definition. For example, Rowland (#455) has taken issue with the inclusion of eschatology in Collins's definition of apocalypse as "a genre of narrative literature with a literary framework, in which a revelation is mediated by an otherworldly being to a human recipient, disclosing a transcendent reality which is both temporal, insofar as it envisages eschatological salvation, and spatial insofar as it involves another, supernatural world" (#466, p. 9). D. Hellholm ("The Problem of Apocalyptic Genre and the Apocalypse of John," in *Early Christian Apocalypticism: Genre and Social Setting*, ed. A. Y. Collins, 13–64. Semeia 36 [Decatur, GA: Scholars Press, 1986]) has noted that Collins does not define the purpose of apocalyptic. A. Y. Collins added a statement of purpose to the previous definition, stating that apocalypse was "intended to interpret the present, earthly circumstances in light of the supernatural world and the future, and to influence both the understanding and the behavior of the audience by means of divine authority" ("Introduction: Early Christian Apocalypticism," in *Early Christian Apocalypticism*, 7). The definition of apocalyptic has been further refined due to greater precision in terminology. According to a convention adopted by many scholars, the term *apocalypse* properly refers to a specific genre, while *apocalyptic eschatology* designates a theology typical of apocalyptic writings but much more widely shared (as for example at Qumran). *Apocalypticism* has in view the social milieu in which apocalypses were written, as shaped by apocalyptic eschatology. In addition to sources below, introductory material can be found in commentaries and Bible companions: J. J. Collins, "Old Testament Apocalypticism and Eschatology," in *The New Jerome Biblical Commentary*, ed. R. E. Brown, J. A. Fitzmyer, and R. E. Murphy, 298–304 (Englewood Cliffs, NJ: Prentice Hall, 1990); J. C. VanderKam, "Apocalyptic Literature," in *The Cambridge Companion to Biblical Interpretation*, ed. J. Barton, 305–22 (Cambridge University Press, 1998); J. J. Collins, "Apocalyptic Literature," in *The Blackwell Companion to the Hebrew Bible*, ed. L. G. Perdue, 432–47 (Oxford: Blackwell, 2001); F. J. Murphy, "Introduction to Apocalyptic Literature," in *The New Interpreter's Bible: General Articles and Introduction, Commentary, and Reflections for Each Book of the Bible . . .* , ed. L. E. Keck et al. (Nashville: Abingdon, 2001), 7:1–16. In addition, see Carmignac (#540), Collins (#519), Tigchelaar (#492), and Collins (#493).

454 D. S. Russell. *The Method and Message of Jewish Apocalyptic: 200 BC–AD 100*. Philadelphia: Westminster, 1964.
    An influential study that defines apocalyptic as having "the prophetic tradition as its father and faith in the ultimate triumph of God in times of peril and persecution as its mother" (104). Three major sections investigate the nature and identity of apocalyptic, its method, and its message.

455 C. Rowland. *The Open Heaven: A Study of Apocalyptic in Judaism and Early Christianity*. New York: Crossroad, 1982.
Major study of the phenomenon of apocalyptic during the Second Temple period that understands apocalyptic as essentially concerned with the revelation of divine mysteries, without any consistent emphasis on or understanding of eschatology. Treats the content of the heavenly mysteries, after which a discussion of the origins of apocalyptic follows, giving a relative chronology of apocalyptic literature and stressing the difficulty of precisely dating most of it.

456 P. D. Hanson. *Old Testament Apocalyptic*. Interpreting Biblical Texts. Nashville: Abingdon, 1987.
Presents his theory of the nature and origin of apocalyptic in a brief and accessible form (for more complete discussion see #497). Organized in two sections, the first of which defines apocalyptic. A second section investigates the human crisis behind apocalyptic, the vision of new creation, and an affirmation of God's reign over hostile powers.

457 M. G. Reddish. *Apocalyptic Literature: A Reader*. Nashville: Abingdon, 1990.
Intended for the nonspecialist, this work anthologizes selected examples of Jewish and Christian apocalypses, which are organized into three sections: apocalypses without otherworldly journeys, apocalypses with otherworldly journeys, and related texts. Provides an introduction to apocalyptic and a brief bibliography of texts and secondary studies.

458 D. S. Russell. *Divine Disclosure: An Introduction to Jewish Apocalyptic*. Minneapolis: Fortress, 1992.
Introduction to Jewish apocalyptic subdivided into eight sections: identification and definition of the literature, birth and growth of apocalyptic, apocalyptic groups and books, reception and expression of apocalyptic, revelation of divine secrets, dualism and apocalyptic, consideration of the "Son of Man" and messianic concerns, and apocalyptic from a Christian perspective.

459 J. J. Collins. *The Apocalyptic Imagination: An Introduction to the Jewish Matrix of Christianity*. New York: Crossroad, 1984.

Second edition: *The Apocalyptic Imagination: An Introduction to Jewish Apocalyptic Literature*. Grand Rapids: Eerdmans, 1998.

Premier introduction to apocalyptic literature by one of its most prominent interpreters. After an orienting chapter on the apocalyptic genre, C. surveys the literature in approximately chronological order, including such related genres as oracles and testaments. A new chapter on NT eschatology and a rewritten chapter on Qumran are featured in the second edition.

460   S. L. Cook. *The Apocalyptic Literature*. Interpreting Biblical Texts. Nashville: Abingdon, 2003.

Introduces biblical apocalyptic literature with two grounding theses: (1) interpreters must seek the literal sense of apocalyptic, by which C. means "the sense of the text in its full symbolic richness, scriptural context, and witness to theological reality"; and (2) apocalyptic is not limited to persecuted minorities but can serve the interests of the central elite (58).

461   G. Carey. *Ultimate Things: An Introduction to Jewish and Christian Apocalyptic Literature*. St. Louis: Chalice, 2005.

Intended for a general audience, this work serves as an introduction to apocalyptic literature with emphasis on its religious, social, and literary backgrounds. Beginning with proto-apocalyptic in the Hebrew Bible, C. casts his net widely to include texts influenced by apocalyptic eschatology as well as apocalypses, including much of the NT. Includes judicious bibliographies after each chapter and an epilogue briefly treating the modern meaning of apocalyptic texts.

6.2 Assessments of Research

Since introductions to apocalyptic generally include some review of scholarship, this section and the previous one share substantial overlap. The following sources focus on interacting with and articulating the relevance of past scholarship for the contemporary discussion of apocalyptic. In addition to sources below, see Hupper (#15) and Thompson (#523) for further bibliographic citations.

462 F. J. Murphy. "Apocalypses and Apocalypticism: The State of the Question." *CurBS* 2 (1994) 147–79.

Surveys important issues and studies in apocalypticism under the rubrics of definition, genre, worldview, social movements, origins, and the nature of apocalyptic discourse. Suggests that the greatest advance in the study of apocalyptic is the appreciation of apocalypses "as legitimate and powerful responses to a changed and changing world" (172).

463 D. C. Sim. "Jewish and Christian Apocalypticism in the Ancient World: Problems and Prospects." Pp. 491–504 in *Religion in the Ancient World: New Themes and Approaches*. Edited by M. Dillon. Amsterdam: Hakkert, 1995.

Discusses the problematic implication of Hanson's suggestion that related terms be used to describe a genre (apocalypse), an outlook (apocalyptic eschatology) and a social movement (apocalypticism) because the use of related terms implies that there may be a closer connection between social groups and written apocalypses than was actually the case. The social movement called apocalypticism expressed itself in other ways besides apocalypses, while apocalyptic eschatology is not reflected in every apocalypse.

464 P. B. Decock. "Some Issues in Apocalyptic in the Exegetical Literature of the Last Ten Years." *Neotestamentica* 33.1 (1999) 1–33.

Reviews research on apocalyptic over the ten-year period up to 1999.

465 J. N. Oswalt. "Recent Studies in Old Testament Apocalyptic." Pp. 369–90 in *The Face of Old Testament Studies: A Survey of Contemporary Approaches*. Edited by D. W. Baker and B. T. Arnold. Grand Rapids: Baker Academic, 1999.

Begins with a discussion of what precipitated the twentieth century's resurgence of interest in apocalyptic. Proceeds to the two foci of scholarly attention in recent decades: definition and derivation. By "derivation" O. refers to the origin of apocalyptic. The majority of the chapter summarizes scholarship on the relationship (or lack of) between prophecy and apocalyptic, as well as other factors that gave rise to apocalypticism and its literature.

6.3 Collected Essays

The essays cited below attest to the growing interest in apocalyptic and related topics. Especially noteworthy is the volume edited by Hellholm (#468), which is the result of a wide-ranging conference seeking to define more closely the threads connecting Jewish apocalyptic with its cousins in its larger sphere of influence. Many of these essays are seminal for ongoing research. In addition to sources below, see Wright and Wills (#495) and Collins and Flint (#525).

466   J. J. Collins (ed.). *Apocalypse: The Morphology of a Genre.* Semeia 14. Missoula, MT: SBL, 1979.
Landmark collection of essays that has provided the basis for research on apocalyptic. The programmatic first essay, "Apocalyptic: Toward the Morphology of a Genre" (J. J. Collins), opens by differentiating the genre (apocalyptic) from an outlook (apocalyptic eschatology) and a sociological ideology (apocalypticism) and further defines the characteristic features of the genre. C. also contributes essays titled "The Jewish Apocalypses" and "Persian Apocalypses." Other contributions include: "The Early Christian Apocalypses" (A. Y. Collins); "The Gnostic Apocalypses" (F. T. Fallon); "Greek and Latin Apocalypses" (H. W. Attridge); and "Apocalypses and 'Apocalyptic' in Rabbinic Literature and Mysticism" (A. J. Saldarini).

467   P. D. Hanson (ed.). *Visionaries and Their Apocalypses.* Philadelphia: Fortress, 1983.
Includes eight essays following an introduction by the editor: "What Is Apocalyptic? An Attempt at a Preliminary Definition" (K. Koch); "Old Testament Apocalyptic Reexamined" (P. D. Hanson); "Apocalyptic Eschatology as the Transcendence of Death" (J. J. Collins); "New Light on the Third Century" (M. Stone); "Enoch and Apocalyptic Origins" (M. Stone); "Wisdom and Apocalyptic" (J. Z. Smith). Two additional essays treat NT apocalyptic.

468   D. Hellholm (ed.). *Apocalypticism in the Mediterranean World and the Near East: Proceedings of the International Colloquium on Apocalypticism, Uppsala, August 12–17, 1979.* Tübingen: Mohr, 1983.

Consists of thirty-five essays divided into three main sections: "The Phenomenon of Apocalypticism"; "The Literary Genre of Apocalypses"; and "The Sociology of Apocalypses and the *Sitz im Leben* of Apocalypses." Includes essays on apocalyptic in Iran, Egypt, Judaism, Qumran, Pauline Christianity, the book of Revelation, Gnosticism, etc. Essays include: "The Genre of Palestinian Jewish Apocalypses" (E. P. Sanders); "Survey of the Problem of Apocalyptic Genre" (L. Hartman); "The Genre Apocalypse in Hellenistic Judaism" (J. J. Collins); "Social Aspects of Palestinian Jewish Apocalypticism" (G. W. E. Nickelsburg); "Introductory Remarks on Apocalypticism in Egypt" (J. Bergman); "The Phenomenon of Early Christian Apocalyptic: Some Reflections on Method" (E. S. Fiorenza); and "Apocalyptic in the Hellenistic Era" (J. G. Griffiths).

469 J. J. Collins and J. H. Charlesworth (eds.). *Mysteries and Revelations: Apocalyptic Studies since the Uppsala Colloquium.* JSPSup 9. Sheffield: JSOT Press, 1991.
Includes eight essays dedicated to a closer understanding of Jewish apocalyptic, in commemoration of the ten-year anniversary of the Uppsala colloquium (see Hellholm [#468]). For an annotated essay see Collins (#502). Other essays are also noteworthy, for example, "Revelation and Rapture: The Transformation of the Visionary in the Ascent Apocalypses" (M. Himmelfarb).

470 J. J. Collins. *Seers, Sybils and Sages in Hellenistic-Roman Judaism.* JSJSup 54. Leiden: Brill, 1997.
A collection of twenty-one previously published articles and two new essays organized around five topics. The introductory article is "Before the Canon: Scriptures in Second Temple Judaism." Part 1 has six articles on apocalypticism, including one previously unpublished: "The Christian Adaptation of the Apocalyptic Genre." Part 2 has four articles on Daniel. Part 3 has three articles on the Sibylline Oracles, including one previously unpublished: "The Jewish Adaptation of Sibylline Oracles." Part 4 has four articles on apocalyptic in the Dead Sea Scrolls. Part 5 has five articles on wisdom and apocalypticism.

471 R. J. Bauckham. *The Fate of the Dead: Studies on the Jewish and Christian Apocalypses.* Supplements to Novum Testamentum 93. Leiden: Brill, 1998.

Collection of fourteen essays, nine of which had been previously published. Articles include: "Descents to the Underworld"; "Early Jewish Visions of Hell"; "Visiting the Places of the Dead in the Extra-Canonical Apocalypses"; "The Conflict of Justice and Mercy: Attitudes to the Damned in Apocalyptic Literature"; "Augustine, the 'Compassionate' Christians, and the Apocalypse of Peter"; "The Apocalypse of Peter: A Jewish Christian Apocalypse from the Time of Bar Kokhba"; "A Quotation from 4QSecond Ezekiel in the Apocalypse of Peter"; "Resurrection as Giving Back the Dead"; "The Apocalypse of the Seven Heavens: The Latin Version"; "The Four Apocalypses of the Virgin Mary"; and "The Ascension of Isaiah: Genre, Unity and Date."

472 J. J. Collins, B. McGinn, and S. J. Stein (eds.). *The Encyclopedia of Apocalypticism*. Vol. 1: *The Origins of Apocalypticism in Judaism and Christianity*. Vol. 2: *Apocalypticism in Western History and Culture*. Vol. 3: *Apocalypticism in the Modern Period and the Contemporary Age*. New York: Continuum, 1998. Condensed into one volume: *The Continuum History of Apocalypticism*. New York: Continuum, 2003.

Eminent compendium of essays from leading scholars, addressing topics essential to the study of apocalyptic. Topics range from the roots of apocalypticism to the influence of apocalypticism through the centuries and into the present. For annotated essays see Hultgård (#483) and Collins (#493). See also "The Roots of Apocalypticism in Near Eastern Myth" (R. J. Clifford); "Apocalypticism in the Dead Sea Scrolls" (F. García Martínez); and "Messianism and Apocalypticism" (J. C. VanderKam) The majority of the rest of the essays address apocalypticism and apocalyptic movements since the biblical period.

473 G. Carey and L. G. Bloomquist (eds.). *Vision and Persuasion: Rhetorical Dimensions of Apocalyptic Discourse*. St. Louis: Chalice, 1999.

Includes five essays on Second Temple apocalyptic: "Destruction, Construction, Argumentation: A Rhetorical Reading of Isaiah 24–27" (D. C. Polaski); "Is Daniel also among the Prophets? The Rhetoric of Daniel 10–12" (J. Kaltner); "Fourth Ezra: Reaffirming Jewish Cultural Values through Apocalyptic Rhetoric" (D. A. deSilva); "The *Ascension of Isaiah*:

Characterization and Conflict" (G. Carey); "Methodological Criteria for Apocalyptic Rhetoric: A Suggestion for the Expanded Use of Sociorhetorical Analysis" (L. G. Bloomquist). Four additional essays treat NT apocalyptic.

474 D. Flusser. *Judaism of the Second Temple Period: Qumran and Apocalypticism.* Edited by S. Ruzer. Jerusalem: Yad Ben Zvi and Magnes, 2002.

Consists of twenty-two essays, representing F.'s seminal insights into the religious concerns of the Qumran portion of the Essene sect. For example, in the early days of the Qumran community, an apocalyptic fervor was common. Later that tended to be replaced by pacifism.

475 C. Rowland and J. Barton (eds.). *Apocalyptic in History and Tradition.* JSPSup 43. Sheffield: Sheffield Academic Press, 2002.

After an introduction by the editors, essays include: "Millennium and Utopia: Images of a Fuller Presence" (P. S. Fiddes); "Temporality and Politics in Jewish Apocalyptic Literature" (J. J. Collins); "Expectations about the End of Time in the Hebrew Bible: Do They Exist?" (B. Becking); "Exile and Return from Jerusalem" (D. J. Bryan); "The Satirical Nature of the Book of Daniel" (D. Valeta); "The Apocalypse in History: The Place of the Book of Revelation in Christian Theology and Life" (C. Rowland). Other essays discuss apocalyptic in the NT, in the Middle Ages, and in the nineteenth and twentieth centuries.

476 L. L. Grabbe and R. D. Haak (eds.). *Knowing the End from the Beginning: The Prophetic, the Apocalyptic, and Their Relationship.* JSPSup 46. London: T & T Clark, 2003.

Consists of twelve essays: "Introduction and Overview" (L. L. Grabbe); "Prophecy, Apocalypse, and Eschatology: Reflections on the Proposals of Lester Grabbe" (J. J. Collins); "Transformations of Apocalypticism in Early Christianity" (D. E. Aune); "The Changing Face of Babylon in Prophetic/Apocalyptic Literature: Seventh Century BCE to First Century CE and Beyond" (A. O. Bellis); "The Eschatology of Zechariah" (J. J. Collins); "Mythological Discourse in Ezekiel and Daniel and the Rise of Apocalypticism in Israel" (S. L. Cook); "Prophetic and Apocalyptic: Time for New Definitions, and New Thinking" (L. L. Grabbe); "Neither Prophecies nor Apocalypses: The Akkadian Literary Predictive Texts" (M. Nissinen); "Apocalypse, Prophecy, and the New Testament" (C. Rowland); "The Priesthood and the Proto-Apocalyptic Reading of Prophetic and Pentateuchal Texts" (M. A. Sweeney); "Are You the One? The Textual Dynamics of Messianic Self-Identity" (J. D. Tabor); Appendix: "Poets, Scribes, or Preachers? The Reality of Prophecy in the Second Temple Period" (L. L. Grabbe).

7

Definition and Identification

For definitions of the terms apocalyptic, apocalypse, apocalypticism, and apocalyptic eschatology, see §6.1 "Introductions." See also articles in Collins (#466).

7.1 Apocalyptic in the Ancient Near East

Apocalyptic eschatology was often characterized in the past as a degenerate form of Judaism, particularly in light of the influence of foreign thought, especially Persian dualism. More recently, it has been described positively, even though the impact of surrounding cultures is patent to many scholars. The difficulties with the parallels to Persian sources, many of which date from later than the formative period of Jewish apocalyptic, have led to casting the net more widely in search of potential influences. One of the more profitable discoveries is the evidence for connections between Jewish apocalyptic and certain pseudonymous Babylonian compositions (see Hallo [#477], Sparks [#486], and Longman [#481]). In addition, VanderKam (#479) has documented connections between Enoch, containing the earliest extant Jewish apocalypses, and Mesopotamian traditions of primeval kings. Daniel, the earliest canonical apocalyptic composition, also shares traditions with Mesopotamia, especially in the first half of the book. In addition to sources below, see Collins and Flint (#525), various essays in Hellholm (#468), and the essay by Clifford in Collins, McGinn, and Stein (#472).

477 W. W. Hallo. "Akkadian Apocalypses." *Israel Exploration Journal* 16 (1966) 231–42.

Considers Akkadian literary texts containing prophecies after the fact (*vaticinia ex eventu*) as one significant analogy in explaining the rise of Jewish apocalyptic, while acknowledging that such literary prophecies in no way challenge the uniqueness of biblical prophecy.

478 J. J. Collins. "Jewish Apocalyptic against Its Hellenistic Near Eastern Environment." *Bulletin of the American Schools of Oriental Research* 220 (1975) 27–36.

Examines the phenomenon of apocalyptic against the ideological background of the ANE in the Hellenistic period, finding that many of the features of apocalyptic that distinguish it from prophecy are characteristic of this period. Jewish apocalyptic sometimes directly borrows concepts from the ANE, but more often shows parallel developments that are due to similar conditions.

479 J. C. VanderKam. *Enoch and the Growth of an Apocalyptic Tradition.* Catholic Biblical Quarterly Monograph Series 16. Washington, DC: Catholic Biblical Association of America, 1984.

Argues that the figure of Enoch was modeled on legends about the seventh Mesopotamian king Endmeduranki and that permissible Mesopotamian techniques of divination were influential on early apocalyptic. The Astronomical Book (1 En. 72–82) is comprehensible against the background of Mesopotamian "scientific" omen interpretation. Later Enoch compositions took this Mesopotamian base and added Hellenistic and biblical elements, with the result that Enoch became a primeval hero who outshone the worthies of other peoples.

480 H. S. Kvanvig. *Roots of Apocalyptic: The Mesopotamian Background of the Enoch Figure and of the Son of Man.* Wissenschaftliche Monographien zum Alten und Neuen Testament 61. Neukirchen-Vluyn: Neukirchener, 1988.

K. conducts an extensive search for the roots of two early components of apocalyptic: the Enochic literature and the Son of Man figure in Dan. 7. Concludes that there is no common source for apocalyptic, yet the roots in different kinds of Mesopotamian traditions are clear.

481 T. Longman. *Fictional Akkadian Autobiography: A Generic and Comparative Study.* Winona Lake, IN: Eisenbrauns, 1991.
Provides a discussion of five texts that constitute fictional Akkadian autobiography with a prophetic ending (131–90). Includes thorough discussion and translation of the texts, interaction with previous scholarship, and treatment of their relationship to biblical prophecy and apocalyptic.

482 J. C. VanderKam. "Prophecy and Apocalyptics in the Ancient Near East." Pp. 2083–94 in vol. 3 of *Civilizations of the Ancient Near East.* Edited by J. Sasson. New York: Scribners, 1995. Reprinted in VanderKam's *From Revelation to Canon: Studies in the Hebrew Bible and Second Temple Literature,* pp. 255–75. JSJSup 62. Leiden: Brill, 2000.
Brief overview of prophecy in Mesopotamia, Egypt, and Israel and Judah, and of apocalypticism in Egypt, Persia, and in Jewish texts, summarizing the relationship between the two. Bibliography focuses on prophecy and apocalyptic outside the Bible.

483 A. Hultgård. "Persian Apocalypticism." Pp. 39–83 in *The Encyclopedia of Apocalypticism.* Vol. 1: *The Origins of Apocalypticism in Judaism and Christianity.* Edited by J. J. Collins. New York: Continuum, 1998.
Surveys the religious literature of the Zoroastrians and finds that typical apocalyptic ideas, such as "the end and renewal of the world, the apocalyptic time reckoning, the signs and tribulations of the end, the struggle of God and his Messiah against evil, personified in the figure of Satan and his demons" were all present in Iran (39). Concludes that "the emergence of an apocalyptic eschatology among Jews and Christians in the Hellenistic and Roman periods was propelled by the fruitful encounter with a religion deeply concerned with the struggle of good and evil and firmly assured of the ultimate restoration of the world" (81).

484   K. van der Toorn. "Scholars at the Oriental Court: The Figure of Daniel against Its Mesopotamian Background." Pp. 37–54 in vol. 1 of *The Book of Daniel: Composition and Reception*. Edited by J. J. Collins and P. W. Flint. VTSup 83. Leiden: Brill, 2001.
Investigates Dan. 6 against the background of the conduct of wise men at Mesopotamian courts, especially a disgraced scholar's metaphorical reference to competing wise men as lions. Argues that Daniel has understood the metaphor literally, providing evidence of more contact with ANE traditions than usually assumed.

485   P. Niskanen. *The Human and the Divine in History: Herodotus and the Book of Daniel*. JSOTSup 396. Sheffield: Sheffield Academic Press, 2004.
Against the neglect of historical information in Daniel and dismissal of the book's relationship to Greek sources, N. addresses both of these lacunae, especially focusing on the similarities in historiography between Daniel and Herodotus. Arguing for the influence of Greek historians on Jewish historiography in general and Daniel in particular, N. finds that Daniel does not describe an apocalyptic end but uses cosmic imagery to describe God's action, an action in which the wise (*maskilim*) should be actively engaged.

486   K. Sparks. "Apocalyptic and Related Texts." Pp. 240–51 in *Ancient Texts for the Study of the Hebrew Bible: A Guide to the Background Literature*. Peabody, MA: Hendrickson, 2005.
Helpful overview of comparative texts from the ANE with up-to-date bibliography and descriptions of the nature of each text. Concludes with four features of ANE comparative texts worthy of note, finding that the Babylonian Dynastic Prophecy and the Demotic Chronicle stand in the closest relationship to Daniel.

7.2 Old Testament Origins of Apocalyptic: Cult, Wisdom, Prophecy

In the search for the origin of Jewish apocalyptic, many scholars explored the connection between apocalyptic and prophecy, finding that apocalyptic was an offspring of prophecy in a new age. G. von

Rad, on the other hand, famously considered the eschatology of apocalyptic to be incompatible with that of prophecy and suggested instead that the origin of apocalyptic should be sought in wisdom circles. Other scholars (e.g., Müller #488) have more clearly argued that mantic wisdom, a special kind of wisdom concerned with discerning the will of the divine through the interpretation of dreams, omens, and other revelatory experiences, is the most important formative influence on apocalyptic. VanderKam (#490), joined by other researchers, has stressed that both mantic wisdom and prophecy played a role in forming apocalyptic. In addition to sources below, see Clements (#21) and §7.3, concerned with the nature of the Jewish social movements that produced apocalypses.

487   R. G. Hamerton-Kelly. "The Temple and the Origins of Jewish Apocalyptic." *VT* 20 (1970) 1–15.
Argues that two attitudes toward the temple existed in postexilic Judaism: one in which the temple is made from a heavenly design, represented by P, and one in which the temple exists already and will someday be revealed, represented by Ezekiel. Contends that apocalyptic arose out of the group that opposed the second temple because they believed in the superiority of the heavenly temple, and that priestly elements were thus significant in the development of apocalyptic.

488   H.-P. Müller. "Mantische Weisheit und Apokalyptik." Pp. 268–93 in *Congress Volume: Uppsala 1971*. Edited by G. W. Anderson et al. VTSup 22. Leiden: Brill, 1972.
Acknowledges that seeing apocalyptic as an outgrowth of mantic wisdom does not solve all problems and that prophetic impulses clearly influenced apocalyptic. Argues nevertheless that the pluralism of the genre, incorporating ideas from widely diverse sources, speaks for mantic wisdom as a primary influence on apocalyptic.

489   J. Barton. "'The Law and the Prophets': Who Are the Prophets?" Pp. 1–18 in *Prophets, Worship and Theodicy: Studies in Prophetism, Biblical Theology and Structural and Rhetorical Analysis and on the Place of Music in Worship*. Papers Read at the Joint British-Dutch Old Testament Conference Held at Woudschoten, 1982. Oudtestamentische Studiën 23. Edited by A. S. van der Woude. Leiden: Brill, 1984.

Seminal discussion of the relationship between prophecy and apocalyptic, probing the questions, "Did apocalyptic writers regard themselves as prophets, and their books as prophecy? Did their contemporaries think of them as prophets?" (2). Concludes that the OT canon of Josephus and of the NT was essentially bipartite, Torah and prophecy, meaning that anything included apart from Torah was considered prophetic; that the prophetic books were a combination of narrative, prediction, and moral teaching; and that the apocalyptists considered themselves to be writing prophecy.

490 J. C. VanderKam. "The Prophetic-Sapiential Origins of Apocalyptic Thought." Pp. 163–76 in *A Word in Season: Essays in Honour of William McKane*. Edited by J. D. Martin and P. R. Davies. JSOTSup 42. Sheffield: Sheffield Academic Press, 1986. Reprinted in VanderKam's *From Revelation to Canon: Studies in the Hebrew Bible and Second Temple Literature*, pp. 241–54. JSJSup 62. Leiden: Brill, 2000.

Suggests directions for further research into the origin of apocalyptic, whether arising out of prophecy or wisdom traditions. Concludes: "Given the divinatory aspects of prophecy in Israel, one ought to avoid drawing a sharp distinction between mantic wisdom and biblical prophecy as candidates for the leading influences on apocalyptic thought and procedure . . . the term prophecy should not be limited to what the few great literary prophets taught or did" (254).

491 J. J. Collins. "The Sage in the Apocalyptic and Pseudepigraphic Literature." Pp. 343–54 in *The Sage in Israel and the Ancient Near East*. Edited by J. G. Gammie and L. G. Perdue. Winona Lake, IN: Eisenbrauns, 1990.

Discusses the changing perception of the ideal sage in apocalyptic literature, especially Daniel and 1 Enoch, concluding that the most significant distinction between apocalyptic sages and sages in wisdom literature is the former's reliance on supernatural revelation. Notes the tension between the mantic wisdom given to the apocalyptic sage in 2 Baruch and 4 Ezra and the Torah revealed through Moses.

492 E. J. C. Tigchelaar. *Prophets of Old and the Day of the End: Zechariah, the Book of Watchers, and Apocalyptic*. Leiden: Brill, 1996.

Using texts which are generally considered more or less datable (Zech. 1–8, 9–14, and 1 En. 1–36), T. approaches the definition of apocalyptic historically by thoroughly exegeting these (proto-)apocalyptic texts. In addition to defining apocalyptic using the means of revelation and the contents of revelation, as is generally done, T. suggests another feature: "revelation stems from the interpretation of tradition" (260). Challenges fuzzy thinking about seeing apocalyptic as the literature of persecuted people.

493 J. J. Collins. "From Prophecy to Apocalypticism: The Expectation of the End." Pp. 129–61 in *The Encyclopedia of Apocalypticism.* Vol. 1: *The Origins of Apocalypticism in Judaism and Christianity.* Edited by J. J. Collins. New York: Continuum, 1998.

Considers the origin of apocalypticism by tracing the development of the concept of the end of the world in three periods. Finds increased use of cosmic imagery expressing eschatological expectation in postexilic prophecy, but not at the level of the end-of-the-world language in apocalyptic. In Hellenistic Judaism a distinctive worldview developed involving final judgment on nations and individuals. Though only a few apocalypses are preserved from the Roman period, the spread of apocalyptic ideas is documented in a wide range of Jewish literature, meaning that apocalypticism was not the property of any one group.

494 M. Sæbø. "Old Testament Apocalyptic in Its Relation to Prophecy and Wisdom: The View of Gerhard von Rad Reconsidered." Pp. 78–91 in *In the Last Days: On Jewish and Christian Apocalyptic and Its Period.* Edited by K. Jeppesen, K. Nielsen, and B. Rosendal. Aarhus: Aarhus University Press, 1994. Reprinted in Sæbø's *On the Way to Canon: Creative Tradition History in the Old Testament,* pp. 232–47. JSOTSup 191. Sheffield: Sheffield Academic Press, 1998.

Challenges von Rad's contention that the roots of apocalyptic are to be found in wisdom literature. Instead, "there was a progressively stronger tendency of *learnedness* that represented a specific tradition of *sapientializing* . . . and that the new phenomenon of Danielic apocalyptic was created and developed in the matrix of this learned or *didactic eschatology*" (247).

495   B. G. Wright III and L. M. Wills (eds.). *Conflicted Boundaries in Wisdom and Apocalypticism*. SBLSymS 35. Atlanta: SBL, 2005.

> Part 1 ("Issues and Outlook") begins with a lead article, "Wisdom and Apocalyptic in Early Judaism: Some Points for Discussion" (Nickelsburg), followed by response. Parts 2 and 3 examine the relationship of wisdom to apocalyptic in early Judaism and early Christianity.

7.3 Social Setting of Apocalyptic

What kind of people produced apocalypses? Hanson (#497) theorized that tension between priestly and prophetic groups led to apocalyptic. Many other scenarios have been proposed. For some scholars, marginal and oppressed groups are the most natural candidates to have written apocalypses, since these validated the groups' sense of importance and encouraged them in their difficulties. Cook (#503) and other scholars have questioned whether only marginal social movements could have written apocalypses, attributing them instead to influential persons. Grabbe (#501) has stressed anthropological models as being more helpful, over against reconstructing a group based on inferences from an apocalyptic text. But Sim (#504) faults him for overreliance on this method. Collins (#502) argues that apocalypses are likely to have arisen from a variety of life settings and that each apocalypse needs to be approached through its own evidence. Daniel in particular has led some scholars to see scribes or wise men in a foreign court behind its composition (Collins #499 and Redditt #529; but see Henze #507 for a refutation of this view). In addition to sources below, see Collins and Flint (#525) (especially the essays by R. Albertz, and L. L. Grabbe).

496   O. Plöger. *Theology and Eschatology*. Translated by S. Rudman. Richmond: John Knox, 1968. Original title: *Theokratie und Eschatologie*. Wissenschaftliche Untersuchungen zum Neuen Testament 2. Neukirchen-Vluyn: Neukirchener, 1962.

> Describes apocalypticism as the outgrowth of prophecy that resulted from tension between the priestly hierarchy and lay observant Jews who came to see themselves as the remnant described in the prophets. Examines Isa. 24–27, Zech. 12–14,

and Joel, tracing the development of eschatology's significance compared to the static orthodoxy fostered in cultic circles.

497 P. D. Hanson. *The Dawn of Apocalyptic*. Philadelphia: Fortress, 1975. Revised edition: *The Dawn of Apocalyptic: The Historical and Sociological Roots of Jewish Apocalyptic Eschatology.* Philadelphia: Fortress, 1979.
Seminal study placing the origins of apocalyptic in the circle of Deutero-Isaiah's disciples who are responsible for Isa. 56–66 and Zech. 9–14. Contends that apocalyptic developed in tandem with the growing realization that salvation could only occur by God's supplanting the present evil order with a new one and highlights the expression of this realization through the reemergence of ancient myth. Apocalyptic is thus primarily Jewish in origin. See the review by R. P. Carroll, "Twilight of Prophecy or Dawn of Apocalyptic," *JSOT* 14 (1979) 3–35. See also #456.

498 R. R. Wilson. "From Prophecy to Apocalyptic: Reflections on the Shape of Israelite Religion." *Semeia* 21 (1982) 79–95.
On the basis of sociological study, contends that apocalyptic arises in a group on the periphery of society, that the group has a program for meeting the difficulties of its members, and that it provides its members with practical ways to reach that program. The shape given by each group to its apocalyptic program depends on the makeup of its members, and so a diverse group will incorporate many elements corresponding to the background of its participants. Traces the development of Daniel as it mirrors the changing nature of the group.

499 J. J. Collins. "Daniel and His Social World." *Int* 39 (1985) 131–43. Reprinted in *Interpreting the Prophets*, pp. 249–60. Edited by J. L. Mays and P. J. Achtemeier. Philadelphia: Fortress, 1987.
Finds that the authors and tradents of the court tales in Daniel were likely upper-class Jews in the service of a foreign king in the eastern diaspora who were interested in the interpretation of dreams and omens. The redactors of the visions are not interested in political or military solutions to their plight but in teaching the people and in persevering until the end. Daniel offers "an act of the imagination which affirms

the freedom of the human spirit in defiance of any force of oppression" (260).

500 P. R. Davies. "The Social World of the Apocalyptic Writings." Pp. 251–71 in *The World of Ancient Israel*. Edited by R. E. Clements. Cambridge: Cambridge University Press, 1989.

After defining the problem and briefly reviewing the history of research on the social setting of apocalyptic, D. emphasizes the scribal affinities of apocalyptic using Sirach (Ecclesiasticus) as an example. Finds that the apocalypses in our possession do not come from sectarian groups (although they do illuminate scribal disagreements) but from millenarian groups. Apocalyptic arose in opposition to Hellenistic reforms.

501 L. L. Grabbe. "The Social Setting of Early Jewish Apocalypticism." *Journal for the Study of the Pseudepigrapha* 4 (1989) 27–47.

Offers a series of proposals drawn from previous study of apocalyptic texts and anthropological research aimed at more carefully defining the social setting of apocalypticism. In contrast to the often circular reasoning of those who describe apocalyptic movements only from the texts they produce or honor, G. proposes that sociological research into millenarian groups can serve to illustrate the diversity of early Jewish apocalypticism.

502 J. J. Collins. "Genre, Ideology and Social Movements in Jewish Apocalypticism." Pp. 11–32 in *Mysteries and Revelations: Apocalyptic Studies since the Uppsala Colloquium*. JSPSup 9. Edited by J. J. Collins and J. H. Charlesworth. Sheffield: JSOT Press, 1991.

Reacts to scholarly critiques of the definition of apocalyptic genre in #466. Finds that apocalypses have abstract, general content in common, which is distinguishable from other Jewish works, often including emphasis on personal eschatology and the judgment of the dead. Accepts the helpfulness of historical development in studying the apocalyptic genre, although he resists finding one life setting for all apocalypses. An appendix reviews VanderKam's and Kvanvig's arguments (#479, #480) for highlighting the Babylonian parallels to the Enoch tradition.

503 S. L. Cook. *Prophecy and Apocalypticism: The Postexilic Social Setting*. Minneapolis: Augsburg Fortress, 1995.
Argues from three proto-apocalyptic texts (Ezek. 38–39, Joel, and Zech. 1–8) that apocalyptic did not originate among the powerless but from a circle of Zadokite priests who held sway in late exilic and early postexilic Judah. Concludes that Jewish apocalyptic is essentially a native development within Judaism and that positive expectation, not negative escapism, characterizes biblical apocalyptic.

504 D. C. Sim. "The Social Setting of Ancient Apocalypticism: A Question of Method." *Journal for the Study of the Pseudepigrapha* 13 (1995) 5–16.
Critiques Grabbe's analysis (#501), faulting him for ignoring evidence for social setting in apocalypses themselves while privileging anthropological studies of later millenarian movements. S. argues that anthropological models "must be used with great caution and must be considered as supplementary to the usual methods of historical reconstruction" (15).

8

Conception and Communication

8.1 Literary Considerations

On the whole the pressing issues of definition and derivation have consumed much scholarly attention, so that literary considerations of apocalyptic works (including redaction criticism) have not been especially prominent. Recent work represents valuable correctives to this inattention, focused particularly on the book of Daniel. In addition to sources below, see Carey and Bloomquist (#473) regarding the rhetorical nature of apocalyptic discourse.

505 A. Lenglet. "La structure littéraire de Daniel 2–7." *Biblica* 53 (1971) 169–90.

Discerns a concentric literary structure within Dan. 2–7, in which chaps. 2 and 7 describe dreams of the four kingdoms, chaps. 3 and 6 describe acts of martyrs, and chaps. 4 and 5 are concerned with judgment on foreign kings. Suggests that the divine wish to be recognized as God by foreign rulers might constitute one reason for the Aramaic language of the middle section, and implies that the whole book originates from the hand of a single redactor in the Maccabean period.

506 D. N. Fewell. *Circle of Sovereignty: Plotting Politics in the Book of Daniel.* Nashville: Abingdon, 1988. Second edition: 1991.

Offers a literary reading of Daniel attuned to the political aspects of the book, especially focusing on the theme of divine and human sovereignty. Six chapters focus on the narratives in the first half of Daniel, while (in the second edition) a final chapter explores chaps. 7–12.

507 M. Henze. "The Narrative Frame of Daniel: A Literary Reassessment." *Journal for the Study of Judaism* 32 (2001) 5–24.

Against the consensus view, H. argues that Dan. 1–6 is fiction designed to draw the reader into the narrative, not merely a reflection of the lives of its authors. To determine the message of the tales, the reader must compare them to other texts of the same genre and read them in light of the book of Daniel as a whole.

508 S. Beyerle. *Die Gottesvorstellungen in der antik-jüdischen Apokalyptik.* JSJSup 103. Leiden: Brill, 2005.

Seeks to understand the redaction history of certain apocalypses based on different ways that God and his attributes are described. Focuses primarily on Daniel and 1 Enoch, noting distinct characteristics of theophanies as well as elements of the theology of divine sovereignty, judgment, and restoration, and of personal eschatology.

8.2 Visions and Revelations

A common type of apocalypse involves a visionary ascent to a non-human realm, either heaven or hell. M. Himmelfarb has produced several substantive works examining visionary tours of both heaven and hell in Jewish and Christian apocalypses. Another important question involved in apocalyptic visions is whether these descriptions resulted from personal experience or instead represent mostly literary creations. Stone (#511) emphasizes elements of personal experience in apocalyptic visions.

509 M. Himmelfarb. *Tours of Hell: An Apocalyptic Form in Jewish and Christian Literature.* Philadelphia: Fortress, 1983.

Examines Jewish and Christian apocalypses in which tours of hell are found, featuring first a discussion of relevant texts. Next H. considers the origin of such tours, arguing for the existence of a "tour apocalypse" in which the seer is granted a tour of either heaven (developing from 1 En. 14) or hell (developing from 1 En. 17–36). Examines punishments that the apocalypses pictured the wicked suffering, while a final chapter explores the development of the tradition.

510   M. Himmelfarb. *Ascent to Heaven in Jewish and Christian Apocalypses.* New York: Oxford University Press, 1993.
Investigates eight apocalypses that involve an ascent to and tour of heaven, claiming that a righteous individual can become the equal of the angels. Considers (1) the priestly and temple background of the ascent vision in the Book of the Watchers, whose influence colors the remaining ascent apocalypses; (2) the permeability between the divine and human realms; (3) the nature of pseudonymity in these apocalypses; and (4) other matters connected with their study.

511   M. E. Stone. "A Reconsideration of Apocalyptic Visions." *Harvard Theological Review* 96 (2003) 167–80.
Defends the thesis that the religious experience of the visionary is one significant component of understanding the visions in 4 Ezra and in pseudonymous apocalypses more generally. Suggests that some apocalyptic circles may have deliberately sought to cultivate ecstatic techniques, although these experiences can only be described in traditional language.

8.3 Ideology and Theological Themes

Apocalyptic concepts and ideas were not confined to the apocalypses of the Second Temple period but occur in other literature as well. Many of these distinctive theological ideas, such as dualism, have been treated in introductions to apocalyptic, but other distinctive features are reflected below, such as the use of numerical symbolism (A. Collins [#512]), the view of history (Helberg [#514], Venter [#517]), and the growth in angelic speculation (Olyan [#513]). The theme of divine rule despite the power of nations who do not acknowledge God is significant in apocalyptic literature, as Seow

(#516) and others point out. In addition to sources below, see the essays in Collins and Flint (#525) and the essay by VanderKam in Collins, McGinn, and Stein (#472).

512 A. Y. Collins. "Numerical Symbolism in Apocalyptic Literature." Pp. 1222–87 in Vol. 2.21.2 of *Aufstieg und Niedergang der Römischen Welt*. Edited by H. Temporini and W. Hasse. Berlin: de Gruyter, 1984.

Surveys the different suggestive functions numbers can assume in apocalyptic literature, noting that they can occur in attempts to calculate the end of time or to discern a pattern in history, and they can even be projected into the future. A second section traces numbers as signs of cosmic order, examining the influence of Pythagorean philosophy on apocalyptic and similar ideas. A final section investigates the use of numbers in Revelation.

513 S. M. Olyan. *A Thousand Thousands Served Him*. Tübingen: Mohr Siebeck, 1996.

Theorizes that the names of angels and the designations of angelic brigades were derived from textual exegesis, arguing against the idea that the notion of a remote God was responsible for the increased attention paid to angels. Divine attributes, rare words, Ezekiel's description of the divine throne, and other factors served in part as catalysts for increased Jewish attention to angelology.

514 J. A. Helberg. "The Determination of History according to the Book of Daniel: Against the Background of Deterministic Apocalyptic." *ZAW* 107 (1995) 273–87.

Contends that the apocalyptic of Daniel is not deterministic but that the book visualizes divine sovereignty and God's covenant bond with his people as vital. God overrides the sins of his people through punishment and restoration, overrides the times through his decree, and frustrates the purposes of evil kings. Believers are called to perseverance, repentance, and faithful keeping of the Law.

515 J. Barton. "Theological Ethics in Daniel." Pp. 661–70 in vol. 2 of *The Book of Daniel: Composition and Reception*. Edited by J. J. Collins and P. W. Flint. VTSup 83. Leiden: Brill, 2002.

Reprinted in Barton's *Understanding Old Testament Ethics: Approaches and Explorations*, pp. 154–61. Louisville: Westminster John Knox, 2003.

Finds that despite the apocalyptic genre of Daniel, its ethics largely conform to other Jewish works of its time, insofar as it emphasizes submission to God and to the Law, for example, in Daniel's obedience to food laws and the necessity of prayer. Gentiles behave ethically inasmuch as they avoid the sin of hubris against God, but the focus is on Jewish obligation to renewed fidelity.

516 C. L. Seow. "The Rule of God in the Book of Daniel." Pp. 219–46 in *David and Zion: Biblical Studies in Honor of J. J. M. Roberts*. Winona Lake, IN: Eisenbrauns, 2004.

Finds that there is a strong coherence in the portrayal of the rule of God in Daniel, and specifically in the image of the one who comes on the clouds (chap. 7), as well as the stone cut apart from human hands (chap. 2). These two figures emphasize the divine origin of the present rule and its subjection to the plan of God, who will institute an eternal kingdom.

517 P. M. Venter. "Reviewing History in Apocalyptic Literature as Ideological Strategy." *Hervormde Teologiese Studies* 60 (2004) 703–23.

Analyzes select apocalyptic reviews of history in Dan. 2 and 7, as well as 1 Enoch, to determine their ideology. In Dan. 2, the historical review intends to teach the readers that the end of their political distress is assured, while Dan. 7 stresses divine sovereignty over the world kingdoms. Similar ideologies are discerned in 1 Enoch's historical reviews in the Apocalypse of Weeks, the traditional biblical history, and the Animal Vision.

9

Composition and Compilation

9.1 Daniel as a Whole

Daniel may be divided into two parts: the court tales (chaps. 1–6) and the apocalyptic visions (chaps. 7–12), although many scholars see a more complicated history of growth in the book. Daniel is important for the history of apocalyptic (although portions of 1 Enoch are generally considered older). The sources cited below are concerned with works which treat the book of Daniel as a whole, either by providing an introduction to the book (Davies [#520], LaCocque [#522]) or by tracing the process of its development (Davies [#520], Gammie [#518]). On a somewhat different subject, Koch's famous article (#521) explores the differences in understanding Daniel between the Jewish and Christian traditions due to their distinct histories. An important two-volume collection of essays (Collins and Flint [#525]) includes most of the noted scholars working today on Daniel and serves as an indispensable first stop for research. See also ##484–85, 506, 514–17.

518 J. G. Gammie. "The Classification, Stages of Growth, and Changing Intentions in the Book of Daniel." *JBL* 95 (1976) 191–204.

Against the tendency of interpreters to highlight the Maccabean *Sitz im Leben* of all of Daniel, G. notes weaknesses with this emphasis, especially the overall friendly relationship of the king to the Jews in the first six chapters of the book. Argues for a three-stage process of growth for Daniel and finds evidence that the first stage could not have been composed later than Ptolemy IV Philopator (221–204/03 BC).

519 J. J. Collins. *Daniel with an Introduction to Apocalyptic Literature.* Forms of Old Testament Literature 20. Grand Rapids: Eerdmans, 1984.

Defining apocalyptic as a macrogenre which can include many elements, C. provides a succinct introduction to the genre, distinguishing two kinds of apocalypses (historical apocalypses and otherworldly journeys) and discussing the media and content of revelation for each. While treating the social setting of apocalyptic, C. stresses that "apocalyptic literature is not all the product of a single movement" and also notes two related genres, oracles and testaments (21). Three chapters on Daniel treat the book as a whole, the court tales, and the visions.

520 P. R. Davies. *Daniel.* OTG. Sheffield: JSOT Press, 1985. Reprinted 1998.

Reliable introduction to the critical issues surrounding the interpretation of Daniel, with brief dismissal of the traditional dating in the sixth century (17–18). Successive chapters treat the historical background of the book, its languages, story cycle, vision series, portrait of God, the Jew in a foreign court, the Jewish people, the Son of Man, the Holy Ones, the wise, and the book's authors.

521 K. Koch. "Is Daniel also among the Prophets?" *Int* 39 (1985) 117–30. Reprinted in *Interpreting the Prophets*, pp. 237–48. Edited by J. L. Mays and P. J. Achtemeier. Philadelphia: Fortress, 1987.

Contends that Daniel should be regarded as a prophet and more than a prophet. Argues that the placement of Daniel among the prophets, as in the LXX and Christian Bibles, is original and that Daniel's placement among the Writings in rabbinic Bibles resulted from a change from emphasizing the book's eschatology to understanding Daniel as a role model. Finds that Daniel was more than a prophet because he provided the key (*pesher*) for understanding the enigmatic words of older prophets.

522 A. LaCocque. *Daniel in His Time.* Studies on Personalities of the Old Testament. Columbia: University of South Carolina Press, 1988. Original title: *Daniel et son temps.* Geneva: Labor et Fides, 1983.
Provides an introduction to interpreting the book of Daniel as a product of its era. Includes discussions of historical background, social and spiritual milieu, literary characteristics, elements of apocalypticism in Daniel, use of symbolic language, and major theological lessons. Concludes: "Daniel personally is a type and figure of Hasidic perfection" (196).

523 H. O. Thompson. *The Book of Daniel: An Annotated Bibliography.* New York: Garland, 1993.
Alphabetical arrangement of 1,851 entries, mostly in English. Focuses on publications of the previous fifty years but includes materials from the nineteenth century and first half of the twentieth century that continue to influence current scholarship. Annotations vary from a word or two to a paragraph. Includes a separate listing of the specific volumes of journals that are cited in the bibliography (keyed to authors' names). Dissertations are listed separately. Indices include author/editor, Scripture references, and subject.

524 A. S. van der Woude (ed.). *The Book of Daniel in the Light of New Findings.* Leuven: Leuven University Press, 1993.
Collection of thirty essays presented at the Colloquium Biblicum Lovaniense (August 1991). Essays are classified in five categories: (1) Bilingualism and Greek Versions; (2) Literary-, Form-, and Tradition-Critical Problems; (3) Literary and Sociological Approaches; (4) General Historical and Religio-historical Problems; and (5) Other Studies. See for example, "'You Are Indeed Wiser than Daniel': Reflections on the Character of the Book of Daniel" (M. A. Knibb). Offers these essays in the hope "that the present publication will help and stimulate further research" (xviii).

525 J. J. Collins and P. Flint (eds.). *The Book of Daniel: Composition and Reception.* 2 vols. VTSup 83. Formation and Interpretation of Old Testament Literature 2. Leiden: Brill, 2001.

Consists of thirty-two essays on the book of Daniel organized in eight sections: (1) general topics; (2) the ANE background of Daniel; (3) exegesis of specific passages in Daniel; (4) Daniel's social milieu; (5) Daniel's literary context, including Qumran; (6) Daniel's reception in Judaism and Christianity; (7) textual studies on Daniel; and (8) Daniel's theology. For annotated essays, see Barton (#515); Collins (#526); Kratz (#532); DiLella (#537); Flint (#538); Ulrich (#539); Dunn (#546); Evans (#547); and van der Toorn (#484). In addition see, for example, "The Book of Daniel in Its Context" (M. A. Knibb); "The Anzu Myth as Relevant Background for Daniel 7?" (J. Walton); "The Social Setting of the Aramaic and Hebrew Book of Daniel" (R. Albertz); "A Dan(iel) for All Seasons: For Whom Was Daniel Important?" (L. L. Grabbe); "Stages in the Canonization of the Book of Daniel" (K. Koch); "Daniel in the New Testament: Visions of God's Kingdom" (C. A. Evans). Other essays are of similar scope and quality.

526 J. J. Collins. "Current Issues in the Study of Daniel." Pp. 1–15 in vol. 1 of *The Book of Daniel: Composition and Reception.* Edited by J. J. Collins and P. W. Flint. VTSup 83. Formation and Interpretation of Old Testament Literature 2. Leiden: Brill, 2001.

Survey of significant issues in Daniel research by a knowledgeable interpreter of the book. Discusses Daniel's text, its composition and genre, its social setting, the history of its interpretation, and its theology and ethics.

9.2 Daniel 1–6

The stories about Daniel and his companions in the courts of foreign kings, commonly referred to as *court tales,* are identified by many scholars as the earlier component of Daniel. Foundational to this designation is the study of Wills (#528), who argued that the court tales constituted a distinct genre. Collins (#527) traces the composition of these court tales and their collection as a unit to a Jewish group in the eastern diaspora. These court tales emphasize the superiority of Jewish conduct and wisdom in contrast to those of their foreign counterparts, an emphasis intended to bolster the morale and the distinctive identity of a community being tempted to conform to foreign ways (Kirkpatrick [#530]). For this reason, the portrait of Daniel in the court tales is taken by many as a kind of ideal scribal figure, a model for others to follow (see §7.3 and Collins [#491]). In addition to sources below, see ##499, 505, 507, 524, and 525.

527   J. J. Collins. "The Court-Tales in Daniel and the Development of Apocalyptic." *JBL* 94 (1975) 218–34.
Traces the origins of the court tales in Daniel to diaspora Jews concerned with maintaining their own identities and with succeeding in a foreign court. Distinguishes three types of such tales: (1) those which emphasize the wisdom of the courtier (Dan. 2); (2) those which emphasize his deliverance after trial (Dan. 1, 3, 6); and (3) those which emphasize the content of a message (Dan. 4 and 5). Originating separately, these tales came to be ordered according to the chronology in Dan. 2 and were probably collected before 165 BC. After discussing three instances of influence of the court tales on the following visions, C. finds that the visions seem to have arisen from a Jewish group that had returned to Palestine from the diaspora.

528   L. M. Wills. *The Jew in the Court of the Foreign King: Ancient Jewish Court Legends*. Harvard Dissertations in Religion 26. Minneapolis: Fortress, 1990.
Identifies a genre of wisdom court tales as a "legend of a revered figure set in the royal court which has the wisdom of the protagonist as a principal motif" (37). Interprets Dan. 1–6 and Esther in light of this genre. After examining such court legends in Greek and ANE literature, W. engages in a redaction-critical study of the Old Greek of Dan. 4–6 and explores the Mordecai-Haman narrative. Concludes that the hero of the ruled ethnic group promotes that group's self-concept, emphasizing that the wise person receives a proper reward.

529   P. L. Redditt. "Daniel 11 and the Sociohistorical Setting of the Book of Daniel." *Catholic Biblical Quarterly* 60 (1998) 463–74.

Argues that Daniel was composed by Jewish courtiers at the Seleucid court. After a short review of scholarship on the issue, R. theorizes that chaps. 1–6 and 7–12 arose within the same group. Maintains that since chap. 11 contains coded information about the history of the Seleucid-Ptolemaic wars in addition to what concerned Jerusalem, it would be most understandable to wise men at the Seleucid court. Considers the self-understanding of such a group as reflected in the book.

530   S. Kirkpatrick. *Competing for Honor: A Social-Scientific Reading of Daniel 1–6*. Biblical Interpretation Series 74. Leiden: Brill, 2005.
Finds that Daniel's tales are designed around the social model of honor and seek to persuade hearers that the Judeans are superior to their foreign counterparts, because their God is superior. Thus, Dan. 1–6 models resistance to foreign domination.

9.3 Daniel 7–12

In the visions constituting the second half of the book, Daniel receives revelation of historical events concerning his own time and the future. One significant element of Daniel's visions is his need for an angelic interpreter who explains to him the meaning of the visions he is having. Scholars interested in the composition of these visions have generally understood chap. 7 as the earliest vision, in part because it is written in Aramaic like most of chaps. 2–6, while the rest of the book is in Hebrew. Daniel 7 also reintroduces the theme of four world empires (chap. 2), though with significant differences. The political dimension of these chapters has attracted enormous scholarly attention as scholars seek to understand the historical point of view in light of events known from other sources. In addition to the sources below, see essays in Collins and Flint (#525) and in van der Woude (#524).

531   J. J. Collins. "New Light on the Book of Daniel from the Dead Sea Scrolls." Pp. 180–96 in *Perspectives in the Study of the Old Testament and Early Judaism: A Symposium in Honour of Adam S. van der Woude on the Occasion of His 70th Birthday*. Edited by F. García Martínez and E. Noort. VTSup 73. Leiden: Brill, 1998.

Once the full texts of the DSS were released to the public, it quickly became clear that four (or five) additional scrolls had a genetic relationship with the book of Daniel. Finds that two texts, the *Prayer of Nabonidus* and 4Q248, were possible sources from which the biblical author drew. Also finds two texts that were possibly influenced by Daniel. Offers a close reading of each text, concluding that direct dependence is less important than filling in the literary context of the respective texts.

532 R. G. Kratz. "The Visions of Daniel." Pp. 91–113 in vol. 1 of *The Book of Daniel: Composition and Reception*. Edited by J. J. Collins and P. W. Flint. VTSup 83. Formation and Interpretation of Old Testament Literature 2. Leiden: Brill, 2001.
Drawing on internal evidence from Daniel, K. traces the development of the book from the first collection (chaps. 1–6) with the addition of chap. 7. The original portion of chap. 8 is a translation of chap. 7 into Hebrew with updated material, while chaps. 10–12 expand the book into Maccabean times. Dan. 9:1–10:1 is the latest portion, complete with a final calculation of the date of the end. Dan. 7–12 makes the same point in four different ways and shows an increase of visions.

533 H. S. Kvanvig. "Throne Visions and Monsters: The Encounter between Danielic and Enochic Traditions." *ZAW* 117 (2005) 249–72.
Argues for the dependence of Dan. 7 on the Book of the Watchers and the Book of the Giants in 1 Enoch, which lends both visions a similar worldview in which the cosmos is beset by an attack of demonic forces. Distinguishes the two visions since early Enoch traditions emphasize the uncontrolled rebellion, while Dan. 7 stresses divine sovereignty.

10

Transmission and Interpretation

10.1 Language, Texts, and Translations

The book of Daniel poses various problems regarding language and text. Along with Ezra, which also contains significant portions in Aramaic, the section of Daniel in Aramaic (2:4b–7:28) has been subject to intense debate for what it tells scholars about dating Daniel. Stefanovic (#535), for example, argues that the Aramaic rules out a Maccabean date, going against the majority view. On the other hand, the Old Greek translation of Daniel—the most ancient Greek version of the book, known to scholars from just a few manuscripts—preserves a much different text, especially in chaps. 4–6. That raises the question whether this Greek translation is a paraphrase or another version of the book. Jeansonne (#534) finds that the translator of the Old Greek was careful and reproduced faithfully the text known to him. The difference between the Old Greek and the Hebrew/Aramaic text of Daniel led to a wave of additional translations, including that of Theodotion, the Hexaplaric Recension, and the Lucianic Recension, as outlined by DiLella (#537). An additional difference between the Hebrew and Greek versions is the existence of three long additions to the Greek text of Daniel, which are now counted among the Apocrypha. A comprehensive

though somewhat dated treatment of these additions is found in
C. A. Moore, *Daniel, Esther, and Jeremiah: The Additions*, Anchor
Bible 44 (Garden City, NY: Doubleday, 1977). The copies of Daniel
found at Qumran are analyzed by Flint (#538) and Ulrich (#539).

534 S. P. Jeansonne. *The Old Greek Translation of Daniel 7–12.*
Catholic Biblical Quarterly Monograph Series 19. Washington,
DC: Catholic Biblical Association of America, 1988.
Comparison of the Old Greek of Dan. 7–12 with the MT,
stressing that the translator rendered his source as accurately
as possible and did not seek to shape his work in light of an
overriding theological motivation. Examines Dan. 8:1–10
to assess what level of variation could occur in an accurate
translation in the Old Greek, conceding that mechanical er-
rors and subsequent changes by copyists and revisers should
not be mistaken for misleading translation.

535 Z. Stefanovic. *The Aramaic of Daniel in the Light of Old
Aramaic.* JSOTSup 129. Sheffield: JSOT Press, 1992.
Challenges the Maccabean dating of Daniel by appealing to
Old Aramaic inscriptions which S. argues have significant
overlap with Daniel's Aramaic. Concludes that Old Aramaic
can no longer be treated as a unity and seeks to answer common objections to a Persian date for Daniel based on linguistic
evidence.

536 T. J. Meadowcroft. *Aramaic Daniel and the Greek Daniel: A
Literary Comparison.* JSOTSup 198. Sheffield: Sheffield Academic Press, 1995.
Applies the tools of literary criticism to a comparison of the
Aramaic sections of the MT (chaps. 2–7) with the earlier LXX
translation. Taking each chapter as an independent narrative,
and finding a chiastic structure in which chaps. 4 and 5, 3 and
6, and 2 and 7 are closely related, M. argues that differences
between the versions arise from differences in the *Vorlage*
of the LXX and the MT, not free translation. Argues that in
the LXX the narrator is more overt and omniscient than in
the MT, while the MT version is more subtle and ambiguous
than the LXX version. Divergences in the portrait of Daniel as
a wise man in the two versions are described as the product
of "differing, if not competing, wisdom circles" (16).

537 A. A. DiLella. "The Textual-History of Septuagint-Daniel and
     Theodotion-Daniel." Pp. 586–607 in vol. 2 of *The Book of
     Daniel: Composition and Reception.* Edited by J. J. Collins
     and P. W. Flint. VTSup 83. Formation and Interpretation of
     Old Testament Literature 2. Leiden: Brill, 2001.
     Discusses the complicated textual history of the Greek versions
     of the book of Daniel, covering five topics: (1) the Old Greek
     version of Daniel; (2) the relationship of Theodotion's version
     of Daniel to the Old Greek; (3) the additions to Daniel; (4) the
     Hexaplaric Recension; and (5) the Lucianic Recension.

538 P. W. Flint. "The Daniel Tradition at Qumran." Pp. 329–67 in vol.
     2 of *The Book of Daniel: Composition and Reception.* Edited by
     J. J. Collins and P. W. Flint. VTSup 83. Formation and Interpreta-
     tion of Old Testament Literature 2. Leiden: Brill, 2001.
     Offers an analysis of seventeen scrolls found at Qumran,
     divided into three parts: (1) analysis of the texts of Daniel
     itself; (2) transcriptions, translations, and commentary on
     noncanonical scrolls related to Daniel; and (3) considerations
     of Daniel's authoritative status and popularity at Qumran.

539 E. Ulrich. "The Text of Daniel in the Qumran Scrolls." Pp.
     573–85 in vol. 2 of *The Book of Daniel: Composition and
     Reception.* Edited by J. J. Collins and P. W. Flint. VTSup 83.
     Formation and Interpretation of Old Testament Literature 2.
     Leiden: Brill, 2001.
     Describes the major witnesses to Daniel and the variants
     discovered in the Qumran scrolls. Argues that four literary
     editions of Daniel existed in antiquity: (1) the foundational
     text for the later editions, no longer extant; (2) the MT, with
     its unique text for chaps. 4–6; (3) the Old Greek, with its
     unique text for chaps. 4–6; and (4) the longer Greek edition
     including three substantial additions.

10.2 Second Temple Jewish Literature and New Testament

E. Käsemann's renowned but controversial comment that apocalyptic is "the mother of Christian theology" highlighted the influence of apocalyptic eschatology on Christianity. The book of

Revelation was deeply influenced by Daniel (Beale [#541]), and Dan. 7 provided the "Son of Man" designation that has proven so elusive for scholars of the NT (Burkett [#545]; Dunn [#546]). Another prime example of apocalyptic ideas influencing a movement is evident in the Qumran scrolls. While not producing many apocalypses of their own, the Qumran sectarians clearly treasured portions of 1 Enoch and Daniel, and their own writings are suffused with apocalyptic ideology and expectation. Thus Carmignac (#540), Collins (#531, #541), and García Martínez (#542) consider Qumran highly significant for understanding early Jewish apocalypticism, given the evidence available. Early Jewish and Christian apocalyptic expectation also included a historical component indebted in part to Daniel. In addition to sources below, see Bauckham (#471) and the essay by García Martínez in Collins, McGinn, and Stein (#472).

540 J. Carmignac. "Qu'est-ce que l'apocalyptique? Son emploi à Qumran." *Revue de Qumran* 10 (1979) 3–33.
    In an effort to define the concept of apocalyptic more closely, C. briefly outlines fourteen of its characteristics, after which he discusses the genre and theology of apocalyptic and their intersection. After defining apocalyptic, C. surveys the affinities of seventeen texts with apocalyptic theology, emphasizing that the Qumran sectarians' worldview is not entirely compatible with it.

541 G. K. Beale. *The Use of Daniel in Jewish Apocalyptic Literature and in the Revelation of St. John.* Lanham, MD: University Press of America, 1984.
    Studies "the usage of Daniel in early Jewish and Christian apocalyptic in order to obtain a better interpretative understanding of these writings and to observe any possible relationships which might exist among them" (2). After analyzing the use of Daniel in Jewish apocalyptic texts, especially Qumran, B. addresses the use of Daniel in Rev. 1, 4–5, 13, and 17, concluding that the author of Revelation respects the context of Daniel from which he quotes.

542 F. García Martínez. *Qumran and Apocalyptic: Studies on the Aramaic Texts from Qumran.* Leiden: Brill, 1992.
    Previously published in Spanish and thoroughly revised, the seven essays in this volume concern Aramaic texts from

Qumran, contending that Qumran manuscripts and apocalyptic are mutually interpretive. Articles treat 4QMess ar and the Book of Noah, the Aramaic fragments of Enoch, the Book of Giants, the Prayer of Nabonidus, 4QPseudo Daniel ar, 4Q246, and the New Jerusalem texts.

543 J. J. Collins. *Apocalypticism in the Dead Sea Scrolls.* New York: Routledge, 1997.

Analysis of apocalypticism at Qumran finding that although few, if any, apocalypses have been preserved, Qumran texts "are informed by an apocalyptic worldview, and influenced by the apocalypses of Enoch and Daniel, which were also prominent at Qumran" (150). Considers distinctive beliefs at Qumran concerning creation, the periodization of history, the Messiah, the eschatological war, resurrection, and the heavenly world.

544 P. B. Munoa. *Four Powers in Heaven: The Interpretation of Daniel 7 in the Testament of Abraham.* JSPSup 28. Sheffield: Sheffield Academic Press, 1998.

Theorizes that Dan. 7:9–17 influenced the portrayal of the judgment scene in *Testament of Abraham* 11:1–13:7, as proven by parallels in themes, vocabulary, and structure. The exalted portraits of Adam and Abel mesh well with other depictions of these figures in Middle Judaism, and such exalted figures combine with the ongoing exegesis of enigmatic apocalyptic texts to serve the needs of the interpretive community.

545 D. Burkett. *The Son of Man Debate: A History and Evaluation.* Society for New Testament Studies Monograph Series 107. Cambridge: Cambridge University Press, 1999.

Reviews the history of debate concerning the meaning of Jesus's self-designation as Son of Man from the patristic period up to 1996. B.'s final chapter presents ten conclusions, including the statement: "The Son of Man debate thus serves as a prime illustration of the limits of New Testament scholarship" (124).

546 J. D. G. Dunn. "The Danielic Son of Man in the New Testament." Pp. 528–49 in vol. 2 of *The Book of Daniel: Composition and Reception.* Edited by J. J. Collins and P. W. Flint. VTSup

83. Formation and Interpretation of Old Testament Literature 2. Leiden: Brill, 2001.

Acknowledges that Dan. 7 influenced the synoptic tradition, identifying three possibilities: (1) it could have come from Jesus's hope to be vindicated by the human-like figure (Dan. 7:13); (2) it appeared as a post-Easter development of Jesus's own use of the figure; and (3) Jesus was influenced by Dan. 7 to define his mission. Revelation was also influenced by Son of Man imagery, but probably drew directly from Daniel without being influenced by the synoptic tradition.

547 C. A. Evans. "Daniel in the New Testament: Visions of God's Kingdom." Pp. 490–527 in vol. 2 of *The Book of Daniel: Composition and Reception*. VTSup 83. Formation and Interpretation of Old Testament Literature 2. Edited by J. J. Collins and P. W. Flint. Leiden: Brill, 2001.

Focuses on two of the most important themes/images in the book of Daniel that have contributed to NT theology: visions of throne(s) and kingdom. Building on a list of quotations from numerous canonical and noncanonical texts and an examination of references to kingdom in Daniel, E. finds that "Daniel's semantics are unexceptional" (501). The majority of the essay explores the significant influence of the Danielic kingdom on later interpretation, including Qumran, Josephus, 4 Ezra, Jesus, the Evangelists, and Paul.

10.3 Apocalyptic in Jewish and Christian Traditions

The legacy of early apocalyptic did not end with the destruction of the second temple, but continued in diverse modulations and incarnations. Apocalyptic traditions resurfaced in the heikhalot literature, a mysterious mystical literature concerned with the journey to see God in heavenly palaces (Gruenwald [#548]). Other Jewish compositions continued the apocalyptic trend (Reeves [#554]). Similarly, in the Christian world, apocalyptic conceptions resurfaced again and again (McGinn [#550]; Ridyard [#552]). Manichaeans incorporated much of the thought-world of apocalyptic (Koenen [#549]). Islam too made use of apocalyptic motifs (Amanat and Bernhardsson [#551]). The figure of Daniel served as the focal point for many elaborations down through the centuries, as traced by DiTommaso (#553). In many ways, then, apocalyptic has never really died out. In addition to sources below, see various essays in Collins, McGinn, and Stein (#472).

548   I. Gruenwald. *Apocalyptic and Merkavah Mysticism.* Arbeiten zur Geschichte des Antiken Judentums und des Urchristentums 14. Leiden: Brill, 1980.
Valuable for discussion of the relationship between apocalyptic and esoteric mystical practices as known from later Jewish texts (the Heikhalot). Discusses the relationship of apocalyptic to wisdom and prophetic literature and the relation of apocalyptic to Scripture, after which G. discusses diverse Second Temple texts that reflect merkavah experiences (*1 Enoch, Apocalypse of Abraham, Ascension of Isaiah*). The second half of the work introduces the works of merkavah mysticism as the author defines them and considers their relationship to Tannaitic and Amoraic sages.

549   L. Koenen. "Manichaean Apocalypticism at the Crossroads of Iranian, Egyptian, Jewish, and Christian Thought." Pp. 285–332 in *Codex Manichaicus Coloniensis: Atti del Simposio Internazionale (Rende- Amantea 3–7 settembre 1984).* Edited by L. Cirillo. Cosenza: Marra Editore, 1986.
Considers the portrayal of the life of the prophet Mani as preparation for the coming end of the world. Explores the indebtedness of Manichaean apocalypticism to Jewish and Christian apocalypses, as well as to Egyptian and Iranian influences.

550   B. McGinn. *Visions of the End: Apocalyptic Traditions in the Middle Ages.* Second edition. New York: Columbia University Press, 1998.
Combines an anthology of scores of texts relating to medieval apocalyptic traditions from AD 400–1500 with critical introductions to those texts. The second edition includes a brief introduction to classical and patristic apocalypticism, a new preface, and a supplementary bibliography.

551   A. Amanat and M. T. Bernhardsson (eds.). *Imagining the End: Visions of Apocalypse from the Ancient Middle East to Modern America.* New York: I. B. Tauris, 2002.

Includes fifteen essays originally presented in a seminar at Yale in 1998 on millennialism from ancient to modern times, divided into four sections: (1) origins; (2) Judaism, Christianity, and Islam; (3) medieval and early modern periods; and (4) modern times. A. contributes a prefatory essay titled "Introduction: Apocalyptic Anxieties and Millennial Hopes in the Salvation Regions of the Middle East."

552 S. J. Ridyard (ed.). *Last Things: Apocalypse, Judgment and Millennium in the Middle Ages*. Sewanee Medieval Studies 12. Sewanee, TN: University of the South, 2002.

Collection of six essays treating apocalyptic and millenarian themes in the Middle Ages, including "Defining Justification: Faith, Deeds, and the Parables of *Pearl* and *Piers Plowman*" (A. Bruce); "A Glorious Vision of Heaven: The Chapel of Henry VII at Westminster Abbey" (V. K. Henderson); "Dante's Prophecy of Peripety (*Par.* 27.142–48): An Astrological *Fortuna*" (R. Kay); "Meditating on Passion, Meditating on Judgment: The First and Second Comings of Christ in Medieval Imagination" (R. Keickheffer); "Thomas Aquinas on Both Ends of the World" (R. McInerny); "The First-Fruit of the Last Judgment: The *Commedia* as a Thirteenth-Century Apocalypse" (J. C. Nohrnberg).

553 L. DiTommaso. *The Book of Daniel and the Apocryphal Daniel Literature*. Studia in veteris testimenti pseudepigrapha 20. Leiden: Brill, 2005.

Surveys the literature that grew up around the figure of Daniel in the postbiblical period, distinguishing three types: legenda, apocryphal apocalypses, and prognostica. Draws ten conclusions regarding geographical and chronological trends in this literature. Concludes with a comprehensive inventory and bibliography of Daniel literature extant in Aramaic, Greek, Latin, Syriac, Ethiopic, Coptic, Hebrew, Persian, Arabic, Turkish, and other medieval languages.

554 J. C. Reeves. *Trajectories in Near Eastern Apocalyptic: A Postrabbinic Jewish Apocalypse Reader*. Atlanta: SBL, 2005.

Consists of nine Jewish apocalypses and apocalyptic collections from the second half of the first millennium AD together with an introduction to, translation of, and a commentary on each work. Three thematic excursuses explore Metatron as an apocalyptic persona, the eschatological appearance of the staff of Moses, and the children of Moses.

10.4 Homiletics and Interpretive Issues

Fifty years ago scholars tended to denigrate the significance of apocalyptic for the Christian faith. Today interest in apocalyptic has reawakened, as the feverish pace of scholarly publication demonstrates. Representing this recent trend, Boeve (#556) gives three reasons for the continued relevance of apocalyptic. But how should pastors and leaders of faith communities make use of what can be baffling and esoteric material? The following sources provide practical advice and examples of sermons prepared from apocalyptic texts.

555 L. P. Jones and J. L. Sumney. *Preaching Apocalyptic Texts*. St. Louis: Chalice, 1999.
Three chapters introduce the problem of preaching apocalyptic texts, the nature of apocalyptic thought, and the characteristics of apocalyptic preachers. Next, J. and S. present short exegeses of five OT and NT passages (Dan. 7; 1 Thess. 4:13–5:11; Mark 13; and Rev. 5 and 14) along with two examples of sermons on each passage.

556 L. Boeve. "God Interrupts History: Apocalypticism as an Indispensable Theological Conceptual Strategy." *Louvain Studies* 26 (2001) 195–216.
Explores three characteristics that render apocalyptic scenarios relevant in contemporary society: (1) fear of judgment provoked by oneself; (2) the anxiety engendered as the inevitable result of individuals seeking greater and greater thrills; and (3) doomsday scenarios as a symptom of and response to escalating insecurity. Argues that apocalypticism is still relevant for Christian theology and that apocalyptic provides an essential strategy for transcending modern societal anxieties.

557 D. Jonaitis. *Unmasking Apocalyptic Texts: A Guide to Preaching and Teaching*. New York: Paulist, 2005.

Considers how to communicate the hope, drama, and imagination of apocalyptic texts in preaching and teaching using the model of tragic drama. Apocalyptic passages from both testaments are examined with a three-step process: identifying the historical situation of the passage, determining how each text gives hope to its audience, and finding ways to communicate that hope to a present-day audience. Intended primarily for preachers in liturgical churches, but more widely applicable.

558 L. D. Bierma (ed.). *Calvin Theological Journal* 41.1 (2006). Collects five plenary and seminar presentations and five sermons delivered at the third Bible and Ministry Conference conducted under the theme "Preaching Apocalyptic Texts" at Calvin Theological Seminary (2005). Articles include "Preaching Apocalyptic? You've Got to Be Kidding" (G. D. Fee); "Preaching Old Testament Apocalyptic to a New Testament Church" (D. I. Block); "The Purpose of Symbolism in the Book of Revelation" (G. K. Beale); "The Slaying of Superman and the Sure Salvation of the Saints: Paul's Apocalyptic Word of Comfort (2 Thess. 2:1–17)" (J. A. D. Weima); and "Charting the Future or a Perspective on the Present? The Paraenetic Purpose of Mark 13" (D. B. Deppe).

Name Index

Aaron, C. L., Jr. 187
Achtemeier, E. 186
Achtemeier, P. J. 69, 86, 123, 132, 175, 181, 209, 218
Ackerman, S. 97
Ådna, J. 174
Albertz, R. 70, 220
Albright, W. F. 65, 142
Alexander, P. S. 45
Amanat, A. 230
Anderson, B. W. 63, 92
Anderson, G. W. 107, 205
Arnold, B. T. 27, 195
Attridge, H. W. 196
Auld, A. G. 42, 44, 49, 56, 67, 147
Aune, D. E. 75, 199
Austin, J. L. 176

Baer, D. A. 170
Bailey, D. P. 173–174
Baker, D. W. 27, 195
Bakhtin, M. 90
Balentine, S. E. 42
Baltzer, K. 50, 73
Barstad, H. M. 36, 44, 55, 119, 147

Barton, J. 21, 72, 90, 102, 107, 118, 192, 199, 205, 215
Bastiaens, J. C. 120
Bauckham, R. J. 197
Bauer, A. 184
Baumann, G. 65, 88
Baumgartner, W. 124
Beal, T. K. 152
Beale, G. K. 227, 233
Beaton, R. 174
Becking, B. 70, 128, 199
Bedford, P. R. 73
Beentjes, P. C. 49, 120
Begrich, J. 60
Behrens, A. 84
Bellinger, W. H., Jr. 85, 108
Bellis, A. O. 60, 199
Ben Zvi, E. 30, 56, 60, 67, 70, 79, 85, 139, 150, 153, 160
Berchman, R. M. 35
Bergen, W. J. 66, 67
Berges, U. 49, 57
Bergman, J. 197
Bernhardsson, M. T. 230
Berry, D. K. 166
Betz, O. 108

Beuken, W. A. M. 121, 176
Beyerle, S. 213
Bibb, B. D. 60
Bierma, L. D. 186, 233
Blank, S. H. 50
Blenkinsopp, J. 23, 29, 46, 54, 74, 94, 111, 114, 115
Block, D. I. 109, 136, 137, 233
Bloomquist, L. G. 198, 199
Boccabello, J. S. 165
Boccaccini, G. 74
Boda, M. J. 91, 164, 165
Bodi, D. 62, 134
Boeve, L. 232
Bolin, T. M. 152
Bosma, C. J. 186
Bosman, H. J. 121
Botha, P. J. 150
Bowden, J. 92
Brenneman, J. E. 53
Brenner, A. 184
Brensinger, T. L. 86
Brettler, M. Z. 93
Bright, J. 99
Brooke, G. J. 172
Brown, R. E. 192
Brownlee, W. H. 172

Broyles, C. C. 119, 120, 169, 172
Bruce, A. 231
Brueggemann, W. 21, 48, 92, 152, 185, 186
Bruster, T. K. 187
Bryan, D. J. 199
Bultmann, C. 49
Burkett, D. 228
Buss, M. J. 30
Butterworth, M. 162

Callender, D., Jr. 136
Carey, G. 194, 198, 199
Carmignac, J. 227
Carpenter, E. E. 177
Carr, D. M. 117, 118
Carroll R., M. D. 109, 149, 184
Carroll, R. P. 42, 44, 52, 73, 104, 106, 111, 122, 123, 125, 127, 176, 209
Carson, D. A. 89
Carter, C. E. 41
Chapman, S. 80
Charlesworth, J. H. 197, 210
Charpin, D. 62
Childs, B. S. 80, 173, 176, 181, 182
Chilton, B. 35, 169
Chisholm, R. B., Jr. 24, 93
Christensen, D. L. 157
Cirillo, L. 230
Cleaver-Bartholomew, D. 159
Clements, R. E. 29, 51, 79, 105, 108, 120, 210
Clifford, R. J. 198
Clines, D. J. A. 28, 39, 50, 53, 73, 79, 94
Coggins, R. J. 53, 89, 146, 162
Collins, A. Y. 192, 196, 215

Collins, J. J. 107, 192, 193, 196, 197, 198, 199, 202, 203, 204, 206, 207, 209, 210, 215, 218, 220, 222, 223, 226, 228, 229
Collins, T. 49, 83, 164
Conrad, E. W. 116, 118, 120, 141, 182
Cook, S. L. 56, 137, 194, 199, 211
Cooper, A. 50, 86
Coote, R. B. 66
Corral, M. A. 136
Craig, K. M., Jr. 152, 153
Creach, P. L. D. 187
Crenshaw, J. L. 21, 30, 52, 56, 63, 79, 96, 123, 141
Crim, K. 83
Cross, F. M. 61
Crowley, J. E. 60
Cryer, F. H. 39
Curtis, A. H. W. 126

Dangl, O. 159
Daniels, D. R. 142
Darr, K. P. 86, 135
Davies, G. I. 142
Davies, P. R. 30, 42, 43, 44, 47, 70, 79, 117, 206, 210, 218
Davis, E. F. 133
Day, J. 64, 89, 98, 107, 108
Decock, P. B. 195
Deist, F. E. 43
de Jonge, H. J. 165
Dell, K. J. 148
de Moor, J. C. 48, 57, 96, 176
Dempsey, C. J. 101, 185
Denova, R. I. 172
Deppe, D. B. 233
de Pury, A. 57
de Regt, L. J. 57

deSilva, D. A. 198
DeVries, S. J. 83
De Waard, J. 170
Diamond, A. R. P. 29, 88, 124, 127
Dick, M. D. 97
Dijkstra, M. 120
DiLella, A. A. 226
Dille, S. J. 88, 177
Dillon, M. 195
DiTommaso, L. 231
Domeris, W. R. 97
Doyle, B. 87
Duguid, I. M. 108
Duhm, B. 94, 115
Dunn, J. D. G. 228
Durand, J.-M. 34

Eagleton, T. 94
Eaton, J. H. 25, 59
Eidevall, G. 143
Emmerson, G. I. 117
Eng, M. 30
Epp-Tiessen, D. 54
Eskenazi, T. C. 73, 106
Evans, C. A. 119, 120, 169, 172, 173, 220, 229

Fallon, F. T. 196
Farmer, W. R. 108
Fee, G. D. 233
Feldman, L. H. 172
Fenton, T. L. 49
Ferris, P. W. 83
Festinger, L. 52
Fewell, D. N. 213
Fiddes, P. S. 199
Finamore, J. F. 35
Fiorenza, E. S. 197
Fishbane, M. 89
Fitzgerald, A. 111
Fitzmyer, J. A. 192
Fleming, D. E. 45, 60
Flint, P. W. 169, 204, 215, 220, 223, 226, 228, 229

Floyd, M. H. 79, 85, 91, 164
Flusser, D. 199
Forbes, C. 76
Foster, P. 165
Fowl, S. E. 79
Freedman, D. N. 30
Frey, R. 30
Friebel, K. G. 110
Fritz, V. 43
Fuller, R. 140

Gaines, J. H. 153
Galambush, J. 60, 106, 111
Gallagher, E. V. 35
Gammie, J. G. 63, 206, 217
García Martínez, F. 198, 222, 227
Gelston, A. 169
Gerstenberger, E. S. 92
Geyer, J. B. 112
Gitay, Y. 30, 47, 51, 120, 177, 179, 182
Gitay, Z. 30
Glazier-McDonald, B. 166
Glazov, G. Y. 51
Gordon, R. P. 26, 28, 42, 43, 46, 53, 64, 79, 86, 89, 110, 115, 169, 175, 181
Gorea-Autexier, M. 62
Gottwald, N. K. 94, 95, 129
Goulder, M. 122
Gowan, D. E. 23, 95
Grabbe, L. L. 39, 40, 46, 60, 61, 69, 70, 71, 111, 199, 200, 210, 211, 220
Graham, M. P. 67, 70, 140
Gray, R. 72
Green, D. E. 70
Greenberg, M. 132
Greenspahn, F. E. 98

Griffin, W. P. 95
Griffiths, J. G. 197
Gruenwald, I. 230
Gunkel, H. 43, 60, 82

Haak, R. D. 111, 159, 199
Hagstrom, D. G. 154
Hahn, S. 100
Hallo, W. W. 202
Halperin, D. J. 134
Hämeen-Anttila, J. 36
Hamerton-Kelly, R. G. 205
Hannah, D. D. 174
Hanson, K. C. 43, 84
Hanson, P. D. 108, 193, 196, 209
Haran, M. 68
Harrelson, W. 63
Hartman, L. 197
Harvey, J. E. 58
Hasse, W. 215
Hauser, A. J. 180
Hay, D. M. 35
Hayes, R. 90
Hays, J. D. 109
Heim, K. 106
Heintz, J.-G. 144
Helberg, J. A. 215
Hellholm, D. 192, 196
Henderson, V. K. 231
Hengel, M. 174
Henze, M. 213
Heschel, A. J. 22
Hess, R. S. 106, 107, 109
Hiebert, T. 158
Hilber, J. W. 61
Hill, S. D. 66
Himmelfarb, M. 197, 213, 214
Hoch, A. I. 187
Höffken, P. 122
Hoffman, Y. 108
Hofius, O. 174
Holladay, W. L. 122, 125, 127, 161

Hollander, H. W. 165
Holliday, J. S., Jr. 43
Holt, E. K. 88, 143
Hooker, M. D. 76, 108, 174
Hoppe, L. J. 106
Horbury, W. 109
Hostetter, E. C. 22
House, P. R. 90, 92, 96, 119, 138, 139, 140, 141, 157, 160, 166
Houston, W. 175
Howard, V. P. 187
Huffmon, H. B. 36
Hugenberger, G. P. 108, 110
Hultgård, A. 203
Hupper, W. G. 26
Hurvitz, A. 55
Hutton, R. R. 25, 51

Irvine, S. A. 61, 62

Jacobsen, D. S. 187
Janowski, B. 173
Janzen, W. 101
Jaruzelska, I. 62
Jeansonne, S. P. 225
Jeffers, A. 34
Jemielity, T. 179
Jenner, K. D. 121
Jeppesen, K. 28, 207
Jeremias, J. 90
Jobes, K. 168
Jobling, D. 94, 177
Johnson, A. R. 59
Johnstone, W. 49
Jonaitis, D. 232
Jones, B. A. 139
Jones, L. P. 232
Joyce, P. M. 107, 108, 133, 176

Kaltner, J. 27, 30, 37, 80, 198
Kamp, A. 154
Karp, A. 35
Käsemann, E. 226

Kay, R. 231
Keck, L. E. 21, 192
Keefe, A. A. 185
Keickheffer, R. 231
Kelle, B. E. 144
Kessler, J. 111, 163
King, P. J. 126, 142
Kirkpatrick, S. 222
Kitz, A. M. 40
Klein, R. W. 104
Knauf, E. 70
Knibb, M. A. 172, 219, 220
Koch, K. 21, 69, 96, 196, 218, 220
Koenen, L. 230
Koet, B. J. 174
Kohl, M. 69, 94, 99, 182
Kohn, R. L. 57, 137
Kratz, R. G. 223
Kugel, J. L. 50, 86
Kugler, R. A. 56
Kuntz, J. K. 87
Kutsko, J. F. 136
Kvanvig, H. S. 202, 223

Laato, A. 96, 120, 176
Labahn, A. 88
Labahn, M. 173
LaCocque, A. 219
Lapsley, J. E. 102, 136
Leavitt, J. 51
Leclerc, T. L. 102
Lee, N. C. 130
Leene, H. 49, 57, 120
Leiter, D. A. 31
Lemaire, A. 62
Lemche, N. P. 70
Lenglet, A. 212
Lescow, T. 150
Lessing, R. R. 180
Levenson, J. D. 132
Levine, B. A. 30
Levison, J. R. 47
Levy, D. 66
Linafelt, T. 130, 152
Linville, J. R. 48, 61

Longman, T. 12, 203
Lust, J. 132, 171

Ma, W. 95
Macchi, J.-D. 57
MacIntosh, A. A. 64
Magonet, J. 151
Malamat, A. 35
Maloney, L. 88
Mandolfo, C. 177
Manning, G. T., Jr. 174
Marinković, P. 73
Markschies, C. 174
Martens, E. A. 92
Martin, J. D. 206
Martin, S. C. 103
Mason, R. A. 72, 91, 109, 145, 155, 162, 164
Masson, M. 62
Mathewson, D. 175
Matthews, V. H. 24
Mayer, W. 70
Mayes, A. D. H. 28, 50
Mays, J. L. 27, 43, 69, 86, 101, 123, 132, 175, 181, 209, 218
McConville, J. G. 24, 108, 126
McCullough, J. C. 175
McEvenue, B. 120
McGinn, B. 198, 230
McInerny, R. 231
McKane, W. 64, 127
McKay, H. A. 28, 39, 50, 53
McKeating, H. 134
McKenna, M. 25
McKenzie, A. M. 187
McKenzie, S. L. 56, 67, 70, 140
McLaughlin, J. L. 111
Meadowcroft, T. J. 225
Mein, A. 49, 104
Melugin, R. F. 108, 118, 120, 148, 177, 182
Menken, M. J. J. 174

Meyers, C. L. 41
Middlemas, J. 71, 107
Milbank, J. 94
Miller, C. W. 130
Miller, P. D., Jr. 186, 27
Millot, L. 144
Möller, K. 149
Moore, C. A. 225
Morgan, D. F. 64
Morris, G. 143
Morse, B. 131
Motyer, J. A. 114
Mowinckel, S. 43, 58, 84, 107, 122
Moyise, S. 174, 175
Muddiman, J. 165
Muenchow, C. 129
Muffs, Y. 44
Muilenburg, J. 178
Müller, H.-P. 205
Munoa, P. B. 228
Murphy, F. J. 192, 195
Murphy, R. E. 192

Na'aman, N. 71
Nardoni, E. 103
Nelson, R. D. 61
Neusner, J. 35
Newsom, C. A. 86, 94
Newsome, J. D. 22
Nicholson, E. W. 99, 123
Nickelsburg, G. W. E. 197, 208
Niditch, S. 82
Nielsen, K. 82, 88, 207
Niskanen, P. 204
Nissinen, M. 36, 37, 40, 48, 80, 111, 200
Nogalski, J. D. 23, 60, 96, 138, 140, 141, 164
Nohrnberg, J. C. 231
Noort, E. 222
Noth, M. 66
Nurmela, R. 91, 164

O'Brien, J. M. 59, 166
O'Connell, M. J. 26

O'Connor, K. M. 125, 127, 131
Odell, M. S. 61, 85, 136
Ollenburger, B. C. 93
Olyan, S. M. 215
Orlinsky, H. M. 50, 65
Orton, D. E. 30, 34, 68, 124, 154, 159, 162
Oswalt, J. N. 186, 195
Overholt, T. W. 38, 39, 43, 44, 66

Paas, S. 112
Park, A. W. 148
Park, J. 31
Parker, S. B. 34
Parke-Taylor, G. H. 128
Parpola, S. 35
Patrick, D. 100
Patton, C. L. 56, 61, 136, 137
Paul, S. 201
Pearson, B. W. R. 169
Peckham, B. 45
Perdue, L. G. 21, 63, 64, 192, 206
Person, R. F., Jr. 55, 152, 91, 164
Petersen, D. L. 21, 25, 27, 41, 42, 47, 48, 49, 58, 71, 82, 85, 86, 101, 140, 164
Pierce, C. 176
Pierce, R. 178, 179
Pippin, T. 94
Pleins, J. D. 102
Plöger, O. 208
Podhoretz, N. 25
Pohlmann, K.-F. 43
Polaski, D. C. 121, 198
Polley, M. E. 147
Porter, S. E. 12, 79, 169
Porton, G. G. 172
Prévost, J.-P. 25
Prinsloo, W. S. 145
Pulikottil, P. 170

Quinn-Miscall, P. D. 121

Ramírez, G. 30
Reddish, M. G. 193
Redditt, P. L. 91, 140, 141, 146, 164, 166
Reeves, J. C. 231
Reid, S. B. 30, 47, 67, 95, 177
Reimer, D. 90
Rendtorff, R. 94, 99, 182
Renkema, J. 57
Rentería, T. H. 66
Renz, T. 106, 135
Reventlow, H. G. 108
Richards, K. H. 27, 73, 86, 106
Ridyard, S. J. 231
Robinson, T. H. 79
Rofé, A. 23, 65
Römer, T. 56, 57, 126
Roncace, M. 62
Rooker, M. F. 133
Rose, W. H. 109
Rosenbaum, S. N. 147
Rosendal, B. 207
Ross, J. F. 43
Rouillard-Bonraisin, H. 62
Rowland, C. 193, 199, 200
Russell, D. S. 192, 193
Ruzer, S. 199
Ryou, D. H. 161

Sæbø, M. 207
Saldarini, A. J. 196
Salters, R. B. 129
Sanders, E. P. 197
Sanders, J. A. 104
Sandoval, T. J. 177
Sandy, D. B. 87
Sasson, J. 153, 203
Satterthwaite, P. E. 107
Sawyer, J. F. A. 25, 29
Schaaf, J. L. 58, 82

Schaper, J. 61, 81
Schart, A. 84, 91, 141, 146, 164
Schearing, L. S. 56
Schenker, A. 171
Schibler, D. 108
Schmidt, H.-C. 43
Schmidt, W. H. 26
Schniedewind, J. J M. 73
Schoors, A. 120
Schramm, L. J. 67
Schultz, R. L. 91, 108, 141
Schwartz, B. 136
Scott, J. M. 104
Seeligmann, J. H. 23
Seibert, E. A. 31
Seitz, C. R. 116, 125, 187
Seow, C. L. 216
Sérandour, A. 62
Sharp, C. J. 128
Shaw, G. 35
Shead, A. G. 170
Shelley, A. C. 187
Sheppard, G. T. 118
Sherwood, Y. 143
Silva, M. 168
Sim, D. C. 195, 211
Simon, U. 67
Smith, D. L. 29
Smith, G. V. 22
Smith, J. Z. 196
Smith, P. A. 118
Smith-Christopher, D. L. 104, 105
Snyman, S. D. 150
Soggin, J. A. 64
Sommer, B. D. 47, 90
Sparks, K. 37, 204
SO'Connoronk, K. 176
Stacey, W. D. 110
Stalker, D. G. M. 92
Steck, O. H. 23, 105
Stefanovic, Z. 225
Stein, S. J. 198
Stevenson, K. R. 135

240

Stiebert, J. 112
Stone, B. W. 29
Stone, M. E. 196, 214
Strong, J. T. 136
Stuhlmacher, P. 173, 174
Stuhlmueller, C. 92
Stulman, L. 27, 29, 30, 31, 37, 80, 124, 127
Sumney, J. L. 232
Sweeney, M. A. 27, 70, 85, 96, 116, 117, 118, 119, 120, 140, 141, 145, 157, 158, 161, 177, 182, 200

Tabor, J. D. 200
Tate, M. E. 119
Temporini, H. 215
Terblanche, M. D. 57
Terrien, S. 63
Thackeray, H. J. 169
Thiel, W. 108
Thompson, H. O. 126, 148, 163, 166, 219
Tiemeyer, L.-S. 112, 164, 167
Tigchelaar, E. J. C. 91, 164, 206
Todd, J. A. 66
Tollington, J. E. 163
Tournay, R. 59
Tov, E. 168, 169
Trible, P. A. 152, 180, 183
Tromp, J. 105, 164
Trotter, J. M. 74
Tucker, G. M. 43, 177
Tuckett, C. 164, 165, 174
Tuell, S. S. 134, 136, 137

Tull, P. K. 85
Turner, J. D. 35
Turner, W. C. 187

Uehlinger, C. 71
Uffenheimer, B. 108
Ulrich, E. 169, 226

Valeta, D. 199
VanderKam, J. C. 192, 198, 202, 203, 206
van der Kooij, A. 121, 165, 169
van der Toorn, K. 36, 80, 204
van der Wal, A. 155, 156
van der Woude, A. S. 186, 205, 219
van Deventer, H. J. M. 57
VanGemeren, W. A. 22
van Grol, H. 121
Van Hecke, P. J. P. 88
Van Leeuwen, R. C. 63, 64
Van Rooy, H. F. 57
van Rooy, H. V. 73
Van Ruiten, J. 120
Van Wieringen, A. L. H. M. 180
Varughese, A. 31
Venter, P. M. 216
Vervenne, M. 120
Villard, P. 62
von Rad, G. 92, 94, 112

Wagenaar, A. 155
Wagner, J. R. 173, 174
Walton, J. 201, 220
Watson, D. F. 180

Watts, J. D. W. 90, 111, 114, 119, 139, 157, 166
Watts, R. E. 173
Webb, R. L. 76
Weber, M. 43, 49
Weems, R. J. 184
Weigl, M. 157
Weima, J. A. D. 233
Weinfeld, M. 101, 108
Wellhausen, J. 99, 149
Wenham, G. J. 106, 107
Weren, W. 120
Westermann, C. 81, 83, 129
White, H. C. 81
Whybray, R. N. 116
Wilk, F. 173, 175
Wilkerson, D. 39
Willey, P. T. 90
Williams, C. H. 174
Williams, M. J. 25
Williamson, H. G. M. 28, 42, 64, 89, 107, 108, 109, 117, 176
Wills, L. M. 208, 221
Wilson, R. R. 21, 27, 38, 41, 53, 69, 209
Witherington, B., III 76
Witvliet, J. D. 187
Wong, K. L. 96
Wright, B. G., III 208

Yee, G. A. 142

Zapff, B. M. 155
Zerbe, G. 54
Zevit, Z. 61, 98
Zuck, R. B. 93
Zucker, D. J. 25